Training for the
U P H I L L
A T H L E T E

patagonia®

Training for the
UPHILL
ATHLETE

A MANUAL
FOR MOUNTAIN
RUNNERS AND SKI
MOUNTAINEERS

Steve House | Scott Johnston | Kílian Jornet

patagonia

Training for the Uphill Athlete
A Manual for Mountain Runners and Ski Mountaineers

Patagonia publishes a select number of titles on wilderness, wildlife, and outdoor sports that inspire and restore a connection to the natural world.

Hardcover edition
Printed in Canada on 100 percent post-consumer recycled paper

Editor – John Dutton
Photo Editor – Kyle Sparks
Book Designer – Faceout Studio
Project Manager – Jennifer Patrick
Photo Production – Sus Corez
Production – Rafael Dunn, Natausha Greenblott
Creative Directors – Christina Speed, Bill Boland
Creative Advisor – Jennifer Ridgeway
Director of Books – Karla Olson

FSC
www.fsc.org
MIX
Paper from responsible sources
FSC® C016245

ENVIRONMENTAL BENEFITS STATEMENT

Patagonia Inc saved the following resources by printing the pages of this book on chlorine free paper made with 100% post-consumer waste.

TREES	WATER	ENERGY	SOLID WASTE	GREENHOUSE GASES
319 FULLY GROWN	26,000 GALLONS	134 MILLION BTUs	1,100 POUNDS	138,000 POUNDS

Environmental impact estimates were made using the Environmental Paper Network Paper Calculator 4.0. For more information visit www.papercalculator.org.

Cover photos: (front) Kílian Jornet in Switzerland. Photo: Steve House
(back) Kim Strom runs a rocky ridgeline above Saas-Almagell, Switzerland. Photo: Dan Patitucci
Paperback 978-1-938340-84-0
E-Book 978-1-938340-85-7
Library of Congress Control Number 2018965947

CONTENTS

SECTION THREE

CHAPTER SIX

CHAPTER SEVEN

Nose to the Wind

The wind had made its presence known all night, the tiny tent shaking off its layer of breath-turned-frost with each gust. The icy flakes settled, then melted onto the only part of me sticking out of the sleeping bag: my nose. I was tired when I woke, but no more than Marko, whom I followed out the tent door at dawn. We snapped on crampons, shouldered our summit packs, and climbed into the storm.

All our known world was below us, invisible but pulling on us, like gravity. Marko climbed steadily, quickly. I, more slowly and erratically. Soon he was also invisible to me, somewhere above me. The loneliness of being lost in between my partner and my world was crushing. I sped up for a moment and then stumbled, gasping, coughing, and wheezing. With only footprints in the snow—no one had ever passed here before (or since)—and the occasional parting of clouds to reveal Marko's green jacket, the mark of an alien in the black-and-white world of 23,000 feet in the Himalaya, I could see enough to know he was there. I could follow, but I couldn't keep up.

Two hours later we turned around, our summit attempt abandoned after five hard-fought days of climbing. A lifetime goal became the newest addition to the dusty, cluttered shelf of abandoned dreams.

I'd climbed thousands of mountains and I'd never trained. I'd earned sponsorships and attention and money as a climber. And I'd never trained. I'd outpaced partners, put up first ascents, gone sixty hours up the steepest, iciest wall in North America. And I'd never trained. Now I had to turn around on the biggest, highest, hardest mountain I'd ever attempted—because I had never trained.

When I came home I found a coach and I started training. Six months later I was sick, IVs in my veins, fever on my brow. I didn't eat for twenty-one days

Kílian Jornet runs down the Täschhorn, Switzerland. Photo: Steve House and went from 165 pounds to 135 pounds. Once I started to come around, Scott Johnston—my friend, climbing partner, and a former World Cup cross-country ski racer—called me over to his house and cooked a hamburger.

Sitting it in front of me, he said, "You know why you got sick, right? She [your coach] doesn't understand climbing; she doesn't understand what goes into your job. She overtrained you. Badly. You have to layer training volume on gradually."

So began my first of thousands of lessons on endurance training and physiology, lessons that eventually would become our first book together, *Training for the New Alpinism*. Needless to say, Scott became my coach. My fitness blossomed. Less than two years later, I turned pro climber—no other work. My climbing career went world-class, and I never found myself overtrained, ill, or injured again. Until I fell 100 feet from a mountain in Canada.

I like to say that the only people who are not enthusiastic about training are those who haven't trained correctly. The only people who hate lunges are those who've never done enough of them to experience what strong legs feel like on the trail. The only ones who hate long, slow, aerobic capacity–building runs and skis are those who have never known what it feels like to sail up the mountain, nose to the wind, with ease. Relaxed, poised, moving fast and flying.

The fitness world is a minefield of snake-oil salesmen, fads, and claims that are too good to be true that are just that. While I recovered from my fall, healing dozens of fractures, punctured lungs, and a shaken identity, Scott and I began to try to answer the most common question I got as a professional climber: How do you train? When we published *Training for the New Alpinism* in 2014, its success far exceeded our expectations. We'd figured on enough alpinists to sell maybe 1,000 copies. We sold 50,000.

Eventually we learned that we had been right. Fifty thousand alpinists did not buy our book. Ten thousand did, with the other 40,000 copies going to mountain runners, ski mountaineers, and skimo racers who lacked a training guide of their own and figured alpinism was the closest thing. They bought in, literally and figuratively, to the no-nonsense, no-fads, no-promises approach of *Training for the New Alpinism*.

I met Kílian Jornet in my home mountains in early winter of 2014. He and Emelie Forsberg were there to ski some of the famous Colorado powder. We teamed up and I guided them to a classic steep descent near Telluride—the San Joaquin Couloir. We skinned from the valley at the first December light, scrambled up the shoulder, and were back in the valley before noon. At the bakery, we ate muffins, our first food of the day, and Kílian told me how much he'd enjoyed *Training for the New Alpinism*. I told him how surprised we'd been by the response, and by the adoption of the book by so many mountain athletes.

Steve House and Kílian Jornet on top of the Täschhorn, Switzerland. Photo: Steve House Collection

"Yes," he said. "There's nothing like it for us."

"We should write that book together!" I almost shouted. Kílian had told me about his university studies in exercise physiology earlier that morning while we were skinning.

Kílian demurred. "I don't want to write," he said, then excused himself to do another workout, steep Zone 3 intervals.

On the drive home I called Scott and a plan was born. At the 14,000-foot camp on Denali that June, I shared our progress with Kílian. That August, with an outline, a publishing agreement, and a lot of emails, Kílian and I met again, this time in Zermatt, Switzerland. We squeezed in some peak-bagging—nothing technical. Fortunately for me, fresh snow blanketed the Alps that August; I had the impossible task of trying to keep up with Kílian on steep trails and ridges. We spent three rainy days camped in my van, frying up big pans of rösti (Swiss potatoes and cheese) and discussing the book, training techniques and their relative value, training mistakes, how to organize and present so much information, and more. Our only problem was parking the van someplace acceptable to the Swiss.

Armed with Kílian's insights, Scott wrote, and wrote, and shared drafts with the two of us. Our network of advisors grew; Luke Nelson and Mike Foote joined as trusted reviewers. In the meantime, our business, Uphill Athlete, was growing—more site visits, more questions, more requests for training plans and coaching. When the book deadline was a distant date it was easy to attend to more pressing challenges. As the deadline neared, Scott immersed himself in writing, and the conversations among the three of us became more frequent. We addressed the same questions we have grappled with for years now: How deep do we go into physiology? How do we teach enough material that people can truly self-coach? How do we address complications such as the power needed for a vertical-kilometer race and the aerobic capacity needed for the Tor des Géants?

The final result: my climbing-training journey and Scott's thirty-plus years of athletic and coaching experience, combined with the insights from Kílian and his years in the snow and on the trail. Everything we learned while writing *Training for the New Alpinism*, and all we continue to learn through writing training plans, coaching climbers, coaching skimo racers, and coaching mountain runners—it is in your hands. *Training for the Uphill Athlete* is a distillation of hundreds of thousands of hours of racing, training, and coaching experience. Just as *Training for the New Alpinism* was built on applying conventional sport methodologies to the unconventional sport of climbing big mountains, this book, too, targets athletes in unconventional sports but uses many of the training methods developed and thoroughly tested in the conventional endurance sports.

This book is a carefully selected blend of information aimed at empowering you to make informed decisions using a proven structure of established knowledge.

We know this works because everything in this book is what Scott, Kílian, and I each have lived—from being world-class athletes to becoming world-class coaches and moderators of a top online training resource.

The book also includes stories from other athletes besides Kílian. Do not be tempted to match these athletes' or Kílian's training (volume, technique, or most other aspects of their training). Instead, try to understand the theory behind what they are saying and the workouts they describe and apply the same principles at your own level. Blindly copying the workouts of world-class athletes is a bad idea.

Training for the Uphill Athlete is the anti-fad. It contains proven training knowledge that you can apply to yourself, so you can get better, every day for decades to come. The only promise is that of smart, hard, consistent work. So please read carefully, make informed training decisions, and get out with your nose to the wind. Enjoy the power of the uphill athlete.

See you in the mountains,

Steve House
Ridgway, Colorado
May 2018

CHAPTER ONE

How to Use This Book

The three sports of mountain running, skimo, and ski mountaineering (skimo and ski mountaineering differ in the tempo and hence intensity of uphill skinning due to the weight of the equipment needed for ski mountaineering) are complementary in most of the demands made on the body. Many skiers run for training and increasingly, runners are finding their way to skiing as a fun and valuable addition to their training. All three of us have used the complementary nature of these sports for many years. It was only natural to combine the topics of training for each into one book. Where the three sports' training converges, we try as much as possible to combine them in the discussion. Where differences cause the training to diverge, we make clear why and how to apply different training techniques. Despite the heavy emphasis on competition, the methods explained in this book work equally well for the recreational level or noncompetitive mountain athlete too. Your body faces the same physiological limitations regardless of whether you have a race number on or are only interested in the more solitary challenges of a big day in the mountains. We think both sets of readers can learn from these pages.

We wrote this book to share three lifetimes of knowledge and experience on the science and methodology of endurance training. But we need to start with a disclaimer: Collectively, the three of us have made all the training mistakes, and a few of them more than once. We know from painful firsthand experience just as much about how *not* to train effectively as we have learned about how to train correctly. There are many more ways to train wrong than right. While learning from your own mistakes is the best teacher, it is painful and, perhaps more importantly, a terrible waste of time. By steering you around the pitfalls

Mountain running is a great complement to skimo racing and ski mountaineering. Hal Koerner running ridges in Castle Valley, Utah. Photo: Dan Patitucci

and danger areas, we hope to save you wasted days and weeks, to say nothing of the disappointment and even heartbreak of ineffective training. Over the accumulated decades that we have been training and coaching, we have been able to refine our approach and want to share this with you.

Physical training is often presented in a very formulaic, cookbook approach: follow the recipe and your fitness cake will turn out perfectly. The reality is that we are very complex organisms and identical recipes will not work for everyone. Of course, all humans share the same physiological systems, but the responses (both in quantity and in kind) to identical training inputs can vary a great deal among any group. Said another way: If a coach has ten athletes perform the identical training session and measures certain physiologic systems, he will see ten different responses. While it is important to give general guidelines and training prescriptions for athletes to follow, unless they have some idea of their individual response, they will be flying blind.

As a consequence, this book is not a cookbook. You will not find a recipe to make one cake. What you will find is an explanation of some of the underlying systems that account for the variation among athletes. You'll learn how to determine what your individual responses to training are and what they mean. In total, our goal is to convey a set of tools that will allow you to operate within a fairly narrow range of training options but be able to individualize the minutiae of training so that it yields the best possible results for you.

The study of any subject is best managed within a framework. We hope to establish that framework within which to dissect what is a complex topic. Even though none of this material is difficult to grasp, there are a lot of topics covered and there's no way one could absorb all the information presented here in one reading. It is our hope that you will use this book as a reference manual to guide your training over many seasons as you apply what we have spent decades learning. No single part of the book is meant to stand alone. Each section is supported by the preceding ones and as such, supports the subsequent parts.

We start in Section One with a look at The Physiological Basis of Endurance Training. Despite the limitations of idealized scientific studies, they can still provide us with a better understanding of the *whys* even if they can't help us so much with the *whats* or *hows*. These *whats* and *hows* are where endurance training becomes more art than science. And like any subject, it can be learned only by study. This section provides the theoretical framework for what is to come.

In Section Two, The Methodology of Endurance Training, we identify and explain numerous concepts that, if understood and applied correctly, will make you a better athlete or coach. These are the tools in your toolbox. Knowing which tool is appropriate for each task is what makes the artisan a master. The range of topics here is as broad as it is deep and this is the area of the book that will likely be the one you go back to over and over again to refresh your knowledge.

As fall transitions to winter, Davide Stofie does a ski-bounding workout in Passo Oclini in South Tyrol, Italy. Photo: Federico Modica

Section Three is devoted to Strength Training for the Uphill Athlete. We demystify strength in terms most applicable to endurance athletes (as opposed to weight lifters).

By the time we get to Section Four we will be focusing on How to Train. Here we talk about ways to categorize, design, and structure workouts, as well as how to mix them depending on what you want to achieve. All the previous information will be brought into play as we show you how to progress from very basic but essential aerobic-capacity building to the speed endurance required for your event. And finally, we offer several example plans you can use for guidance or apply directly to your own training.

The Physiological Basis of Endurance Training

CHAPTER TWO

The Physiology of Endurance

"All models are wrong. Some are useful."

– George Box, mathematician

Please don't rush past these important pages in your hurry to see what workouts you need to do to beat Kílian in his next race. You won't find that info. As we say numerous times throughout this book: There is no single recipe for maximizing fitness. Only you can optimize the ideal plan for yourself. We have included these early chapters exactly because of this individualistic nature of training. We *know* that you need to have this information to make good decisions about your training plans.

In this chapter we will take a look at the physiology underlying the production of the energy that enables endurance exercise. It will help to have a basic understanding of how this physiology works so that you have an intellectual framework for making decisions when it comes to designing and implementing your own or others' training. Blindly following any training scheme without understanding the underlying principles will handicap, if not undermine, your performance. What follows is a look at the physiology of endurance.

The Evolution of Endurance

For thousands of years, several coevolving protohuman species existed alongside and competed with *Homo sapiens* as hunter-gatherers. The fact that we won the

Previous page: Luke Nelson runs along the northern reaches of Eysturoy Island, Faroe Islands, Denmark. Photo: Kelvin Trautman

Opposite: Kílian Jornet running in the mountains above Åndalsnes, Romsdal, Norway, two weeks before heading to Cho Oyu and Everest in March 2017. Photo: Jordi Saragossa

evolutionary contest is partly due to our species' endurance capacity. Scarcity was the normal state of affairs, and competing for and obtaining calories required a lot of time and a lot of calories, so protoman's metabolism evolved to give those with the most economical use of those precious calories the best chance to pass their genes on to the next generation.

Most days involved many hours of low-intensity searching for food with occasional short bursts of high-intensity effort sprinkled in during the heat of the hunt or when the need arose to overpower a targeted prey or out-compete another predator or scavenger. The components of the early hominid diet were high in animal fats and protein, with a smattering of complex carbohydrates from plant sources. Early man's physiology developed a caloric fuel tank in the form of fat stores (both intramuscular and subcutaneous) for the excess calories consumed during times of plenty. Fat could sustain our ancestors on those long days of hunting and gathering as well as give a greater chance for survival in times of food shortages. We evolved to store fat in vast quantities to last many hungry days before incurring permanent damage to our bodies. The well-adapted hunter-gatherer could go longer between meals and operate at higher intensities on fats, thus conserving the scarce and precious stores of glycogen that came from carbohydrates. Another interesting aspect of this topic is our ability to recover muscle glycogen stores quickly during periods of rest (e.g., hours instead of days). This is not the case for most other animal species; thus, we could run our prey into the ground since we needed only a short period of time to recover.

Fat is a complex molecule with many chemical bonds, each bond containing usable energy. Even a lean, well-trained endurance athlete can carry up to 100,000 calories stored as readily accessible fat. Carbohydrates, being simpler molecules with less energetic bonds, yield about half the calories per gram than fat does. We have a much smaller carbohydrate-storage capacity of no more than 2,000 calories, even in a well-trained athlete. Our body's strategy during times of excess is to store any calories we consume, from whatever source, as fat. On a purely physiological level, this explains the modern-day obesity epidemic; many humans consume an abundance of calorie-dense foods and are rarely exposed to food shortages.

According to one popular theory of evolutionary biology, early hominids exploited their endurance and lack of hair (which allowed them to avoid the overheating fate of their prey) to run their next meal to the point of exhaustion. This helped them rise to the top of the food chain despite their relative physical weakness. It was by virtue of their endurance that our predecessors could get close enough to kill an otherwise much more powerful animal once the prey became too tired to defend itself. The theory goes on to say that the high-protein diet resulting from successful hunts allowed increased brain capacity and complexity, and consequently, a cognitive revolution, which in turn led to all the subsequent cultural advances and evolutionary traits we have inherited. It follows then that you can read the words on this page precisely because our species survived by utilizing its inherent ability to sustain a long duration of low- to moderate-intensity work. We are the product of an evolutionary heritage that has predisposed us to endurance.

(Liedenberg, 2008; Billat, et al., 2003)

Endurance and Fatigue

Endurance training is aimed at improving our ability to run, climb, or ski for an extended period of time. Endurance is ultimately limited by our bodies' predictable fatigue response to these activities. It is fatigue that limits endurance. Because of this, a brief discussion of fatigue is in order.

Within athletics, endurance is the maximum sustainable work rate (e.g., speed or power) an athlete can maintain for the duration of an event before fatigue dictates a reduction of the work rate. Fatigue in our sports is manifested as reduced stride length and slower stride rate. Several interconnected physiological systems work together to dictate endurance performance in events of differing durations and intensities. For example, a vertical-kilometer (VK) race is run at a very different intensity than a 50K trail run. However, both events will still test whatever the specific endurance/fatigue limit of the runner allows. The type of endurance needed and the type of fatigue experienced are relative to the specific event.

We don't need an exercise scientist to tell us that fatigue causes us to slow down. Proper training makes you more fatigue resistant and thus forestalls the slowdown. We are very complex organisms and multiple adaptations to several of our bodies' systems are required to improve our resistance to fatigue. Simplifying: that dreaded reduction in speed that we all loathe is caused principally by 1) your body's inability to meet the energy demands of the exercise. This is caused by 2) a depletion or an accumulation of certain metabolites, or 3) a reduced motor nerve signal.

We can group these several physiological systems, roughly, as you see below. What we are doing is creating a model, an artificial delineation and segregation of these systems that are, in reality, intimately interconnected and interdependent. This simplified model format is commonly used in science to allow complex systems and ideas to be broken into their constituents, which may then be better understood. The art of coaching comes, in part, from an understanding of the interconnectedness and interdependence of these systems.

The Brain and Central Nervous System

The brain is the master control. It exists in a complex web of feedback and feed-forward messages. The Central Governor Theory, developed by Tim Noakes, MD, PhD, postulates that the brain is the ultimate arbiter of fatigue and regulator of endurance. Despite not being able to physically locate the "governor" inside the brain, this model currently does the best job of explaining all of the limitations of endurance performance. In brief, it states that no matter the source or type of fatigue, the response of the brain is always the same: a reduction of muscle activation (reduced power output), causing you to slow down. The theory goes on to say (and some evidence suggests) that training results in raising of the governor's limit so more work can be done before the state of alarm is reached and the governor kicks in.

The Oxygen-Delivery System

The heart, lungs, and blood vessels make up the oxygen-delivery system responsible for supplying oxygen (O_2) to all the cells of the body, including our primary focus: the working skeletal muscles.

Lungs. While we may feel as if we are "out of breath" during strenuous exercise, healthy lungs are actually overbuilt for our needs and have more than adequate gas-exchange capabilities. Human lungs have the surface area of one side of a tennis court.

Heart. From an O_2-delivery standpoint, many scientific investigations have shown that the heart's pumping capacity is the biggest limiter to O_2 delivery in healthy people. However, while the lungs do not adapt after puberty, the heart *can be trained to increase its output for each beat*, which means an increased output of O_2 and improved O_2 delivery to the muscles. This adaptability is limited by your genetics and history of endurance training. The heart reaches full maturation during adolescence, adapting fastest and to the greatest extent during this period. Young, as well as older, untrained individuals can see rapid and significant changes in the heart's stroke volume because the heart muscle is very trainable; but, only up to a genetically predetermined limit. This stroke-volume limitation ultimately sets the absolute upper limit for O_2 delivery and hence becomes a limit to aerobic power output. Athletically mature individuals (those with long endurance-training history) will see small, if any, changes in stroke volume due to training.

Oxygen-Utilization System (Aerobic Metabolic System)

The rate at which your muscles can utilize the O_2 that is delivered to them is another primary determinant of endurance performance. This capacity for O_2 utilization is also the most highly trainable system in the endurance arsenal. It is dependent on the aerobic qualities of the muscles, which can be improved for many years, well into athletic maturity. We'll dig pretty deep into this vital component later in this chapter, so for now, remember that this is the main focus of most endurance training and, to a very large extent, endurance is the consequence of upgrading the aerobic metabolic system with the application of the correct training stimuli.

Muscular System

This is where we can no longer ignore the interplay of the above systems. The brain, through the motor nervous system, controls which muscle fibers are recruited and the duration of their activation. As mentioned above, the particular metabolic qualities that those muscles are adapted for (or not adapted for) play a commanding role in endurance. Different training practices influence which muscle fibers are recruited to do the work and the training stimulus those fibers receive. Long-duration training improves the aerobic qualities primarily of the slow-twitch (ST) fibers. Shorter, high-intensity training improves the anaerobic (or glycolytic) qualities primarily of the fast-twitch (FT) fibers.

Fatigue resistance is the desired outcome of endurance training. Effective endurance training works by causing fatigue to the systems described above. This in turn induces adaptations to occur with these systems. Because these systems are interconnected, monodirectional training (e.g., training primarily one system) will, after some time, inevitably yield diminishing returns. An athlete experiences this as a plateau, and in the worst cases, a degradation, in performance.

The Factors That Determine Endurance Performance

Many factors come together to determine how you will perform in any endurance situation.

Conventional wisdom and research give credence to the notion that endurance performance is supported on a tripod of three main attributes:

1) VO_2 Max: VO_2 max is defined as the maximum volume of oxygen you are capable of taking up and utilizing during intense exercise. This quantity is measured in milliliters of oxygen used in a minute, divided by the body weight (in kilograms). This gives an aerobic power-to-weight ratio and is written as ml/kg/min. This quality is one that responds best to training in the young or the undertrained and can be difficult to change in the well trained. See the "Misunderstanding VO_2 Max" sidebar on pages 56 and 57.

VO_2 max is the product of the heart's output and oxygen utilization of the skeletal muscles. Increasing the working muscle mass results in more oxygen use. Sports like cross-country skiing and skimo, which use all four limbs for propulsion, place a big demand for oxygen delivery from the heart. This results in skiers often having very high VO_2 max measurements. Untrained men and women typically show

(continued on page 32)

Making the Decision

Janelle Smiley

My husband, Mark, and I were walking along a valley road in the Alps, twenty-one days into what would ultimately be a thirty-six-day ski traverse of the range. Of the three women who'd started out as part of our international team, I was the last remaining.

I looked over at Mark. "Do you realize that if I finish this, I'll be the first woman to cross the Alps on skis?"

He lit up with excitement. "Janelle, we are doing this!" he exclaimed. Right then, I made the decision that quitting was not an option. I was going to keep touring unless something maimed me. Before that moment, I was just trying to survive from one day to the next. Now, for the first time all trip, reaching the goal felt real.

Earlier that winter, Mark and I had been invited to join a group of seven athletes—a mix of alpinists and skimo racers—to ski from Vienna, Austria, to Nice, France. It seemed like a dream come true: to be on my skis for up to forty days crossing an entire range.

Ski touring is by far my favorite thing to do, and this big objective would call on both my racing and climbing backgrounds. It was a challenge beyond my ability and beyond what I thought was possible. In my heart I wanted it, but I wasn't convinced I could do it. I'd never gone more than seven days without a rest day, and now I'd hammer for five to six weeks without rest. Could my body handle the workload?

We met our five teammates for the first time during a one-day orientation in January. There were three men—an Austrian, a German, and a Swiss, who were skimo racers—and two women, a Spanish runner and an Italian alpinist. Alpinists and racers don't

necessarily look at the mountains with the same mindset; whereas racers are all about speed, alpinists tend to be about teamwork and managing terrain with an eye for safety. Mark's more of an alpinist, and I straddle the two disciplines.

The team dynamics were tense from the get-go, when the skimo boys—all German speakers—took off from the start line at race pace. As a group, we'd agreed to break the route planning into four sections and then share those plans in advance, which they neglected to do. Two of the skimo boys had planned the first section of the route with race pace in mind. So when they headed out at top speed, speaking a language I didn't understand, I was flying blind. I couldn't take part in any critical decision-making, and I didn't know where I was going except for a line I'd received the night before on my GPS.

The first week was chaotic—a series of ten- to fifteen-hour days spent chasing the racers in whiteout conditions and high winds. If you had to pee or change a layer, they were gone; if you were to fall into a crevasse or break a ski, they'd already be halfway down the mountain. I couldn't do much more than get through each day.

I felt out of control, but I didn't want to quit. I kept going out of curiosity; I wondered when I would break, either mentally or physically. To help manage the mental component, I shifted my mindset to gratitude. I had to find something to be grateful for, otherwise my mind would take me down a destructive hole and I didn't have the mental capacity to go there with so many external stressors.

Janelle Smiley, somewhere in France ... or maybe Italy ... on day twenty-nine of Der Lange Weg (The Long Trail), an iconic ski tour that's reputed to be the world's longest, traversing the Alps from Vienna, Austria, to the beach in Nice, France. The team Janelle was part of succeeded in breaking the forty-day record—set in 1971—by more than three days. Photo: Mark Smiley

Philipp Reiter crossing underneath the north face of the Matterhorn on the biggest day (74 kilometers and 4,500 meters of climbing) of Der Lange Weg 2018 during a significant storm. Photo: Mark Smiley

The group broke up twice that week over differences in attitude and approach, especially toward risk tolerance, but each time we were able to stitch ourselves back together in the interest of pushing on.

Our numbers did eventually dwindle: First the Spanish runner dropped out because she was uncomfortable with the style of travel and its associated dangers. Later the Italian alpinist withdrew due to an overuse injury.

My mental fatigue throughout those first seven days was overwhelming. I'd take my boots off at the end of each day and wonder how I was going to get up the next day and put them on again. Then I'd get up the next morning, decide to put my boots on, and start moving. After a few steps, my body knew what to do and my mind followed along. By the eighth day my body had grown used to the routine of the workload.

We covered so much ground—up mountains, down mountains, through valleys that sometimes expanded, sometimes narrowed. Clouds swirled and danced around the peaks. As the days inched by, I felt my mind quieting. On grades that were perfect for a gentle downhill glide, slow and controlled as if I were on an escalator, I'd watch the mountains go by and do nothing but enjoy their beauty. I fell into trances looking at the snow passing underneath my skis.

I decided to surrender myself to the circumstances— to these strangers in our group, to the mountains, to the variable conditions and harsh weather. I decided to *like* things that were otherwise uncomfortable or frustrating. Instead of turning my back to the wind, I faced into it, making me feel alive. I developed a giddy appreciation for the warmth of my protective layers while in a whiteout. I chose to be thankful for an abrasive teammate; if it hadn't been for his constant pushing, I might never have glimpsed what's possible inside this body and this mind. I continually made the decision to find the good in each situation. I had to— it's what carried me through.

On day twenty-one, when I made the decision to complete the traverse, my curiosity to see if I could do it turned into belief that I would. Fifteen days later, our now-five-person team walked into Nice, skis strapped to our packs. We'd averaged about 35 miles and 8,500 vertical feet each day.

This traverse of the Alps magnified my thinking about how our decisions dictate our outcomes. I still can't believe we pulled it off, but I'd decided I was going to finish, and with that decision came success. ■

Janelle Smiley *grew up in Aspen, Colorado, and lives in Jackson Hole, Wyoming. She is a six-time ski mountaineering champion; she has completed forty-eight of the fifty classic climbs of North America; and in 2018 she became the first woman to cross the Alps on skis. She currently works as a mindset performance coach, helping individuals bring body, spirit, mind, and heart into alignment toward performance goals. Learn more at janellesmiley.com.*

values in the range of 35–40 ml/kg/min and 25–30 ml/kg/min, respectively. The highest VO_2 max values for males are in the range of 90–95 ml/kg/min. Values for females are generally lower due to a lower percentage of lean muscle mass to whole body weight and top out at about 80. To put our aerobic power into context: Thoroughbred race horses usually have about 180 ml/kg/min. Top-flight racing dogs will exceed 250 ml/kg/min. Hummingbirds come in at over 600 ml/kg/min, and the winner is the honey bee with the equivalent of over 6,000 ml/kg/min. Recall our early reference to our relative weakness in the animal kingdom.

2) Movement Economy: Just like a car's fuel economy, this is the measure of how much energy it costs you to move your body a certain distance. And, like your car, it is specifically related to the energy used to move your body at a certain speed (race pace). Intuitively you can see that if athlete A uses 20 percent more energy than athlete B to cover one kilometer in four minutes, then A will need more endurance to sustain that energy output or will tire more quickly. Movement economy combines two components: the mechanical (technique) and the metabolic. Good technique implies an efficient use of the energy needed to move at a given speed. Less energy is wasted compared to inefficient movements. Watch the graceful, floating running style of a sub-2:10 marathoner compared to the plodding of the four-hour competitor. This is technical economy. Metabolic economy, the second component, while invisible to our eyes, is equally as important. Metabolic economy is dictated by the metabolic pathway our muscles use to produce the energy required to sustain the exercise intensity. As we dive into the metabolic systems in the next few pages, you will see that not all metabolism has the same energetic costs or creates the same stress on the system. Keep in mind that both the technical and metabolic components of economy are highly trainable.

3) Lactate Threshold: Also known by the confusing array of names listed below* (thank you, exercise science!). We will discuss Lactate Threshold (LT) in much more detail soon, but for now understand that this is the maximum work rate you can sustain for a long duration. If that sounds like endurance to you, then you're correct. The pace at LT is the best predictor of endurance performance. The rate at which your metabolism can sustainably produce energy is the single largest determinant of your endurance. Luckily, this metabolic effect is perhaps the most adaptable to training of the endurance tripod. Because of this, we're going to roll up our sleeves and dive right in.

*They are, in no particular order, Anaerobic Threshold, Functional Threshold Power or Pace, Critical Pace, Critical Speed, Critical Power, and Second Ventilatory Threshold. While the meaning and even existence of these terms engender serious scientific dispute, we lump them here as having the same basic meaning to the coach and athlete. They represent the maximum pace sustainable for an extended (30–60 minutes) duration.

Endurance Seen Through the Metabolic Lens

We're going to deal first with the last of the above-mentioned three legs of the performance tripod. We will return to the others shortly.

In a healthy and well-trained individual engaging in events lasting less than two hours, endurance is limited primarily by the rate at which the muscle cells can sustainably produce the energy required for their contractions. For events lasting longer than two hours, fuel stores become the major limiter (we'll cover that soon). Training for endurance then must involve optimally organizing and executing a long-term series of workouts to increase the muscles' sustainable metabolic output. Keep this basic idea in mind as we move through the book, and it will help frame why smart training needs to be targeted at enhancing specific metabolic processes rather than the popular, but misguided, method of going as hard as you can, for as long as you can, as often as you can.

ATP's Role in Endurance

What enables endurance? More specifically: What powers the muscular work that propels you up the mountain? The answer can be stated in three letters: ATP.

Adenosine Triphosphate is a short-term energy-storage molecule used by every cell in your body. If any one molecule can be singled out for its life-giving force, ATP is it. The energy released when an ATP molecule's chemical bonds are broken is what powers all the functions of cellular life.

Most importantly for athletes, ATP's energy is used to power muscular contractions. The more work you do, the more ATP you use. The ATP supply, specifically its rate of production, thereby becomes the limiter of the speed you can run for durations exceeding a few seconds. Endurance athletes need to not only improve the rate of metabolic turnover of ATP but, at the same time, they need to ensure that these higher rates can be sustained for as long as needed for their specific event.

Metabolism: The Energy Transfer from Food to Physical Work

The energy in the food you eat is not directly available to the body. The digestive process first breaks down the food into its macronutrients: fat, carbohydrate, and protein. These fats and carbohydrates are further converted into various fatty acids and sugars that can then be used to produce ATP.

Metabolism is the term for the biochemical process of breaking down the molecular bonds in the fats and sugars for the energy needed to assemble the molecule ATP. Think of metabolism as a miniature ATP recycling plant in the

muscle cells. After ATP is broken apart to extract the energy needed for muscle contraction, the metabolic recycling plant using the energy from food reassembles the ATP molecules so the whole process can keep going.

It's a good thing we recycle ATP because it is a heavy molecule. The amount of ATP required to sustain a resting metabolic rate for one day would amount to about 60–70 kilograms. Basically an extra "you" if we had to store and carry all this ATP.

THE TWO METABOLIC PATHWAYS TO ATP PRODUCTION

We rely on two unique metabolic pathways to create ATP. Each process involves multistep chemical reactions. Each pathway yields a different quantity of ATP per unit of the fuel (carbohydrates and fat) consumed. Each pathway can change its rate to meet energy demands up to its maximum limit or capacity. That capacity is what we aim to increase with training.

Anaerobic Glycolysis Metabolic Pathway

This is the method by which carbohydrates fuel you. All the various sugars contained in carbohydrates are converted to glucose by the liver and either used directly or stored in the muscles or liver as glycogen for later use. Anaerobic glycolysis is a ten-step process of breaking apart the glycogen molecule. This process does not require oxygen (hence the modifier anaerobic). The end products of anaerobic glycolysis are a molecule called pyruvate along with two ATP molecules. This ATP can be directly put to use for energy. But it is the fate of that pyruvate that is central to the discussion of endurance, so we'll come back to it after a look at the other metabolic pathway we use to make ATP. Glycolysis can proceed at a much faster rate than the aerobic process (following) so is used when ATP demand is high and exceeds what can be supplied with aerobic metabolism, such as during high-intensity exercise like running very fast.

Aerobic Metabolism

This complex, multistep chemical process occurs inside the muscle cell's mitochondria (see sidebar on page 37) and requires oxygen in order to function. It can use those pyruvate molecules produced by the anaerobic metabolic path mentioned above as well as fat to produce additional ATP. Aerobic metabolism produces roughly seventeen times the amount of ATP that the anaerobic path makes but is a more complex and hence slower process. The relative amounts of fat and sugar that contribute to its prodigious ATP output will become central to our understanding of how training methods affect endurance*. For many years it was thought that, due to its slow rate of ATP synthesis, the aerobic metabolism was incapable of meeting

Previous page: Michele Maccabelli logs vertical meters and long hours by skiing up to Punta Rocca in the Dolomites, Italy. Photo: Martina Valmassoi

the demands of high-energy outputs. Recent studies on elite endurance athletes have shown that the aerobic contribution can be significant right up to the highest intensities in well-trained and fat-adapted athletes. More on this later.

Aerobic metabolism can utilize protein to produce energy. But protein contributes only a tiny fraction of the energy used for exercise.

Mitochondria

Mitochondria are tiny organelles in every cell of your body (besides blood cells) and are considered the powerhouse of the cell. These tiny factories use oxygen in the air you breathe to produce ATP, the essential fuel of life in all the cells of your body. Slow-twitch muscle fibers have a high concentration of mitochondria, predisposing them to aerobic metabolism. This makes these muscles more fatigue resistant than their fast-twitch neighbors. Fast-twitch muscles are less aerobically endowed and have to rely more upon anaerobic metabolism to produce their power.

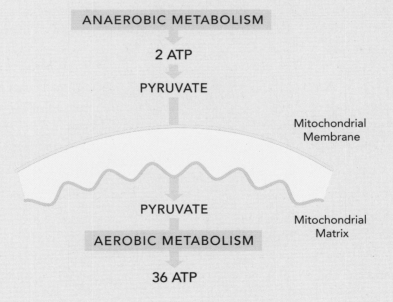

Fig. 2.1 Mitochondria and the Fate of Pyruvate

Pyruvate, the end product of anaerobic metabolism (glycolysis), can either linger in the cytosol of the muscle cell—a metabolic dead end—or it can be transported into the mitochondria where it undergoes aerobic metabolism, which produces a great deal more ATP (energy for muscle work). Mitochondria are the powerhouses of life in all our cells.

The Role of Metabolism in Endurance

The connection between muscle contractions (mechanical work), ATP (chemical energy), and metabolism can now be made more clearly:

- ATP fuels muscle work and is consumed in the process.

- Metabolism is the process whereby ATP is resynthesized.

- The faster ATP is recycled, the more work you can do per second.

- Work per second is defined as power.

- More ATP = more muscle power.

- More muscle power = more speed (all things being equal).

At its most elemental, then: Endurance is the ability to sustain rapid ATP production, predominately through aerobic means, for long durations. When an athlete improves endurance, he or she is able to maintain higher speeds for a longer time. This is how we described the quality "endurance" earlier. It should make more sense to you now.

Because endurance training should enhance the athlete's ability to produce greater speed for longer periods, it follows that endurance training improves the athlete's ability to sustain a high rate of ATP turnover. With this

Energy In from Food

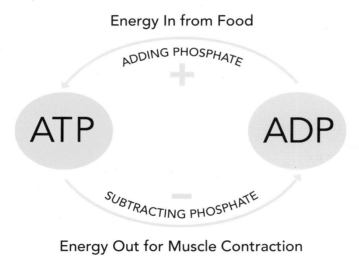

Energy Out for Muscle Contraction

Fig. 2.2 The ATP Recycling Plant
Metabolism functions as a recycling plant. The energy contained in the food you eat is used to recombine the severed phosphate molecule with ADP (adenosine diphosphate), making ATP again. The cleaving of this third phosphate from ATP provides the energy of life—and the energy to run or ski. This continual recycling of ATP, to ADP, and back to ATP is called metabolism. If we couldn't recycle ATP, we'd need massive ATP stores (tens of kilograms) just to get through a normal day, let alone one filled with heavy exercise.

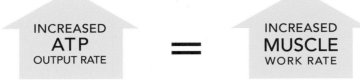

Fig. 2.3 More ATP Equals More Power
The role of all endurance training is to increase the output of the ATP recycling process. The faster your metabolism can recycle ATP, the faster you can run.

understanding of the relationship between metabolism and endurance we can focus our attention more closely on how we can manipulate our metabolism's role in endurance through training.

Now you understand why we say: *Endurance is a metabolic quality.*

Lactate Dynamics, the Key to Endurance

You are much closer to understanding the basis of how you will make coaching and training decisions in the future. You understand why our metabolism determines our endurance. The two metabolic pathways differ in distinct ways. The next several pages will explain these distinctions. This will help you understand how and why you must apply the correct training stimulus to get the desired training effect.

Metabolic Mix

Whether sitting still or running a race, both the anaerobic and aerobic metabolic engines are contributing to your body's energy needs. The relative contribution from each is a result of several factors:

- Intensity: As intensity (speed) increases, so does the demand for ATP. At a certain speed, the aerobic system alone will no longer be able to meet the ATP demands, and ATP from glycolysis will begin to dominate overall energy output.

- Genetics: Those naturally endowed with more slow-twitch muscle fibers will be able to produce more ATP aerobically as speed increases and delay the dominance of glycolysis.

- Training history: Those with a history of high-volume, low- to moderate-intensity training will have slow-twitch muscles that are aerobically well adapted and will be able to sustain higher speeds aerobically. Likewise, those with a history of higher-intensity training will have predisposed their metabolism toward the anaerobic/carbohydrates use.

Lactic Acid: A Metabolic Fork in the Road

Let's revisit the pyruvate molecule that is the end result of anaerobic glycolysis. Pyruvate can take one of two roads: It can enter the muscle cell's mitochondria and undergo additional aerobic metabolism, ultimately producing about thirty-six additional ATP—which is a very desirable outcome from the endurance standpoint. Or, it can linger outside the mitochondrial membrane, in the muscle cell's cytosol, where it will be converted into lactic acid. You have no doubt heard about lactic acid. Its notoriety, while deserved, is somewhat overblown. Lactic acid plays the central role in determining an athlete's endurance, so we will spend some time becoming familiar with it.

When a lactic acid molecule is formed from pyruvate, it immediately dissociates into a lactate molecule and a hydrogen ion. Lactate and pyruvate molecules contain useful energy in their chemical bonds. That hydrogen ion, however, is an acid and its unchecked accumulation will upset the delicate acid/base balance of the cell. The conversion of pyruvate into lactate and that hydrogen ion represents a temporary dead-end to the metabolic process. Excess accumulation of these metabolites causes a reduction of glycolytic ATP production. We feel this as muscular fatigue and a slowing of our pace.

The fate of pyruvate then is a crucial determinant of the endurance performance of an athlete. If pyruvate takes the aerobic fork in the metabolic road and enters the mitochondria, it can produce a bunch of valuable energy to further sustain physical activity. If it takes the dead-end fork in the road, ATP production will eventually slow (eventually halting) and so will the athlete. This is one mechanism of fatigue that all endurance athletes are familiar with.

WHAT DETERMINES THE FATE OF PYRUVATE?

At lower intensities, pyruvate production is small enough that most of it can be taken into the aerobic pathway. In this case the athlete can be said to be operating below his or her aerobic capacity. In other words, there is enough mitochondrial capacity to take up and utilize the pyruvate production, thus preventing its accumulation and subsequent conversion to lactate. In these conditions, lactate production is minimal. Importantly for the endurance athlete, the aerobic metabolism of fat produces no lactate, and its potential metabolic downside. This makes fat the more desirable fuel in endurance sports.

To support higher intensity (speed), ATP turnover must increase. This increase will come from the breakdown of fats and, increasingly, sugars. As speed

Lactate as a Problem
Limited Slow Twitch Equals Aerobic Deficiency

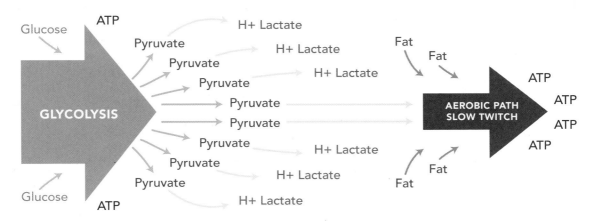

Fig. 2.4 Lactate as a Problem

A metabolic traffic jam occurs when an athlete has insufficient aerobic capacity to shuttle all the pyruvate being produced by the anaerobic metabolism back into the mitochondria where it can contribute to ATP output. This pyruvate back-up converts to lactate and a hydrogen ion and increases the acidity of the cell thereby slowing glycolysis. We perceive this disruption of cellular homeostasis as fatigue—our pace slows and our effort increases.

Lactate as a Benefit
Abundant Slow Twitch Equals High Aerobic Capacity

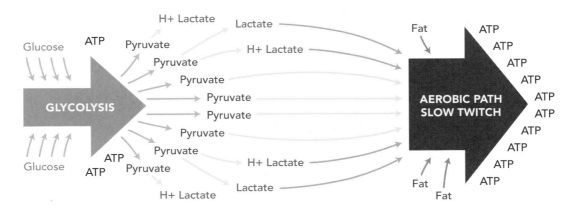

Fig. 2.5 Lactate as a Benefit

An athlete with a high aerobic capacity has the ability to utilize this pyruvate, preventing the back-up and consequent repercussions. Cellular homeostasis can be maintained at higher energy outputs. This means you can run faster for longer before needing to slow down.

continues to increase and meeting the ATP demand relies more on glycolysis, the capacity of the slow-twitch muscle mitochondria to take up pyruvate will eventually be overwhelmed, and lactate and hydrogen ions will accumulate at an ever-increasing rate. The following three scenarios will each play out as you move up the intensity/speed scale from low to high:

1) Low Speed: At low intensities, predominately using slow-twitch (ST) muscle fibers, the rate of ATP production is modest. Much of the ATP will come from the breakdown of fats, which does not produce any lactate. ST fibers have a high concentration of mitochondria and are able to take up the pyruvate from glycolysis for the aerobic metabolism. Any lactate produced can be used in the heart, liver, and adjacent active ST muscles. At this speed, you are operating below your aerobic threshold (AeT). (See note 1 on page 44.) This intensity range represents Zones 1 and 2 in the conventional five-zone system. Zones will be explained in more detail in the Methodology Section on page 84.

2) Medium Speed: As more speed is called for, you begin to recruit some fast-twitch (FT) muscle fibers. FT fibers contract with more force, so are used when extra force is needed. They are less fatigue resistant than ST muscles because they are not as well endowed with mitochondria. They rely largely on glycolysis for their energy needs, producing more pyruvate. So, pyruvate and lactate begin to accumulate. As long as the rate of accumulation does not exceed the rate of removal (by the ST muscles, heart, and liver), this speed can be maintained. This is a comfortably hard pace sustainable for many minutes up to one hour. This intensity range equates to Zone 3.

3) High Speed: As ATP turnover continues to increase, you eventually pass a critical point called the Lactate Threshold (LT). (See note 2 on page 44.) Beyond this intensity, the rate of pyruvate/lactate production exceeds its removal rate. This lactate accumulation—plus those pesky hydrogen ions increasing the acidity of the muscle—plays havoc with the happy condition known as homeostasis in the muscle cells. This leads to a slowing of glycolytic ATP production required by those very same FT fibers that are allowing the high speed. The drop in ATP output means the pace must slow after a few minutes of operating above the LT. If not by consciously slowing, the pace will involuntarily slow. Every endurance athlete has experienced this form of fatigue. This intensity is covered by Zones 4 and 5.

The three numbered paragraphs above, corresponding to different metabolic states inside the working muscles, should form the basis for every zone system used for grading intensities. We will explain a metabolically based zone system later in the book.

Lactate as a Measure of Intensity

Since lactate accumulates in lockstep with pyruvate, it can serve as a marker of intensity. More lactate hanging around in the blood indicates a higher production of pyruvate by the glycolytic metabolism. Coaches and sports scientists have long used lactate concentrations in the bl as a measure of intensity. The subject of lactate measurements can, and does, fill a book (*The Science of Winning* by Jan Olbrecht).

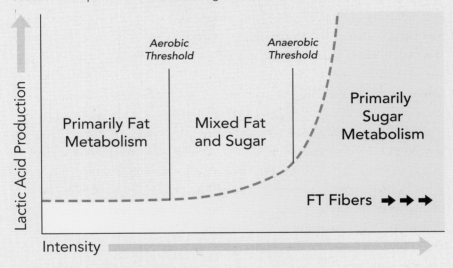

Fig. 2.6 Intensity Versus Lactate
Increasing exercise intensity is fueled by increasing sugar metabolism (glycolysis) and a corresponding drop in the percentage of fat used for fuel (lipolysis). This increased glycolysis means an increase in lactate production. By measuring blood lactate levels, one can get a good idea of where an athlete is operating along this metabolic spectrum.

Fig. 2.7 ST and FTa, and FTb Muscle Fibers
Shown above is the relative amounts of slow- (red) and fast-twitch (pink) muscle fibers in the leg muscles of different running populations. While genetics play a significant role, the type of training one engages in year after year also seems to influence this mix.

Measuring blood lactate after a climb of Mount Bachelor in Oregon. Photo: Steve House Collection

Note 1

The aerobic capacity is indicated by the athlete's AeT. This is sometimes also referred to as Onset of Blood Lactate Accumulation because it is the intensity of work at which blood lactate concentration rises 1mMol/L above baseline levels. This point is best determined with a laboratory test. We'll cover these testing procedures in the Methodology Section on page 152.

Note 2

Lactate Threshold, Anaerobic Threshold, Maximum Lactate Steady State, and Functional Threshold are all names for essentially the same metabolic event. Just remember that this is where lactate production exceeds its rate of removal. Beyond this point, exercise can be sustained for only a few minutes at a time before fatigue will cause slowing.

Summary of Metabolism as It Relates to Endurance

Before moving on to the implications of what you've just read, let's take a moment to restate what we know so far:

- Your speed is a function of your muscles' ATP recycling rate.

- ATP can be produced via aerobic and anaerobic metabolic processes.

- Anaerobic and aerobic ATP output combine to meet energy demands.

- The aerobic pathway is mainly used during lower-intensity, long-duration exercise.

- The anaerobic pathway should* be mainly used for higher intensities.

- The anaerobic ATP production is limited in duration by the accumulation of pyruvate/lactate.

- *ST muscle takes up pyruvate and uses it for fuel in aerobic metabolism.* We'll come back to this very important point.

Should, because as we will soon see, many developing athletes must rely on glycolysis even at very low intensities. We will address the topic of Aerobic Deficiency Syndrome in a few pages.

The Implications for Performance

From a performance standpoint, the metabolic fate of that pyruvate molecule is the essential event in determining endurance in events longer than two minutes. Physiologically speaking, the end goal of most endurance training should be to encourage that pyruvate molecule to enter the mitochondria and undergo aerobic metabolism. How that is achieved is what we are going to spend most of the rest of this chapter and much of this book looking at.

We have talked at length about the pyruvate molecule and this may be confusing to some. "Isn't lactic acid the demon of performance?" Lactic acid gets a bad rap, but it's worth remembering that *lactic acid only forms when pyruvate hangs around and does not enter the aerobic metabolism.* So, elevated pyruvate means elevated lactate. With proper training, you can increase the speed/intensity at which pyruvate production exceeds its removal into the mitochondria, causing that accumulation of lactate. This point is defined as the Lactate Threshold (LT). Elevating the speed at the LT results in improved endurance performance.

We have previously defined this intensity as the LT. There are two ways we can raise the LT:

1. Reduce the production of pyruvate/lactate in the first place.

2. Increase the rate of removal of pyruvate/lactate from the working muscles.

Each of these requires different and to some extent mutually exclusive forms of training. This is the reason that understanding something about intensity and its effect on the metabolic systems with regard to endurance is important if you hope to maximize your performance.

Step 1: Reduce the Production of Lactate

Goal number one for any endurance athlete must be to maximize his or her aerobic capacity. Aerobic capacity is a term used to describe the limit of the aerobic metabolism to produce ATP. It is largely a function of the adaptations in muscle cells and is enhanced through training. Athletes with a high aerobic capacity can maintain relatively high speeds over long distances with a low metabolic cost since they create much of the needed ATP using the aerobic pathway, minimizing lactate accumulation. This system of training was described in detail by Soviet sport scientist Dr. Yuri Verkhoshansky in his article "Block Training System for Middle Distance Runners" in the mid-1980s, in which he coined the term "anti-glycolytic" principle of training.

AEROBIC DEFICIENCY SYNDROME (ADS)

When you exceed the capacity of the aerobic system's production of ATP, you will be forced to rely upon the anaerobic system to make up the deficit. As you now know, that reliance will be self-limiting and you will have to slow down sooner or later. Athletes who overuse high-intensity training methods will usually have a low AeT because their aerobic metabolism has become detrained while the anaerobic metabolic pathway has become very powerful. We call this condition Aerobic Deficiency Syndrome (ADS). It is reflected in a slow (often shockingly slow) AeT pace. These athletes will be dismayed that despite all their hard training, they still can barely get above a jog or even a walk before exceeding their AeT. These athletes typically respond with disbelief: How can they possibly be getting any training benefit from such a slow (perhaps even walking) pace? This low aerobic capacity has only one cure: a high volume of low- to moderate-intensity training. To determine if you have ADS, read "The Ten Percent Test" sidebar on page 91.

To give credit where credit is due: ADS was first described to the author Scott Johnston in 1985 by the coiner of the term, Dr. Phil Maffetone, as he explained a common phenomenon he saw frequently among runners. We have used it since to describe the condition of underdeveloped aerobic conditioning. Maffetone is perhaps most famous as the coach of the legendary Ironman triathlete Mark Allen. He places a very high emphasis on rectifying ADS and maximizing this aerobic capacity during the crucial aerobic base-building period before the athlete engages in high-intensity training. He calls this period the Patience Phase, with good reason. Aerobic adaptations are slow to accumulate, and patience is needed. Approach this training with diligence rather than ferocity, and patience will be rewarded.

This condition is more common than you might think, and we'll examine one athlete's case.

ANTIGLYCOLYTIC TRAINING METHOD

Duration is the single biggest stimulus from any exercise. The more you train a certain way (within your ability to absorb the work), the more adaptation you

A Real-World Example of ADS

We often see athletes who have ADS. Some of them have even managed to achieve fairly high levels of performance despite this handicap. For successful athletes it can be a difficult pill to swallow that they need to take what appears to be a step backward in order to move forward.

A few years ago a top US Cross Country skier approached Scott Johnston for help with his training. Despite his very impressive VO_2 max test numbers (90 ml/kg/min), this skier was suffering from ADS due to the type of training he had been using. His performance progression had stagnated for two years, which is typical for athletes relying too heavily on medium- and high-intensity (Z3–Z4) training. The adjustment to his training was drastic and meant taking two steps backward before he could advance. The hardest thing about this training prescription was the embarrassment he felt by training so slowly.

With the new training Johnston prescribed, during his four-month base period the skier managed to drop his AeT pace from 8:30/mile (5:16/km) to 6:15/mile (3:53/km), with a corresponding heart rate increase from 135 to 158. This occurred as a result of doing *all* his aerobic training under his AeT. His speed was no longer embarrassingly slow and represented a dramatic improvement. He was a fast responder due to the high volume of this low-intensity training he was able to do. He had gotten his aerobic house in order. The implications of an improved AeT for him were:

- He could produce a lot more power/speed aerobically than he could when he started this program. His metabolic efficiency (fat adaptation) was greatly improved. His body experienced less metabolic stress and more energy per gram of fuel.

- His basic aerobic training pace moved significantly closer to his racing pace, so even his easy base training had a more race-specific training effect. This improved mechanical economy at race pace because he was spending more time near to race pace.

- Because of the higher speed that he could now sustain, the neuromuscular stress of even Z2 workouts went up, thus requiring more recovery training between these AeT sessions. In the beginning of this program he could do six to seven Z2 workouts a week; by the end, that had to drop to one or two per week because the pace was now *fast*.

Once this aerobic foundation was created, the next year the skier added more race-specific training. He greatly improved his personal bests and was selected for the 2014 Olympic team.

The lesson is that, if you suffer from ADS, then the AeT pace is going to be very slow and very far from race pace. Accept that this is all the power your aerobic system is capable of in its current deficient state. No ifs, ands, or buts about it. Faking it by running at a faster pace to soothe your ego will only slow the development of that aerobic engine.

Michele Maccabelli finding long runs on the ridges of Monte Baldo, above Malcesine, Lake Garda, Italy. Photo: Martina Valmassoi

will cause. One of the strongest training stimuli for increasing the aerobic recycling rate of ATP is glycogen depletion in the ST muscles. This is best done with long-duration, low- to moderate-intensity training sessions because it takes long durations to deplete the glycogen of these already well-endurance-adapted ST muscle fibers. Short, high-intensity training depletes the glycogen in the less well aerobically adapted FT fibers but is too short in duration to have much training effect on the important ST fibers. This is why endurance training has traditionally contained so much relatively easy intensity training volume.

If you want to reduce the production of lactate, both by using more fat for fuel and by being able to produce more power from the aerobic system, you need to do a lot of long-duration, low-intensity work. This is the reason the common classic training method across all endurance sports is called building an aerobic base. An athlete with low aerobic capacity (small aerobic base) can never fully maximize his or her endurance performance no matter how much high-intensity training is done.

Step 2: Increase the Rate of Lactate Removal from the Working Muscles

When the ability to run or ski fast without producing much lactate is maximized, we can focus on lactate removal improving endurance.

REMOVING LACTATE: THE LACTATE SHUTTLE

From an endurance performance standpoint, being able to make use of pyruvate/lactate in muscles is one of the most important training adaptations. Research done by Dr. George Brooks of the University of California, Berkeley, describes a mechanism he termed the "lactate shuttle," which remains the best explanation for determining the LT. He found several proteins that are responsible for intra- and inter-cellular lactate transport. These transporters shuttle the lactate from where it is accumulating and causing problems to the mitochondria in adjacent ST muscles, where it can be utilized as fuel.

Increased levels of lactate in the muscles acts to signal an increase in these transporter proteins. So, high-intensity training that causes lactate accumulation enhances the lactate-shuttle process.

This mechanism has gone a long way to explaining what endurance coaches have noticed for decades: When a large volume of low- to moderate-intensity (aerobic) work is judiciously supplemented with higher-intensity training, that improves the shuttle process, and hence the highest LT and the best endurance results are obtained. *The key point of misunderstanding for many athletes and coaches is how much of the high-intensity training to apply.* It turns out to be much less than is commonly assumed and we'll come back to this soon.

When steps 1 and 2 are combined, you can see how aerobic metabolism acts like a vacuum cleaner sucking up all that pyruvate and thus reducing the accumulation of lactate. Slow-twitch muscles are the ones with the biggest vacuum cleaners, so they are responsible for the bulk of the lactate removal in the working muscles. The greater the ST fibers' aerobic capacity, the bigger the vacuum cleaner.

Enhanced Lactate Removal and Endurance: The Metabolic Key to Improving Endurance Performance

Given the above discussion, the best method for improving endurance is to do these two things:

1. Increase your aerobic capacity (make a bigger vacuum cleaner) so that you have a larger reservoir of mitochondria in the ST muscles to take up and use excess pyruvate and lactate to produce useful energy.

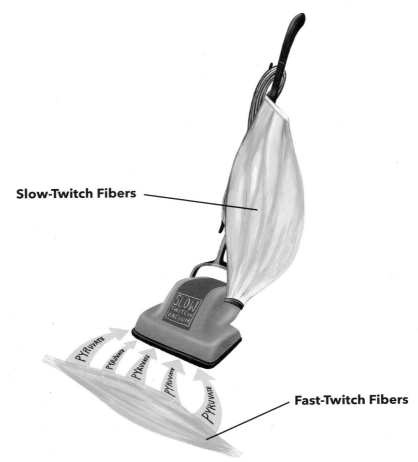

Slow-Twitch Fibers

Fast-Twitch Fibers

Fig. 2.8 A Bigger Vacuum
The aerobic metabolism, especially in the slow-twitch muscles, acts like a vacuum cleaner, sucking up all the "bad" by-products of anaerobic metabolism. The bigger the capacity of this vacuum cleaner (aerobic capacity), the more anaerobic metabolism can contribute to the overall energy production before you slow down.

2. Improve the lactate-shuttle mechanism (make the vacuum more powerful) so lactate that is produced at higher intensities can be effectively converted into useful energy rather than gum up the ATP works.

Achieving this is tricky because doing the first requires one type of training, while doing the second requires a very different kind. Increasing aerobic capacity requires a high volume of low- to moderate-intensity work. Improving the lactate shuttle, on the other hand, requires high-intensity training that produces significant levels of lactate.

The bigger and stronger the vacuum cleaner, the more high-intensity work that can be done, and the more power/speed an athlete can produce for longer.

Nickels and Dimes

Rod Bien

I have run eighteen 100-mile races at this point, and I have thrown up during every single one. Not just once per race, but ten to twenty times per race. When my body becomes stressed, my GI system is the first to shut down. I have tried numerous diet and fueling techniques, but all end with the same result: vomiting. Instead of dropping from races—or quitting the sport altogether—I've come to accept this physiological quirk of mine. In fact, I'm so used to it now that sometimes I'll throw up right in stride.

I've been running ultramarathons for eighteen years, as well as numerous adventure runs. In all of these events, but especially during mountainous 100-milers, I have experienced physical and mental difficulties—including the now-familiar indigestion. But my desire to keep going always overrides any discomfort. I've had to DNF (did not finish) only once, and that was because I felt the outcome could be dangerous.

I've noticed that when runners DNF, their reasons for quitting are often very specific and numerous, with the excuses accumulating from the very beginning. The pity party may start innocently enough: "I had the wrong breakfast." Then a couple miles in: "The trails are muddier than expected and I'm slipping around." At mile 15: "I have a hot spot on my heel." At mile 30: "My crew didn't meet me and I didn't get my normal gels." As the race or adventure goes on and mental strength diminishes further, all of these little items start to "nickel and dime" a runner toward a DNF.

One of the intangibles that separates better endurance athletes from the rest is how we handle these challenges—small to serious—that almost everyone will experience at some point during a difficult race or climb. Around mile 35 during the 2011 San Diego 100, my stomach rebelled, and I dropped from second place to fourth or fifth. Demoralized, I started consulting the "rolodex of excuses" for why I should quit. But instead of settling on one, I decided to problem-solve my way out

of the situation. I nibbled on some avocado. I was still sick, but I concentrated on the fact that I was running through some beautiful mountains and just needed to get to the next aid station, which was five or so miles away. Once I got there, I felt a touch better and focused on the goal of pressing on until the sun started to fade. Once the shadows lengthened, my spirits and stomach rebounded. I ended up finishing in second place with a great race to look back on. Driving away those negative thoughts and concentrating on short-term goals and positive reinforcement got me through.

Part of being a successful endurance athlete is recognizing and trying to solve challenges without letting them stack up against you mentally and physically. It all comes down to outlook: Do you let the trivial issues overwhelm you, or do you shrug them off and keep going? Do you DNF due to stomach issues, or do you throw up without breaking stride?

Going into an endurance event, you need to have a positive attitude and excitement about the adventure—but it is also extremely important to understand that there will be many physical and mental obstacles you will have to overcome along the way. While dealing with them, keep going and do not allow yourself to sink into a dark mental place. Don't nickel and dime yourself out of the satisfaction of crossing the finish line.

By eliminating the negative voices in your head and concentrating instead on what you *can* control, you'll develop the mental tenacity to become a stronger, and ultimately faster, endurance athlete. ▪

Rod Bien is a Patagonia Ambassador and one of the top masters ultrarunners in the country. He has been racing ultramarathons since 2001 and has won races and set course records at 50Ks, 50-milers, and 100-mile endurance races. He is a husband, a business owner, and a very proud parent of three kids.

The greater the aerobic capacity of your ST muscles, the more lactate that can be shuttled into those muscles' mitochondria and turned into useful energy. This allows you to sustain higher outputs for longer. You have no doubt heard the various terms of adulation heaped on amazing endurance athletes: "He has a great aerobic base" or "She has a really big motor." Now you understand the physiology behind those comments. Here is the counterintuitive rub: *To improve your high-intensity endurance you must maximize the aerobic capacity of those unsexy, low-intensity, low-power, slow-twitch fibers.*

THE ALLURE OF HIGH-INTENSITY TRAINING: THE COUNTERINTUITIVENESS OF TRAINING FOR ENDURANCE

The type of training determines the type of adaptations that are induced. The most important adaptations to lower-intensity aerobic training are structural, meaning that you grow new protein structures in your body: denser capillary beds in the trained muscles, increased mitochondrial mass, and changes to the heart. These are slow to occur and take from weeks to months to show significant changes but can continue for years, which is one reason that endurance athletes often have very long careers, continuing to improve even into their forties.

Adaptations to higher-intensity training that enhance the anaerobic metabolic output are of a functional nature. These are changes to the function of pre-existing structures. They are primarily changes in glycolytic enzyme concentrations or to the lactate transporter proteins. These adaptations occur within hours of a workout and can show significant improvements within a few days and weeks.

Due to the rapid response to high-intensity training stimuli, adaptations to this sort of training make themselves felt very quickly, especially as compared to the weeks and months of patience required before seeing significant gains in aerobic capacity. The positive reinforcement of seeing rapid gains leads many athletes and coaches to overuse high-intensity training. This stuff feels like training should feel … hard and tiring. It gives tangible and rewarding results that can be quickly seen and felt. What's not to like about that?

Training dominated by high intensity often fails in the long term to produce the desired results, not so much because the athlete is doing too much high intensity but because that person is doing too little low intensity. The final result of this strategy, usually seen after just a few very exciting and rewarding weeks of high-intensity workouts yielding big gains, is first a plateau and then a reduction in performance. This happens because those lowly, low-power ST fibers are not getting enough training stimulus and so their aerobic capacity begins to drop off. The vacuum cleaner gets smaller. Even though the aerobic capacity plays a supporting role to the anaerobic star of the show, those ST fibers' aerobic-capacity role is critical in setting the endurance limit.

Sabina Parigian rips down the trails of Longs Peak, Rocky Mountain National Park, Colorado.
Photo: Fredrik Marmsater

This performance plateau or drop is often interpreted as a need to add more intensity to the program when, in fact, just the opposite is needed. The aerobic base has eroded and endurance will not improve until that base is restored. Maintaining sufficient aerobic-capacity workouts during the high-intensity phase of the training program is essential to long-term performance gains.

The reason for this confusion is that our intuition is wrong. When an athlete nears the limits of his or her endurance, it is at higher intensity that the limits become apparent. When you can't sustain the pace as the hill becomes steeper or you are unable to make your legs respond to the challenge of outkicking your rival in the last minutes of the race, it is quite intuitive to assume that the endurance limitation is caused by some deficiency in your training at this race-specific intensity. Intuition tells us that if we are weak at something, we need to train it more.

But not if the vacuum cleaner is too small.

The Big Motor

From the above you can see that both low- and high-intensity training are important to proper endurance training. Neither alone will suffice to maximize performance. It is the balance and timing of the application of these methods that is so critical to this end goal.

Increasing aerobic capacity has major benefits to all athletes regardless of the duration of the event they are training for.

- Most interesting to endurance athletes is that increasing the size of the aerobic vacuum as defined by the AeT will have very direct and profound effects on increasing the athlete's endurance or LT (the power of the vacuum).

- You will also see improved recovery rates from workouts, including very high-intensity ones. As you will read in Section Two, this is one of Kílian's biggest advantages over most other athletes. Having a big aerobic motor will allow you to handle more anaerobic work. Since all training adaptations occur in direct relation to the amount of time spent doing the training, this means you can do even more anaerobic work as a result of improving your aerobic system.

The whole fitness house needs to be constructed from the ground up on a solid foundation (high AeT) before worrying too much about the upper floors.

The Other Two Legs of the Endurance Tripod: Economy and VO2 Max

We have devoted a lot of ink on the previous pages to the role of metabolism in endurance. It may seem like we are giving short shrift to movement economy and VO_2 max, but we will address them now in greater detail.

MOVEMENT ECONOMY: THE VALUE OF GOOD TECHNIQUE

The mechanical component of economy, often referred to as technique, varies from sport to sport and is best learned from visual cues and direct coaching, not through a book.

Technique in anything, from playing the piano to running fast on rough terrain, is something that is acquired only through many, many hours of specific practice. We learn through repetition, creating motor nerve–firing patterns that result in the desired movements. By patterns we mean that many thousands of motor units (nerve/muscle combinations) must fire in exactly the right sequence with the right magnitudes to create these skills that we are seeking.

If your training is predominated by running on flat surfaces in urban areas, your nervous system gets hardwired for these types of movement patterns. The motor cortex of your brain has developed a library of what are called engrams to choose from for these firing patterns. It is quite good and efficient and will automatically select the appropriate engram without any conscious effort. But when you switch to rough terrain or downhills or skimo, the library shelves are nearly empty, and you are forced to use the conscious control of your frontal cortex for running. This conscious control is slower, less efficient, and tiring.

Simply stated, you have to run a lot of downhills and rough terrain to become proficient at them. You will not learn to play Chopin by practicing "Chopsticks." You'll have to expand your engram library, which is challenging and time-consuming. But there is no other way to do this. For a discussion of metabolic economy see the next section on fat adaptation.

VO2 MAX

The VO_2 max is the least trainable of the three endurance components for the well trained. Of the three, it has the poorest correlation to performance. The preponderance of evidence indicates that, to a large extent, it is genetically predetermined. Since you can't choose your parents, it seems rather futile to become overly concerned with this number. We have coached athletes competing at the highest levels of international competition who have had exceptionally high VO_2 max values and turned in rather modest results. At the same time, in the same races, we have coached athletes who had rather modest VO_2 max values and achieved exceptional results. This extensive firsthand experience has made us skeptical of the importance placed on a single number as a predictor of performance. More importantly, it should cast doubt on the common practice of training to improve VO_2 max (rather than performance). There is a lot written about the subject, and we provide the sidebar on the next page for those who seek additional info.

Fat Adaptation, Metabolic Economy, and Endurance

Coaches of endurance athletes, across a broad spectrum of sports, have known for many years that well-trained athletes can utilize fats better and at higher (even maximum) intensities than studies indicated was theoretically possible. It was assumed by coaches that this adaptation was an important key to success in endurance sports. But research didn't support the coaches' experiences. Several new scientific studies now substantiate the coaches' beliefs. (See note 3 on page 61 for studies.)

How the Scientists Got It Wrong

For decades, exercise scientists have told us that fat played a significant role in total energy use only during low- to moderate-intensity exercise, and that fat's contribution was theoretically capped at a paltry amount. This meant that energy demand for high-intensity exercise could be met only with carbohydrates. They were partly correct: this is what happens in the general population and, to a lesser extent, in the recreationally trained athletes who were the subjects of their tests.

Misunderstanding VO$_2$ Max

With the way that the term VO$_2$ max gets tossed around in both the popular media and in scientific studies on endurance, you could be forgiven for thinking that this single number was a direct proxy for endurance performance. It might then come as a surprise to learn that VO$_2$ max is not a measure of endurance at all.

Measuring the maximum amount of oxygen that the body could take up and utilize was first carried out by Archibald Hill, PhD, in the early twentieth century. Both the measure itself and the theory that he proposed for the limits it places on human performance won him the Nobel Prize in 1922 and have formed the basis for a huge portion of the study of exercise for the past one hundred years. However, neither Hill's theory nor the numerical quantity were intended to describe endurance. It is only recently that the popular press, and by extension the public, came to see VO$_2$ max as somehow identical to, and indicative of, endurance performance. Despite its popularity as a metric, this single number, while it does relate to endurance potential, does not define aerobic endurance.

The term VO$_2$ max defines the upper limit of an individual's aerobic power. It is analogous to maximum strength in some important ways. Just as you can't exert your maximum strength many times in succession, VO$_2$ max can't be sustained for long. But, just as having a high maximum strength would give you a greater potential of lifting a lighter weight many times in succession (muscular endurance), having a high VO$_2$ max also allows for the potential to develop a high level of aerobic endurance.

Research suggests that the most important factor in determining VO$_2$ max is the amount of oxygen-carrying blood ejected with each heartbeat, called stroke volume.

Long-term studies, along with personal testing by author Johnston, have demonstrated that elite endurance athletes will often show no change (and even a reduction) in VO$_2$ max during a competition season and over their careers while at the same time seeing marked improvements in performance. These gains in performance come from improved economy and speed at the LT (the other two legs of the endurance tripod).

VO$_2$ max is what is called a "first wave response" to training. This term refers to a quality that tends to develop quickly in the young and those new to endurance training. That is largely because the heart responds rapidly to training and increases the aforementioned stroke volume and other characteristics that increase the volume of blood ejected from the heart.

Many scientific studies aimed at endurance will measure changes in VO$_2$ max in test subjects after several weeks of certain training protocols. The VO$_2$ max has become the standard metric for measuring cardiovascular fitness because it is easily measured and can be compared across the test subjects as well as across populations—not because it is the best predictor of endurance. The unintended consequence of this has been to make VO$_2$ max synonymous with endurance in the minds of the lay public. Other factors that have contributed to this misunderstanding are:

- Most studies are relatively short term because it is hard to find subjects willing to engage in invasive studies lasting for months or years. So most tests use training interventions that can show results in a short time. Functional adaptations from high-intensity training occur quickly. The result is often an increase in VO$_2$ max across the study subjects.

- Most studies use recreationally active or untrained individuals since it is hard to find high-level athletes willing to forego their normal training to engage in a study. Almost any training will increase VO_2 max in an untrained population.

- The results of these tests are presented as average changes in VO_2 max. Some subjects may have seen a decrease, but as long as the average is significantly positive, the test can be held up as proof that such and such a training protocol works. The all-important individual nature of training response is not taken into consideration in these studies.

All these factors lead to an overemphasizing of VO_2 max's importance in the public's mind. Many of these studies compare some high-intensity interval training (HIIT) program against lower-intensity, continuous training protocols. This oversimplification and misunderstanding has led to a rash of training schemes promising to raise VO_2 max. Since HIIT affects systems that respond quickly and dramatically (functional adaptations), the HIIT protocols almost always come out looking like a shortcut to fitness. Mix this misunderstanding of these studies with a media bent on discovering the next new thing and a time-crunched public looking for shortcuts, and you have the perfect storm of the HIIT fitness craze. These programs, often gym-based, are social and great for getting people exercising. However, there are no world-class endurance athletes in the major sports of running, rowing, cross-country skiing, or skimo using an exclusive HIIT training program. Enough said?

High-intensity training, while important for any endurance athlete, should be used as a supplement to, and not a substitute for, aerobic base training.

The takeaways from this are important:

1) Beware whenever you read that some study "proves" that such and such HIIT methodology is "the" recipe for successful training because it raised the VO_2 max of its subjects by X percent.

2) Don't believe that there is a newly discovered shortcut to endurance fitness that only these overhyped fitness fads have discovered. If that were true, professional endurance athletes of all stripes would be beating down the doors of their local CrossFit.

3) The history of endurance training is the story of trial and error over hundreds of years by thousands of coaches and millions of athletes. While the evidence is anecdotal, the population size is so big that coaches can weed out what does and doesn't work. New stuff is tried all the time. Good ideas stay, bad ones get rejected are modified until they are good ideas. These ideas must stand the toughest test of all, the stopwatch, in the highest levels of competition.

Note:

Bassett DR Jr, Howley ET, "Limiting factors for maximum oxygen uptake and determinants of endurance performance," *Medicine & Science in Sports & Exercise* 32, no. 1 (Jan. 2000): 70–84.

This scientifically supported understanding became enshrined in sports science literature, and you will still find nutrition and exercise scientists today who are unequivocal in stating that once the athlete reaches his or her LT, fat metabolism will have ceased to contribute any energy to the overall exercise demands.

New studies (see note 3 on the following page) have shown that the rate of fat usage is much higher (up to twice as high) in well-trained athletes and can be sustained to maximum intensities, contrary to the conventional wisdom. To put this correction in perspective, that's like increasing your car's horsepower and its fuel economy at the same time!

Becoming Fat Adapted

Becoming fat adapted is one of the simplest-to-implement training prescriptions you will read in this book, and the returns from it will be significant for the effort involved. Recall from earlier that glycogen depletion is one of the most powerful training stimuli responsible for aerobic adaptations. Glycogen is depleted from the all-important ST muscles during long training sessions. Engaging in these long-duration, low-intensity workouts also enhances fat adaptation. You can boost this adaptation by doing some of your aerobic capacity–building workouts in a fasted state. If you train in the morning before consuming any calories, you will be in a mildly glycogen-depleted state. This will force your muscles to make better use of the available fat for fuel and increase their aerobic capacity. Consuming a diet reduced in carbohydrate calories and increased in fat will also accelerate fat adaptation. Athletes training more than twelve hours per week will see less effect from modifying their diet because the low-intensity training volume is providing ample stimulus for fat adaptation.

Two advantages are gained with improved fat adaptation: The first relates to fuel depletion. Fat stores, even in a lean, well-trained athlete, are virtually limitless (up to 100,000 calories of intramuscular fat). On the other hand, glycogen stores will rarely reach 2,000 calories even in the well trained. Glycogen is a critical nutrient even for the fat adapted. So much so that when you deplete your glycogen stores (bonk) the effect on performance is a dramatic and swift drop in power. Sipping from your limited glycogen reserves while guzzling from the bottomless fat gas tank enables higher outputs for a longer time before the low fuel light comes on.

The second and potentially greater performance benefit is reduced lactate production at submaximal efforts. As you know by now, the unchecked accumulation of lactate in the muscles leads to a type of short-term fatigue that most of us are

Previous page: Pierra Menta 2013, day two, when the race was routed across the wild and rarely seen Roselend side of Beaufortain. During a long, multiday stage race like the Pierra Menta, fat adaptation plays a major role in a successful finish. France. Photo: Jocelyn Chavy

How Much Fat Can Humans Use?

A Consensus View

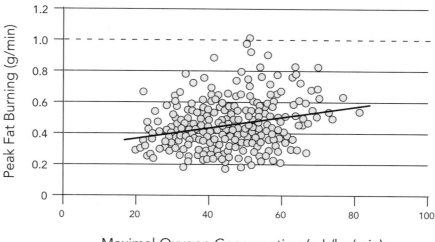

Fig. 2.9 How Scientists Got It Wrong

In the above diagram each dot represents the results of a study done on fat's contribution to metabolism at various intensities. Most of these studies were done on untrained individuals. The horizontal scale shows increasing intensity as a percentage of VO_2 max, while the vertical scale represents fat use. The sloping line shows the average fat contribution in all these studies. The dashed line shows what was considered to be the maximum possible fat use (one gram/minute), which would occur at relatively modest intensity. The dogma that at higher intensities fat's contribution to overall energy production dropped to zero was handed down over decades, even though coaches saw much higher rates of fat use among well-trained athletes.

---

painfully familiar with. You don't need to be an exercise scientist to understand that feeling—if you don't voluntarily dial back the intensity, your body will do it for you. Being able to increase your reliance on fat at higher intensity means lower lactate levels and lower perceived exertion. *Et voilá!* More economy!

Note 3

Yeo et al., "Fat adaptation in well-trained athletes: effects on cell metabolism," *Applied Physiology, Nutrition, and Metabolism* 36, no. 1 (2011).

Seiler et al., "Rethinking the role of fat oxidation: substrate utilization during high-intensity interval training in well-trained and recreationally trained runners," *British Journal of Sports Medicine* 1 (2015).

Volek et al., "Rethinking fat as a fuel for endurance exercise," *European Journal of Sport Science* 15, no. 1 (2015).

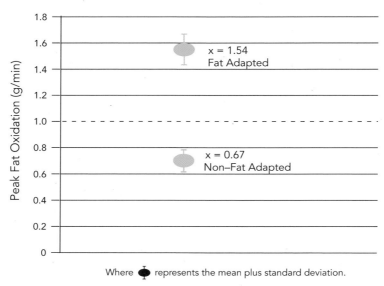

F.A.S.T.E.R. Elite Runner Study
Comparing Fat Usage During Maximum Intensity

Where ◆ represents the mean plus standard deviation.

Fig. 2.10 Fat Usage During Max-Intensity Exercise

Recent studies compared well-trained, fat-adapted endurance athletes (the average fat usage rate represented by the orange oval) to less-well-fat-adapted athletes (their average fat usage rate represented by the green oval). These studies show more than two times greater ability to use fat for energy by well-trained athletes, and they show this fat contribution continues up to much higher intensities than was previously thought possible. Fat adaptation has positive benefits for endurance athletes. Courtesy: Voltek et al.

GRAPHICAL REPRESENTATIONS OF ALL THAT WE HAVE DISCUSSED SO FAR

The charts on the next page show the interaction of the two metabolic systems. The fuel (either carbohydrate or fat) contribution is shown as a percentage of the total energy production (vertical scale) at ever-increasing intensity (horizontal scale). Blue lines represent fat's contribution. The green lines represent the carbohydrate contribution. The sum of the blue and green values at any given intensity will add to 100 percent. These charts show the different metabolic responses to exercise between athletes with different training states to illustrate the point that *endurance is a metabolic quality.*

In these graphs we use heart rate along the horizontal scale as a measure of intensity. The vertical scale is a measure of the percentage contribution of fat versus carbohydrate for fuel.

The comparison of these three charts shows the dramatic differences between the well– and not so well–endurance trained in terms of fat versus carb contributions

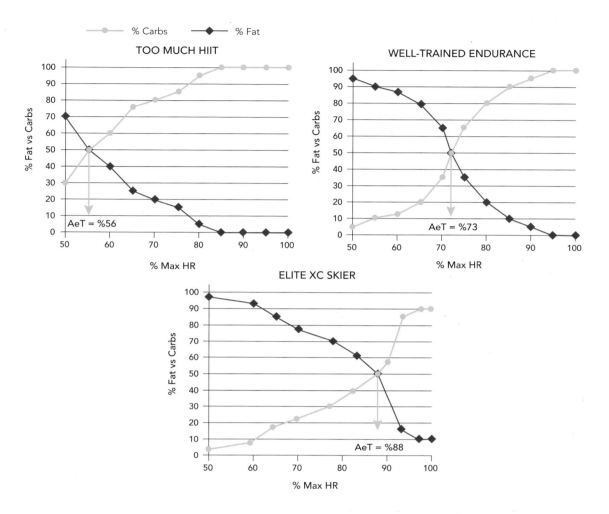

Fig. 2.11 Fat Versus Carb Burning in Athletes with Different Training Backgrounds

This figure shows the results of metabolic efficiency tests done on three different athletes: a top-ranked cross-country skier; a recreational-level competitive runner logging 40 miles/week; and an avid HIIT adherent who did three to four high-intensity interval workouts per week with no other aerobic training. They show the relative contributions from fat and glycogen at varying intensities in a running treadmill test. The green lines indicate carbohydrate use and the blue lines show fat use in the total energy use during the test. The horizontal axes show intensity as indicated by heart rate. The vertical axes show the relative percentage of each fat and carbohydrate. At any intensity the sum of fat and carb contribution will add to 100%. The orange arrow at the crossover point approximately indicates the AeT for each individual. The more the aerobic threshold is shifted to the right, the bigger the athlete's vacuum cleaner and the better his or her endurance performance will be.

at different intensities. Notice that for the cross-country skier, the aerobic (fat) contribution is larger at all intensities than it is for the other two athletes. This well-trained cross-country skier can produce much more power (ATP) from his

Janine Patitucci and Cynthia Alverson in the Italian Dolomites on a sunny summer day.
Photo: Dan Patitucci

aerobic system than the other two. The point where the blue and green lines cross usually corresponds to the AeT. The crossover point of the skier is shifted far to the right side of the chart; this indicates a very big aerobic base.

Enhancing Your Aerobic and Anaerobic Metabolic Pathways

Now that we have covered some of the basics and laid out the role metabolism plays in endurance, we are ready to talk about the principles governing the training methodologies presented in the next chapter.

By improving your ability to produce ATP faster and for longer, you can improve your endurance performance. Since the metabolic pathways are distinct, it should come as no surprise that they respond to distinctly different types of training stimuli. Understanding which stimulus to apply to achieve the desired result is the first step in understanding how to train for any event.

A strong training stimulus that is ideal for causing desirable adaptations to the aerobic system will have a negative effect on the anaerobic system. Any workout that has a powerful anaerobic training effect will diminish the aerobic system's capacity to do work. By now you should be beginning to grasp the complexity of the systems working to supply the divergent energy needs during exercise.

The complexity of our metabolic system is also the beauty of it. We are highly adaptable. We respond to the application of different training stimuli with varied adaptations that have different effects on endurance. We can bias our metabolism toward the maximum anaerobic endurance required by events ranging from one to two minutes in length, or we can bias our metabolism toward events that last many hours and even days. But we can never optimize it to both at the same time. While this is an amazing range of potential specialization, the real lesson is that we have to *target the training we do to get the outcome we desire.*

The Uphill Athlete Training Philosophy

We follow an approach to training for endurance that has stood the test of time in all of the conventional endurance sports for more than sixty years. The following is a distillation of this successful approach:

You will never maximize your endurance potential without first maximizing your basic aerobic capacity (AeT).

In the next section we'll get deep into the various ways to do the above work.

The Roots of My Athleticism

Kílian Jornet

Surrounding my house growing up were mountains and forests. I didn't see my first television until I was five years old. All the time when my younger sister and I were not in school, we would play outside together, climbing trees and jumping from rocks. It makes a big difference to be outside all the time when you are a child—to be in the outdoors, in the forest and in the snow, and get used to that kind of mountain terrain.

My mother and father were both mountain enthusiasts. My father was an alpine guide with a more traditional vision of mountaineering; he taught me technique, safety, and respect for the mountains. My mother was a longtime climber and runner, a bit more disorganized, but very experienced. She was much freer in the mountains. She liked to move fast and light.

When I was three years old, we started to do some summits as a family. We would cross-country ski up, and my parents would carry our alpine skis for the downhill. That was my introduction to ski mountaineering. By the time I was five years old, we were going up 3,000-meter peaks and practicing glacier travel with ropes, crampons, and ice axes. Around that time, I also did my first easy couloirs. In pictures from those days my helmet is so big on me that I look like a mushroom.

We backpacked across the Pyrenees—a forty-day journey—when I was ten. We did something like that every year. That's how I learned about endurance, about how to keep going over many days. By the time I was thirteen, my mother began taking me on longer outings in the mountains, and sometimes I wouldn't bring enough to eat or drink. I remember going for as many as sixteen hours without food and water, just licking water off rocks.

It was around this time that I started training for ski mountaineering. I had been doing long cycling races and 80-kilometer hut-to-hut runs, but without following any kind of a training plan. I entered the Sports Technification Centre in Catalonia, and my coach there sent me a plan every month telling me what I should do each day. There were two coaches, and it was maybe ten people for each coach. From the age of thirteen to seventeen, I learned about volume, intervals, strength, recovery, mountain conditions, and technique.

I was in school then, so I'd train early in the morning or after school, and then in the middle of the day I'd go to the gym or for a run. I used the weekends for longer training. Sometimes I'd bike to school, my skis in my backpack, and then after school I'd bike 60 kilometers to the snow, ski for two hours, and then bike home. Other days I'd run to and from school—25 kilometers each way. Many times my coach was upset with me because I was doing too much, even though I tried to convince her that the cycling was just my transportation to the training. I was very focused—obsessed, really.

I have always been good at recovering, so I was able to assimilate this high volume of work. I think it comes from when I was a kid, playing outdoors all day and doing long hikes starting when I was three.

At the start of each year at the Technification Centre, we would get tested for VO_2 max, recovery, and such things. At the beginning I didn't understand what the results meant, but I learned by talking with my coach. And I was always interested in understanding the reasons behind the workouts—like why she would have me do intervals one day, endurance another day. I'd ask her why it was important to do volume and strength. I was doing a bit more than she told me to, but I respected the interval training and the strength training she gave me. I asked, and she taught.

Kílian Jornet and his sister take a break in the Pyrenees. Photo: Kílian Jornet Collection

When I was seventeen I started university at Font-Romeu in France, taking sports science and studying anatomy and physiology. I learned the theory behind what my coach had been telling me all those years. That's when I started to train myself. In the beginning, I would make a plan for the whole year, mapping out what I would do each week. It worked well and I got good results. But as preparing for the races became more automatic, I stopped planning so far out and in so much detail. I trained more by feel, sensing if I could train more or if I needed rest, if I should push more or less. I had the background to train this way, based on how I was feeling—a lot of years of training with a coach and the knowledge I'd gained from that.

For me, training in the mountains is a hobby. Sometimes I do things for my sponsors, like traveling and photo shoots, but the training is not my job. I take it seriously, but not so seriously that I lose my love of moving fast in the mountains. ■

Kílian Jornet *defines himself as a lover of mountains. He enjoys competition, but above all, he conceives of sport as a way to discover the landscape both inside and outside of himself.*

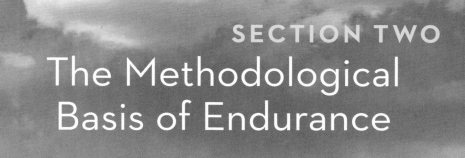

The Methodological Basis of Endurance

CHAPTER THREE

The Methodologies of Endurance Training

In the previous section we explained the basics of what enables endurance and the physiology that supports it. To establish the knowledge for this endeavor, we mentioned early in Section One that we need to ensure we're all speaking the same language. In this section we will establish a common vocabulary of terms and principles and then we'll investigate how these principles improve endurance.

A Little History

What are the methods used to increase endurance? Where do they come from? Why are they successful? Just as with the physiology of endurance, there is an intellectual framework that underlies the whole methodology of endurance training. The better handle you have on this framework, the better you can understand and apply the correct training for your situation.

Over the past one hundred years, a vast body of knowledge concerning the body's response to various forms of endurance training has been amassed. Despite the prodigious amount of scientific research examining the myriad qualities that comprise endurance, it is the coaches and not the scientists who have been at the forefront of establishing the most effective training methods. Through a trial-and-error approach, the coaches of the past have discovered what does and doesn't work. Failed training methods were discarded or modified until the most effective methods rose to the top in an evolution-like process. The scientists came along later to shed light on why those successful coaching methods work, and that in turn supports the intellectual framework. Having an understanding of some of the concepts involved will create some context for your own training decisions.

Previous page: Alyson Dimmitt Gnam and Katie Rogotzke running ridgelines in the Two Medicine region of Glacier National Park, Montana, while a wildfire flares up in the distance. Photo: Steven Gnam

Opposite: Kílian Jornet doing his aerobic-capacity training, Romsdal, Norway. Photo: Sébastien Montaz-Rosset

NOTES FROM KÍLIAN

As a result of the combination of my education in exercise physiology and working with coaches, especially as a junior, I learned what the expected result would be from every training action. What an easy run means for my fitness; what a fast-tempo run means for my fitness. And perhaps most importantly, how it all fits together. How to build a broad base before doing faster, harder work. With both book learning and learning from my coaches, I built up the knowledge that allows me to understand the expected effect on my body that will result from every training day. I understand why I can go long easily. Why I recover well. I've been a student of myself, my own reaction to training, as well as the science.

I also studied a lot about running mechanics during my school years—I really worked hard on my running technique. How to be relaxed. And when I notice I'm not efficient, I can figure out where the problem is coming from and try to fix it.

And then there is stress. I believe it is very important to appreciate how nice it is to be out running in the summers and skiing in the winters. I think it is very important that training is not stressful in and of itself. It should be fun, enjoyable, with good people, and in nice places. This reduction in stress is important to recovery, and therefore progress.

Become a Student of the Sport

Doing an experiment on a sample size of one (yourself) is risky and likely to be misleading. Self-coached athletes owe it to themselves to learn as much as they can about not only what methods do and don't work, but also why. Avail yourself of this knowledge base and hopefully you can avoid making unnecessary mistakes with your training. Rest assured that it has all been tried before.

Important Concepts, Terms, and Principles

Building the knowledge base with which to view training programs, and even individual workouts, allows you to think in terms of cause and effect. It gives a perspective that moves training from blindly following a recipe to making informed decisions. A great deal of coaching (especially of yourself) comes down to artfully applying certain time-tested methods. As with other sciences, our understanding of complex systems is enhanced through the use of simplified models. While we recognize the limitations of models for their predictive ability, they are still useful for understanding systems as complex as the human body and its responses to training.

The Training Effect

"Training is not the work you do but the effect it has on your body."

– Renato Canova

When some of the physiological systems of the body move too far outside their homeostasis (comfort zone), those systems are put into a crisis state. When this destabilization is caused by a training stimulus, it triggers the start of what we have come to know as the Training Effect (see glossary). The stress of training causes certain adaptive responses to occur: first manifested as fatigue and later recognized as adaptations that enable a greater resistance to that same stress when applied later.

The concept of the Training Effect was a consequential offshoot of Hans Selye's Generalized Adaptation Syndrome. Selye, a Viennese medical doctor and chemist, coined the term *stress* as we know it today in the biological context. His theory explained, in a coherent manner, how biological stressors acted upon organisms in both beneficial and detrimental ways.

The following presents the cascade of effects occurring during and after the application of training stressors, or Training Stimuli (glossary), as it is often referred to.

Examples of the Training Effect

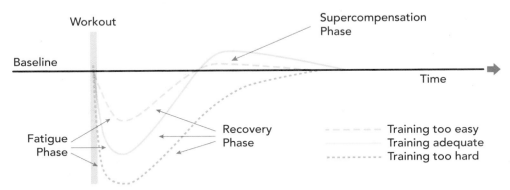

Fig. 3.1 Examples of the Training Effect

The result of a training session is fatigue and a temporarily diminished work capacity. During the recovery phase is when the adaptations occur that increase a person's fitness level. Applying a new training stimulus during the supercompensation phase will, over weeks and months, result in improved fitness. Too frequent training stimuli with insufficient recovery or too infrequently applied training stimuli with too much inactivity will both result in the adaptation process not occurring and the athlete will become less fit.

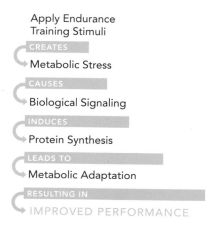

Apply Endurance
Training Stimuli

CREATES

Metabolic Stress

CAUSES

Biological Signaling

INDUCES

Protein Synthesis

LEADS TO

Metabolic Adaptation

RESULTING IN

IMPROVED PERFORMANCE

Fig. 3.2 The Endurance Training Cascade

Endurance training stimuli cause stress that triggers a cascade of events leading to improved performance. These changes go right down to the gene level. Genes are either enhanced or moderated by training stimuli.

Capacity Versus Utilization Training

Imperfect as it may be, one of the more helpful models of training is the distinction made between Capacity Training and Utilization Training. Understanding whether a workout's goal is to increase your capacity for that sort of work or to maximally utilize whatever capacity you bring to the workout can help with placing individual workouts into a plan.

Among endurance sports, USA Swimming has had the most consistent and unparalleled international success for decades. This success has caused the athletic and coaching world to take notice. Bob Bowman, most famous as Michael Phelps' coach for his entire phenomenal career, has used the terms Capacity Training and Utilization Training to describe two different types of training that swimmers can use. Here is how Bowman defines these terms:

- Capacity Training: Training that improves the *long-term* performance *potential* of the athlete. Capacity Training is commonly prioritized during the Base Period. This training acts to improve the fundamental qualities needed to support participation in the event itself and Utilization Training. As such, it is often not sport specific.

- Utilization Training: Training that improves the *near-term* performance *results* of the athlete. Utilization Training is commonly prioritized during the build-up to the competition period or the targeted event. This training models the specific demands of the event an athlete is training for.

Racers climb above the Col du Tourmalet, on the French side of the Pyrenees, during the 2018 Altitoy-Ternua race, the biggest and most popular skimo race in Spain. Photo: Davide Ferrari

A debate has raged in sports for decades: Is it more effective to focus the training of an athlete on the more general qualities (increasing capacity), with a short utilization phase before competition? Or is it better to train primarily by doing event-specific workouts that maximally utilize whatever capacity the athlete currently has?

The sport of running in the US dealt with this debate at the turn of the century after the United States' success of the 1970s and 1980s gave way to an era of disappointing results in the 1990s and early 2000s. The later era coincided with a shift by many coaches and athletes away from a capacity-oriented training system to one relying heavily on a utilization approach. Rowing had this debate back in the 1980s after a dramatic change in the coaching philosophy in Germany, which abandoned the utilization approach in favor of one based on building capacity. This switch soon led to German domination of the sport. Cross-country skiing had a similar internal debate when, in 2004, Norwegian exercise physiologist Dr. Jan Helgerud caused a sensation with his outright denunciation of Capacity Training as useless.

These two training models have been well tested by millions of athletes and thousands of coaches in the ultimate laboratory: the competitive arena. While some noteworthy holdouts exist, the approach of relying primarily upon building capacity before applying limited amounts of Utilization Training has largely won out in

Colin Haley and Sébastien Montaz-Rosset ascending the Argentière Glacier near Chamonix, France. Colin and Ben Tibbetts, supported by Sébastien and Vivian Bruchez, made the first north-south traverse of the Mont Blanc massif: 6,800 meters of climbing and 89 kilometers of ski mountaineering in 32 hours. Viewed as training, this would be considered Utilization Training. Viewed as an objective, this is a huge goal. Photo: Ben Tibbetts

this contest of ideas. Kílian's legendary ability to handle a huge volume of work (and much of it very hard) is a result of his decades of capacity-building training. It can be very tempting to try to simulate the training of elite athletes. Doing so without their years of capacity-building work will mean that you are actually doing Utilization Training. As you read on, you will see why this is not the best path to long-term gains.

Different sports use different terms to describe these concepts, but Bowman's is perhaps the simplest to understand. This is how he explains the terms.

CAPACITY TRAINING

Capacity Training increases the ability to do work in each of the various realms required for the sport. In uphill athletics (mountaineering, mountain running, ski mountaineering, and skimo), here is what we'd call Capacity Training:

- Aerobic Capacity: This training improves the main locomotive muscles' ability to produce ATP via aerobic metabolism. This results from increases in mito-chondrial mass, capillary density, aerobic enzymes, and cardiac output. This should be the top priority for all endurance athletes. An endurance athlete can never have so much aerobic capacity that it is detrimental to performance.

- Anaerobic Capacity: Increases the ability of the glycolytic metabolism to produce ATP. An endurance athlete *can* have too much anaerobic capacity, and this depends very much upon the event being trained for.

- Strength Capacity: Increases the maximum muscular force in sport-specific movements along with local muscular endurance in the main locomotive muscle groups. Greater strength is beneficial up to a point. Excessive strength can cause problems for mountain endurance athletes when they add significant muscle mass. We will discuss this in detail in the section on strength.

- Technical Capacity: Improves the economy (energy cost) of locomotion, balance, and proper movement patterning.

Notes on Capacity Training:

- Its gains in general take a long time to accrue. Its effects tend to be longer lasting than those brought about by Utilization Training.

- It usually involves training each of the above-mentioned qualities in isolation. As such, it will appear as less sport specific and more general in nature; it may not have a direct relation to the competition or event being trained for.

- It is meant to improve the performance *potential* sometime in the future and may even reduce near-term performance. It's analogous to building the Interstate highway system: Tedious and dull during the construction process and may cause a slowdown in traffic but once completed, it allows much more traffic to flow (work to be done) more quickly (utilizing one's capacity).

UTILIZATION TRAINING

Utilization Training is used to increase performance *outcomes* in the short term. For a runner or a competitive ski mountaineer, this type of training would be racing or race-specific workouts. These will maximally utilize whatever capacities the athlete currently has. Extending the Interstate analogy: It dumps a lot of fast-moving traffic on that Interstate system. If the highway system can handle the increased traffic flow, then a lot of work gets done very fast. If the highway system is still under construction with restricted speed limits, then no matter how much traffic hits the highway, the amount of work being done will be severely limited by the capacity of the roads to handle the traffic. Utilization Training is quicker acting than Capacity Training. For maximum effect, it should be sport/event specific. It is usually of an intensity that mimics the event being trained for.

Here's how Utilization Training looks by physiological system:

- Aerobic Utilization training is also called endurance training, LT training, or VO_2 max training (Zones 3, 4, and 5 in a conventional zone system). It increases the athlete's maximum sustained output. While it plays a role in all endurance training programs, this high-intensity training is especially important for events with durations under two hours where the maximum competition speeds are at and above the LT. For long-duration events, over three hours, the Aerobic Capacity and Aerobic Utilization Training are essentially the same because most of the event will be competed at speeds below the LT and nearer to the AeT.

- Anaerobic Utilization increases the fraction of the Anaerobic Capacity that can be sustained in competition. It typically involves training at speeds 5–10 percent faster than competition speeds or under a workload significantly greater than those encountered in the event for a total duration significantly less than the competition distance. This type of work has a strong training effect on muscular endurance capacity.

Notes on Utilization Training:

- Utilization Training will reduce the athlete's capacity and this effect must be offset with Capacity Training *during all phases of the training cycle.*

- The effects of Utilization Training are dynamic and volatile. While rapid gains are seen when implementing Utilization Training, they are often short lived. If you've had back-to-back awesome and horrible races, or find it difficult to string together a full season of good races, one potential cause is too much Utilization Training as compared to Capicity Training.

- Utilization Training will be necessary to enable an athlete to achieve his or her personal best. However, Utilization Training cannot be expected to have its optimal effect if the athlete's capacity is small. Think again of the Interstate highway system.

- Athletes with a large capacity can and must do much more Utilization Training to maximize results. This explains why elite athletes do more and harder training than do novices, who have less capacity. It also explains one of the most common mistakes made in training, which is for amateurs to copy the elites.

It's clear that Capacity Training and Utilization Training both have their places, and are interdependent. But it is Capacity Training that takes the majority of an athlete's time. Only when the capacity for the sort of work needed by your event is sufficient will you maximally benefit from adding Utilization Training. The result of Utilization Training, which can be astonishingly quick and seductively satisfying, is the reason that any endurance athlete is wise to take the long view. Real endurance is built from year to year, not weekly or monthly.

Next page: Katie Bono laying down some aerobic-capacity training while running the Pinnacle Peak Trail in the Tatoosh Range with Mount Rainier, Washington, in the background. Katie holds the female speed record on both Tahoma and Denali. Photo: Jason Thompson

Understanding the Language of Intensity

I monitor intensity with a heart rate monitor. However, I've been doing it so long I don't need a watch anymore; I can tell you my heart rate within a few beats per minute, simply by feel.

– Kílian Jornet

Determining the appropriate intensity for training is of the utmost importance in all endurance sports. This intensity dictates the energy systems and how many and which type of muscle fibers (ST or FT) get recruited to do the work—the effect of the training is directly related to the intensity. The goal of this discussion is to allow you to target your training to achieve the intended outcome.

Intensity can be measured with power meters in cycling and pace in road and track running. Uphill athletes train and race on a variety of terrain and conditions, which makes heart rate (HR) the only practical method of controlling intensity.

A Brief Review of the Metabolic Markers of Intensity

Aerobic Threshold (AeT)

When ventilation is slow and controlled—you can carry on a conversation without needing to catch your breath or can breathe through the nose only—aerobic metabolism is providing the majority of the energy and this intensity can be maintained for hours. This is referred to as the AeT or First Ventilatory Threshold (VT1). The rate of breathing makes a jump above this point. In the majority of endurance-trained athletes, the AeT corresponds to the point where the blood lactate concentration has risen modestly (1mMol/L) above a baseline reading to a value of about 2mMol/L.

Lactate Threshold (LT)

As the speed (intensity) increases, so does the body's energy demands. Eventually the lactate removal rate can't keep pace with the lactate production rate. This point is normally referred to as the LT. It represents the maximum intensity at which lactate levels will remain elevated but stable for up to an hour at a time. Above this intensity, lactate levels climb quickly and the athlete will eventually be forced to slow down.

Every endurance athlete knows this point. Cross it, and you know you can hold that pace for only a short time before you have to dramatically slow or stop. The LT is the best proxy for endurance. Raise it (either speed or heart rate or both), and you improve your endurance performance. Luckily, it is the most trainable of all endurance qualities.

This point corresponds well with a Second Ventilatory Threshold (VT2) where breathing suddenly becomes noticeably deeper and more rapid. Above this, conversation becomes impossible; only a few words can be spoken between breaths. Above the LT, exercise duration will be measured in seconds to minutes. The higher the intensity, the shorter the time.

A Long Road to the Same Place I Started

Dakota Jones

For my first adventure I set out to traverse a range of peaks that stood above my home. At the age of seventeen, I had just discovered that there are whole groups of people who spend their free time going as far and as fast in the mountains as possible. Recently I had come to the surprising conclusion that there was very little I'd rather do than explore wild places on foot. So, I set out on my adventure with a backpack containing some food, some water, and little else.

Four hours into the climb, I emerged from the pathless forest onto a high ridgeline dividing two major drainage basins. Ahead of me stretched the rocky spine of mountains, their sharp summits outlined against the brilliant blue sky. There were four peaks to climb, and the descent lay on their far side.

Not long after, I sat at the base of a steep wall of rock that had stymied my best efforts to climb it. Without rope, experience, or partners, I decided to descend, but not by the way I had climbed, which from this vantage seemed roundabout and overlong. Instead I hiked down into the basin below me, knowing it would drain down to the river I had crossed in the morning. In this way I embarked on my first epic.

The basin below me was calm and still, the lake reflecting the darkening clouds above. Farther on, the creek dropped off in a 300-foot waterfall, and I slid down the cliffs alongside it hanging from tree trunks clinging to the hillside and then dropping to the next one. Below that I marched through a nearly flat valley grown over with bushes taller than me and crisscrossed by invisible logs at knee level. Escaping to the grassy hillsides, I encountered swarms of blackflies that clung to every inch of exposed skin, biting painfully. I was forced to sprint along the hill, jumping between rock outcroppings like a mountain sheep. Lower down, while I was walking knee-deep in the creek, the canyon walls narrowed and became vertical, forcing me to swim through long stretches of icy water. When I reached my car after eighteen hours, dark had long since fallen and I was exhausted, dirty, scratched, and ravenously hungry. But I'd emerged, and my despair instantly transformed to elation.

Many adventures followed, until I became so accustomed to mountain travel that the word *adventure* quit being relevant. Real adventures involve uncertainty, fear, struggle, and the euphoria of overcoming them. But as I pursued a passion for movement and exploration, I got really good at running long distances—good enough to become a professional trail runner. The desire for running success started taking me out of the mountains, as I pursued specific workouts like intervals, at specific elevations, in conjunction with specific food and cross-training routines. Athletes must learn to schedule their lives so as to maximize their time doing beneficial activities (like training, eating, sleeping, etc.) and minimize time doing nonessential things (like having friends, working, and going on adventures). I became a mountain runner who spent very little time in the mountains.

My single-minded focus on running success eventually led me to injury. With a "more is better" attitude, I relied on my physical strength to carry me farther than anyone else, with the result that I played myself out in training and suffered in races. I developed a stress fracture in one foot, and after that healed I strained a hamstring, and while recovering from that I pulled my Achilles tendon. This took place over a matter of years. My career, such as it was, began to fall apart because I simply couldn't do the thing I was best known for. When I was able to train, I returned to the patterns that had injured me before, desperate for a comeback. The mountains were always in the near distance, but adventure had long since taken on a different meaning.

Dakota Jones having a great time running up La Tournette above Annecy, France. Photo: Martina Valmassoi

As you read this book, keep in mind that training to be an uphill athlete is simply a mechanism to make you more able to do what you love. Strength and preparedness will give you the tools to take advantage of opportunities, and in turn you have to remember to continue to take opportunities. It won't help you to be the greatest uphill athlete if you forget to go to the mountains and actually go uphill. I spent so much time training to be a great runner that I never got to actually run, and though my life is centered on mountain adventures, those adventures have been few and far between in recent years. The passion we all feel for exploration in wild places must be the guiding light that directs us through the confusing milieu of culture and sport. Training is important. But it is only a means of facilitating what you love. Don't forget what you are training *for*.

These days I'm trying to strip away some of the certainty in my life and go back to the attitude that sent me on an eighteen-hour hike/climb with little food and no map. I want to remember to laugh and keep moving even when I can't see the ground in front of me. I want to remember what it's like to truly have no idea what might be around the next corner, and if I'm going to make it home in time for dinner. If I train well—not more, but smarter—then I'll be prepared to deal with the unexpected, and my adventures can be adventurous again, and maybe even a little fun. There can be enjoyment in struggle, if you're willing to try something new. And there can be happiness in uncertainty, if you train for it right. At the end of the day, the point is to have a good time. ∎

Dakota Jones is a runner from Durango, Colorado, who's currently having a great time.

A Discussion of Intensity Zones

Each of the intensity HR zones described here has a specific role to play in the overall scheme of the training for any athlete in any endurance sport. The anchors for this five-zone system are the two metabolic markers we covered in the Physiology Section, AeT and LT, and are repeated in the sidebar nearby. These two markers are highly trainable, so these points are not fixed and you can expect to see your zones shift a small amount on a long-term basis due to fitness changes. By basing the scale primarily on these personal metabolic events, you will have a personalized zone distribution offering much more accuracy than those based off percentages of max heart rate. Methods of determining these two markers are addressed in Chapter Five.

Let's be clear that your metabolic response to exercise does not fit neatly into discrete zones with hard boundaries, as is implied by the zone system and chart on the opposite page. Not only is there a great deal of variation between individuals, but there is some variation from day to day for each athlete. A heart rate of 145 on a day when you are fully recovered is going to have a different training effect on the day after a hard effort. As with most of our attempts to understand the very complex human body, the zone system is a flawed model. However, it is a model that can still shed useful light on the control of intensity. Keep in mind that there is no single agreed-upon zone system. Systems range from three zones delineated only by the AeT and LT metabolic markers up to a seven-zone system

(continued on page 89)

Intensity Zone Systems

There is understandably a fair bit of confusion surrounding the several different zone systems in use. Let's start by saying that all of them are flawed to some extent. All zone systems attempt to associate heart rate with intensity. The body's response to exercise will vary from day to day depending on a number of factors—recovery state being the most powerful one affecting where an athlete's zones lie on a given day. This means that the principle metabolic markers that anchor the zones may move around by several beats per minute from day to day. Expecting the same heart rate to represent the same physiological state during every workout is a big assumption. This also should cause you to question the parsing of zones into subzones that purport to define intensity zones to within one bpm; this is what scientists call false precision. Not only are the factors just mentioned at play, but it is impossible to control the heart rate with that level of precision in real-world training. When you read about a seven-zone system, carefully consider whether it can actually aid you in your training.

We suggest using the traditional zone system described nearby, which is anchored by the two primary aerobic metabolic markers: AeT (top of Z2) and the LT (top of Z3). This gives the broad separation of the aerobic zones (Z1 and Z2) for easy to moderate training from the anaerobic zones (Z4 and Z5) where training is very hard and of shorter duration. This leaves Z3 in the middle as hard training.

	Heart Rate	Perceived Effort	Training Effect/ Purpose	Metabolism	Muscle Fiber Recruitment	Training Method
Zone 5	N/A.	Supra max, unsustainable, exhausting.	Power, speed, technique, anaerobic capacity, anaerobic endurance.	ATP/CP and glycolytic, minimal aerobic involvement.	All ST + all FT.	Interval 8–60 sec.
Zone 4	Lactate Threshold to maxHR.	Hard, max sustainable.	Maximal aerobic power, strength/ speed endurance, economy, technique.	Both aerobic and anaerobic capacities maxed out.	All ST + most FT.	Interval 30 sec–8 min.
Zone 3	AeT to Lactate Threshold.	Medium, fun-hard not exhausting.	Aerobic capacity, anaerobic capacity, lactate shuttle, economy.	Glycolytic/ anaerobic begins to dominate.	All ST + some FT.	Interval 10–20min, continuous to 60 min.
Zone 2	AeT-10% to AeT.	Moderate for those with high AeT, easy for those with low AeT.	Aerobic capacity, economy.	Aerobic-fat dominates, maximum fat utilization.	Most ST.	Continuous 30–120 min.
Zone 1	AeT-20% to AeT-10%.	Very easy to easy.	Aerobic conditioning.	Aerobic-fat.	ST.	Continuous 30 min to several hours.
Recovery	Under AeT-20%.	Light.	Recovery.	Aerobic-fat.	ST.	Continuous 20–60 min.

Fig. 3.3 The Five Training Zones

This chart shows a zone system using the AeT and LT as the significant metabolic events as anchors. It also lists the training effects, the metabolic process, and the muscle fibers that dominate each zone, and the training method used to improve this quality. The percentage ranges above and below the AeT and LT are for guidance only and should not be treated as hard boundaries. Only careful lab testing will determine these points. The Recovery Zone is not clearly defined. Its boundary with Zone 1 is indistinct depending on the recovery state of the athlete. Hence it does not get its own numeric zone designation.

Training for Mountain Running Without Mountains or Time

John Kelly

If you're reading this, then chances are that you, like me, would love to live in the mountains, or maybe you already do. I often daydream of escaping, staring longingly at the slideshow of pictures that plays in our living room, hanging where most people would have a TV. The solitude, the serenity, the scenery . . . not to mention the incredible training I could get in. But most of us can't drop everything and move to Montana.

My reality is that I live just outside of Washington, DC, with my wife and three kids, in a congested area where finding a hill with 100 feet of gain is a serious challenge. I also work a demanding job at a tech startup, leaving little time to escape to the mountains.

Most people in the ultrarunning world know me from being the winner and sole finisher of the 2017 Barkley Marathons, a race that boasted over 67,000 feet of elevation gain—more than climbing Everest twice from sea level. Without the proper terrain or time, how did I train for a race like that? Admittedly, not as effectively or enjoyably as I could have if I lived in Montana, but the results prove that it is possible.

My "letter of condolence" accepting me to the 2015 Barkley Marathons was oddly appropriate. The race had long appealed to me and held enormous personal meaning—my family has lived on the land alongside the course for more than 200 years—but to be honest I wasn't expecting to get in. The thought of finishing Barkley was like the thought I had as a kid of striking out the last batter with the bases loaded to win the World Series. But it was fun to dream about.

So there I was with my condolences, absolutely no idea what I was doing, and a nice conversation to have with my wife that started, "Yeah, so remember that thing I said I'd apply for but that almost definitely wouldn't happen?"

I had never trained for anything even remotely resembling Barkley. In my head I frantically went through all the nearby hills. There was one that went up 90 feet in half a mile, or a little slope that went up about 15 feet over 130 feet. I got on Google Earth and scanned everything around for the tightest contour lines I could find. I zeroed in on Mar Lu Ridge: it was about an hour away but had a much more appealing 500 feet up in half a mile.

So I ran them. I ran all the hills. I had no real plan, no real purpose. My mind, overwhelmed with the enormity of Barkley, latched on to the one certainty it could: must run hills. On weekday evenings, I ran the nearby hills. Weekends involved pre-dawn drives to Mar Lu Ridge, with my biggest workout going all the way past sunset: over 40 miles with about 20,000 feet of gain in single digits with a foot of snow. *Perfect miserable conditions for Barkley training!* I thought.

But in the end I still felt unprepared. And worse, it had consumed my life: evenings and weekends were spent training while my wife was home with our infant son. I managed to complete a Fun Run (three out of five loops) that year, which was an incredibly surprising result to nearly everyone. And it was actually a poor nutrition plan rather than physical training that did me in; turns out that you need a bit more than gels and energy bars for thirty-plus hours.

After that experience I knew better what I needed to do, and I knew that I could do it. In 2016 and 2017, my training focused more on time efficiency and effectiveness rather than just volume and elevation. I found a new hill nearby—95 feet in 1/20 of a mile—and used it on the weekends. I no longer lost two hours just driving.

John Kelly, snatching a page from one of the books, before becoming the winner of the Barkley Marathons, 2017, Frozen Head State Park, Tennessee. Photo: Alexis Berg

John Kelly touches the yellow gate, finishing the Barkley Marathons and becoming one of the few finishers in the race's history. John is wearing a beanie he found on the course and the remains of a garbage bag, which he used as a makeshift rain jacket. Photo: Josh Patton

On weekdays all my running was done as my commute— free in my time budget. There wasn't much elevation, but I focused on intensity to maintain the LT needed to survive sixty hours of Barkley hills. I added incline treadmill workouts on weekends so that I could be at home to free up my wife while the kids slept or played. None of these runs were as great as stepping out my back door into the mountains, but it's what I could do consistently and it allowed for more time for family.

By shifting my focus to efficiency, I actually improved the quantity by creating more time for it: my 2017 Barkley training was about 20 miles and 6,000 feet of gain more per week than in 2015. A lot of that gain was on the treadmill, which meant less of the critical but often overlooked downhill running and building of trail muscles. But otherwise my miles were higher quality, with structured workouts tailored toward Barkley's demands.

Training is an optimization problem with a complex set of constraints, unique to everyone. Very few people can spend the optimal amount of time training for mountain ultramarathons: after things like work,

family, and sleep, there simply aren't enough hours left in the day. The best anyone can do, in training or, for the most part, life in general, is to work with the conditions given. But that doesn't mean all of us with busy lives and no mountains must abandon hope; it just makes for a puzzle to solve to fit in the best-quality training possible however we can. And then like Barkley itself, when success does come, it's all the more satisfying knowing the obstacles that were overcome to achieve it. ■

John Kelly is an ultrarunning data scientist with a triathlon habit. He has won the Barkley Marathons, finished in the top ten in the men's 30-34 division at the Kona Ironman, and holds the world record for fastest marathon dressed as a video game character. He also holds a PhD from Carnegie Mellon University and works as the director of analytics at QxBranch. This proud father of three (including twins!) resides in Rockville, Maryland. Follow John's running saga at randomforestrunner.com.

that seems to split metabolic hairs with false precision. We're presenting here the most common five-zone system. Though other zone systems exist, we have found the time-tested five-zone system to be the most useful model to address real-life training decisions. Below we take a more detailed look at what is described in the five-zone chart.

RECOVERY ZONE

Below Zone 1 lies an intensity that plays a minor role in improving aerobic fitness. But, it plays a major supporting role in that it speeds recovery from the more demanding training sessions. You should feel better right after or within a few hours of completing one of these. It can be almost any form of light exercise; you may benefit most from a modality different than your primary one. One of our favorites for hammered legs is a swim. No specific duration is given in the accompanying charts because this is so individual. For some, a fifteen-minute walk before bedtime will be perfect. Some people will use daily foam rolls or yoga. Others may find a one-hour slow jog does the trick. Heart rate for recovery workouts should be at least 20 percent below the upper Zone 1 heart rate.

ZONE 1: AEROBIC CONDITIONING

This intensity forms the base for aerobic development. Undervaluing it will undermine your aerobic development. Throughout your training life, this forms the foundation upon which all higher-intensity training rests. The benefits of Zone 1 include increases in blood volume, mitochondrial mass, and capillary density and aerobic enzymes in the working muscles, all of which improve aerobic metabolism. Long workouts at this intensity also improve fat metabolism. Early on in a running program, it prepares the body for the heavy-impact loading, thus helping with injury prevention. Blood lactate concentrations for this intensity should range between less than 1 to around 1.5mMol/L. Heart rate at the top of Zone 1 will be about 10 percent below your AeT (top of Zone 2).

Aerobic Threshold Speed Is the Single Most Important Measure of a Person's Aerobic System

Without this speed being as high as possible, no amount of high-intensity work will ever give the best endurance results. Kílian understands this concept well, and even in a year with a very full race calendar his training is still dominated by low-intensity aerobic base training. Understanding this fact is critical to maximizing your long-term results.

Recall from the Physiology Section that this unglamorous aerobic base is what allows you to sustain higher speeds for longer times. World-class endurance athletes across many sports typically spend about 80–85 percent of their training volume in Z1 and Z2.

NOTES FROM KÍLIAN

In 2016, I was training a bit more than 1,300 hours. Of this, I had approximately 275 hours spent at a high intensity, mostly Zones 3 and 4, and a bit of Zone 5, almost all while racing. I did a lot of racing that year. While training, I had another 350 hours pushing a bit, comfortable but fast aerobic, Zone 3. The other 675–700 hours were all much easier at an aerobic capacity-building intensity, Zones 1 and 2. This year represented a high proportion of higher-intensity training mostly because I had a heavy race schedule. Note: This breaks out as roughly 20 percent racing, 26 percent at Zone 3, and 54 percent at Zones 1 and 2. Of course, in my younger years, especially as a teenager, I was not racing as much, so my training distribution was more heavily weighted to base aerobic-capacity work.

Duration of Zone 1 work should be a minimum of thirty minutes of continuous activity and can range up to several hours. Due to the duration, training at this intensity can be a significant aid to technique and economy training. It should account for between 50 and 70 percent of the annual aerobic training volume for all mountain athletes.

ZONE 2: AEROBIC CAPACITY

We frequently refer to the importance of the aerobic base when speaking of endurance sports; this is the key to endurance success. Zone 2 intensity requires the maximum output of the fat/oxidative (aerobic) metabolism. It has the greatest effect in raising the AeT, which is one of the most important benchmarks of aerobic development. For all but the elite-level athlete, this may be the most trainable aerobic quality. Raising it will provide the support needed to maximally improve endurance as measured by speed at the LT.

The benefits from Zone 2 training are much as they are for Zone 1, except that they accrue to a larger pool of muscle fibers due to the increased power output and hence greater muscle-fiber recruitment. Training is performed in a continuous mode with durations usually between 30 and 120 minutes. It can and should be utilized mainly through the base phase of training and plays a smaller role once higher-intensity training begins to be included in the plan as competitions near.

Those just starting aerobic training and/or those with Aerobic Deficiency Syndrome (see pages 46/47) can do almost all their aerobic base training in Zone 2 (foregoing Zone 1 completely) because their pace at this intensity is going to be slow enough that their muscles will not get too much of a beating. However, those athletes with a high AeT and whose pace at this threshold is fast will not be able to do much Zone 2 training in a week without risking overtraining. They will need to do much more of their aerobic base work in Zone 1 and even the Recovery Zone. Workouts in Zone 2 for them will be too taxing to do every day and need to be limited to one or two days per week, with a total volume of less than 10 to 15 percent of the weekly volume spent in Zone 2.

ZONE 3: ENDURANCE

While this is considered aerobic training, it is of a different nature than Zones 1 and 2. At this intensity, the increase in speed requires the muscles to up their ATP turnover. Glycolysis becomes the dominant source for ATP, both in the ST muscle fibers and as more FT fibers get recruited. Lactate levels begin to rise with the increased pace. Lactate accumulation remains at levels sustainable for up to an hour in well-trained athletes with no performance degradation. Because of the high energy demands to sustain these speeds and the duration that can be sustained at this intensity, both the aerobic and glycolytic systems get a hefty training stimulus from Zone 3 training. For the less well trained, this intensity will have a strong Muscular Endurance effect because the limit to this endurance is imposed by the aerobic capacity of those FT fibers needed to sustain this output.

The upper end of this intensity zone is defined by the LT (the speed above which lactate begins to accumulate faster than it can be removed). Beyond the LT, every athlete is operating on borrowed time and will be forced to slow the pace. Most athletes very quickly develop an intuitive sense for what this feels like.

Many people see Zone 3 training as the magic intensity, the one-stop shopping of endurance training. They assume that since this zone has such a powerful

The Ten Percent Test

Zone 3 training is most effective when the athlete has sufficient basic aerobic capacity; when the vacuum cleaner is big and powerful. How much capacity is sufficient? When you've raised your AeT to be within 10 percent (elite athletes can have a Z3 spread of 6-7 percent or only 10 beats) of your LT as measured by either heart rate or pace. With more than a 10 percent spread between thresholds, an athlete still has aerobic deficiency and needs to build more aerobic base. Those who have less than a 10 percent spread between thresholds will need to reduce or even drop Z2 training, substituting Z3 workouts.

Here's how to do the Ten Percent Test: Determine your AeT using one of the methods described on pages 152-155 (AeT Testing). Then do the LT test (see page 155).

Calculate the percentage difference between the AeT heart rate and the LT heart rate by dividing the higher heart rate by the lower heart rate. We know this is not the conventional way to calculate percentage, but it works well for our purposes.

Example: Suppose your AeT heart rate is 128 as determined by a laboratory test. Your LT hill-climb test shows an average heart rate of 150. 150/128 = 1.17. This shows that the LT heart rate is 17 percent greater than the AeT heart rate.

You still have a lot of potential to improve your aerobic base with Z1-2 and should not be too eager to move to adding Z3 or higher intensity yet.

training effect, it can be used almost exclusively to make endurance training more time efficient. Tempting as this may be, we strongly caution you to not overuse this intensity because it puts you into the Utilization Training modality, with all the associated pitfalls. Zone 3 training is seductive because it will give an immediate boost to anyone. This intensity should typically make up no more than 10 percent of the total annual training volume. For those with insufficient aerobic base development, as indicated by the Ten Percent Test (see sidebar on previous page), overuse of this intensity can easily lead to a performance decline.

ZONE 4: AEROBIC POWER

As with Zone 3 training, this is another intensity that can elicit seductively rapid gains in fitness and is a necessary component in all endurance programs. This intensity above the LT maximally utilizes both the aerobic and the glycolytic metabolism of the working muscle cells as well as the lactate removal (shuttle) mechanisms. Most of the adaptations from this training accrue quickly. You feel yourself getting noticeably fitter from workout to workout. What's not to like about such rapid gains, right? Read on.

Polarized Training

In a recent study by Stephen Seiler (see note below) that looked at how world-class endurance athletes actually trained across several sports—cross-country skiing, running, cycling, and rowing—he found just the opposite of what the popular press advises. He looked at the actual training logs of many of the world's most accomplished endurance athletes, including multiple Olympic gold medalists, world champions, and Tour de France riders. He found a striking similarity across sports when he examined how much of their training volume consisted of training below the AeT, between the AeT and the LT, and above the LT. His collation of the data from these elites who, as professionals, must choose the best training methods to remain competitive, gave a clear picture of the preferred training intensity distribution. The conclusion he drew was that they tended to train 80 percent of the time below the AeT, roughly 6 to 8 percent between AeT and LT, and 12 to 14 percent at the higher intensity above the LT. This may seem highly counterintuitive given the benefits accrued from Z3. As we mentioned in chapter two, Seiler coined the term *Polarized Training* to describe this system. Another study (see below) by Seiler has shown performance gains using Polarized Training even with recreational runners.

Notes:
Seiler, "What is best practice for training intensity and duration distribution in endurance athletes?" *International Journal of Sports Physiology and Performance*, Vol 5 (2010).
Seiler, "Does Polarized Training improve performance in recreational runners?" *International Journal of Sports Physiology and Performance*, Vol 9 (2014).

The Message of Running

Rickey Gates

Historically, running wasn't about individual accomplishment and the spectacle of winning and losing. It was a means of communication. In 490 BC, before the Battle of Marathon, Pheidippides ran 125-plus miles from Athens to Sparta to enlist help against the coming Persian forces. When the Spartans delayed, he ran back to Athens with the bad news. He wasn't the first to carry crucial information over an ultradistance. The original runners in ancient cultures around the world, from Central and South America to Japan, were messengers.

Today, I see being a messenger as a more valid goal than being a champion. But I don't pass judgment on those who are single-mindedly focused on a race or on a world record, because I went through that same journey before reaching my current philosophy. Early in my running life, I chased the spectacle.

When I was in college, at the University of Colorado, I decided I wanted to make their highly competitive cross-country team. I'd just taken two years off school to travel, and now I fixated on this goal. My training was tightly regimented: I timed and measured every single run. I didn't dare step out the door without a watch. For three Augusts in a row I lined up to race against the team, hoping to finish within a minute of the leaders. I came up short each year.

After my third and final attempt, I realized I'd been training to be a runner I wasn't. Once I got back into the mountains, I saw that I'd been pursuing a goal that was not *my* goal. It wasn't who I was. My true love and appreciation for the sport took off thanks to that failure.

I ditched my watch and I stopped keeping track of miles. I settled on a new objective: making the US Mountain Running Team. To that end, I still needed some sort of program, but instead of being overly strict about it, I decided to run by feel. My plan, which I followed for several years, was simple: go for one run a day. On a day where I had absolutely no interest whatsoever in going for a run, maybe I'd turn around at the base of the driveway. According to my rule, that counted. But most of the time, even if I didn't want to go for a run and yet still made the effort of putting on my shorts and my shoes and heading out the door, I would go much farther than the end of the driveway.

Sometimes we can feel really good, but our minds aren't into it, and sometimes our minds are into it, but our bodies aren't. It's important to keep the mental and the physical in balance and to listen to both.

Based in part on this tuned-in approach, I made the US Mountain Running Team when I was twenty-four. The year after that, I won two national titles: US Mountain Running Champion and US Trail Running Champion. Running in the mountains is me; that's who I am.

Not only did trail and mountain running bring me a newfound appreciation for how I can interact with the environment, it also became a way for me to indulge my passion for traveling. As racing became increasingly less important to me, I embraced running as an opportunity for exploration—at home and abroad. I came to see it as the ideal vehicle for immersing myself in new places and meeting new people.

In 2017 I embarked on a true cross-country adventure: from March 1 to August 1, I traced a 3,700-mile route from South Carolina to San Francisco. Like those ancient runners, I wanted to be a messenger—to use running as a medium of connection and communication. There was no advance training involved; I didn't do much beyond putting on as much weight as I could, because invariably I was going to lose it all (which I

did, plus some). Along with a lightweight pack (and a baby jogger while crossing the desert), I carried a clear message from one state to the next: we may not agree politically, and our backgrounds may be divergent, but I'm a good person and you're a good person and we have more things in common than we do differences. I barely noticed when I crossed state lines.

After stitching that thread of commonality from coast to coast, I hatched a follow-up adventure: Every Single Street. Over forty days in the fall of 2018, I'll run every street in San Francisco—all 1,200 miles. My run across the country was a very long, thin line, and running every street in San Francisco will be like grabbing a crayon and vigorously coloring in this urban grid until there's no white left. I experienced how diverse the country is, and I suspect that a city—a seven-by-seven miles square, the size of San Francisco—can be equally diverse, as long as I allow myself to be curious and open to new people, places, and opportunities.

If there's one word that could be used to describe my running over the years, from my aspiring cross-country days to now, it would be *consistency*. I no longer run every day, but I run often, because without maintaining consistency, I can't mine the depths of this sport.

The very act of running has been my messenger: over my fifteen-year evolution as a runner, running has unlocked its own potential—a potential that lies beyond races and competition. It's not about going faster; it's about slowing down, opening my mind, and engaging with what I see and hear. It's about being a modern-day messenger. ∎

Rickey Gates is piecing together a visual and written journey of his run across America and learning that the journey is actually easier than the telling of it. He lives in Oakland, California, with his girlfriend and motorcycle, the Freedom Machine.

Rickey Gates runs through the desert near Green River, Utah, on day 113 of a five-month run across the United States. He picked up this golf caddy in Moab to help him transport the amount of water necessary to cover ninety miles of desert at a time. Photo: Rickey Gates Collection

Zone 4 workouts, like Zone 3, also have a very powerful muscular endurance training effect. Especially for the less well trained, the duration of Zones 4 and 5 workouts will be limited by a lack of localized muscular endurance. You'll recognize this if your legs are screaming at you but your heart rate tops out in Zone 3 levels. When this happens, you are not getting the intended benefit of a Zone 4 workout. You need to improve your muscular endurance before you will be able to sustain the high heart rates of Zone 4. For more on muscular endurance, see the Strength Section.

ZONE 5: MAXIMUM ANAEROBIC EFFORT

This is maximum intensity and can be maintained for less than eight to sixty seconds. Due to the lag in cardiac response, heart rate is not a good measure of this workload. This intensity requires that your brain recruit the bulk of the pool of motor units available for the task. This intensity taxes the glycolytic metabolic system and the neuromuscular system and is a great stimulus for improving sport-specific strength and technique. And finally, it is the best way to develop anaerobic power endurance critical for short events like the skimo sprint.

Zone 5 training can and should be included in most training periods for endurance athletes. Early in the training cycle it will consist entirely of ten-second, very powerful sprints, usually up a steep hill, and only later will the duration be extended to produce an endurance effect.

The downside to this sort of training is potential injury due to the high loads imposed. A good strength base will help prepare you for this powerful work. It should always be done in interval fashion with very long rest intervals between work bouts. To maximize the power in each repetition, you need to allow enough time for the muscles' ATP stores to replenish. Three minutes is sufficient to restore most of the ATP. If you notice a significant drop in power after a few reps and longer rests don't help, you should conclude the workout. You have fatigued the FT motor units and done the job you intended to do. These workouts can be mentally tough for endurance athletes who think resting is counterproductive and get antsy during the rest intervals.

Continuity, Gradualness, and Modulation

These three words are the principles of all successful training programs. Keep these in mind as you build your program to prevent you from making gross errors.

Correct training places one or more of your body's systems into a crisis state. These stresses impact the body's structural and functional systems. The myriad adaptation processes that occur to both these systems are induced by varying stimuli and take place at varying rates.

A failure to adapt (known as stagnation) can occur or, even worse, can cause overtraining, which is a diminishing level of fitness when these key elements are

Jeff 'Bronco Billy' Browning sees his workout ending sooner than planned as he gets chased out of the alpine by an approaching thunderstorm. San Juan Mountains, Colorado. Photo: Steven Gnam

ignored. It takes time for the body to adjust to the training load you impose. A reapplication of another similar training stress will not give you the benefits you seek if your body's structural and functional systems have not sufficiently adapted to your current training load.

CONTINUITY

Continuity in training refers to maintaining a regular schedule of training with minimal interruption. You have to be motivated and disciplined to fulfill the requirements of the plan you undertake. Obviously, there needs to be some flexibility to account for the unexpected. Lapses in training do happen. They can be managed, but they cannot be overlooked. If you miss a week of training due to work, travel, or sickness, you can't pretend that you actually did all that training and progress to the next part of the plan. Your body will not be prepared for the next step, and you'll likely have setbacks.

How you manage this discontinuity depends on its length and the reason for it. Occasional breaks of a day or two are not much of a problem as long as they do not diminish the training load by more than roughly 5 percent in a month. Frequent or prolonged breaks from training that amount to more than 5 percent of the monthly volume do create a need to adjust your subsequent training by taking a step back in the plan.

GRADUALNESS

The most effective training must be progressive, meaning that the training loads need to *gradually* become larger than those that have come before in order to have a beneficial effect. As your fitness increases, what used to be too much will gradually become not enough.

Gradualness is an acknowledgment of the time your body needs to adapt to the training stimulus. Given the right training stimulus with adequate recovery, your body has a remarkable ability to adapt to frequent gentle nudges. But it does not respond well to infrequent bludgeoning. Occasional bursts (or lapses) of enthusiasm and motivation that result in big changes in training load are a common approach to training by beginners and dilettantes. The outcome of this sporadic exercise (we can't call it training) will never lead to optimal results and can be disastrous. Gradualness is a virtue that cannot be overemphasized.

Once your body is adapted to the stress of the current training load, what used to create a physiological mini-crisis will no longer be enough load to cause your body to keep adapting. Some creative changes to the training load need to be implemented for the next cycle, or progress will stop as you become adapted to this old level of stress. The types of changes vary according to the qualities you seek to develop and tend to fall into two distinct categories: volume and intensity. For a quality such as aerobic capacity, these adjustments are simple and involve mostly an increase in training volume. To effect simultaneous adaptations of different qualities like anaerobic capacity and speed, or aerobic endurance and muscular endurance, more elaborate training methods need to be implemented and must be administrated with care and finesse.

A gradual progression of the training load means different things for different athletes. Beginners and those with a low annual volume of training can progress faster than those with many years of training who are closer to their ultimate potential fitness. As a general rule, beginners (under 350–400 hours each year) can increase training load, as measured by time, by as much as 25 percent per year. Advanced athletes, training more than 500 hours per year, will be unable to make such jumps because they are already operating much closer to their limit. For them, a 10 percent jump in yearly volume should be considered a maximum. Elite-level athletes often make no change in overall annual training volume, instead seeking gains by juggling the type and amount of higher-intensity and specific training.

MODULATION

Modulation refers to the fluctuating level of the training load that allows the body a chance to recover its homeostasis after a build-up period. Modulation allows you to stress the targeted systems, then give them time to adapt before applying a new training load. Depending on the systems you target, this modulation can follow a cycle measured in hours, up to one that's measured in weeks. With care, an athlete can modulate training to allow several systems to adapt at the same time. Being mindful of and recording your daily perceptions of how you feel before, during, and after training in a training log helps you learn how you adapt to the various stressors in your life.

An extreme form of modulation is called overreaching; it is sometimes employed by advanced athletes. This entails a short, planned period of very high training loads preceded by a slightly below average week and followed by a substantial recovery period. Overreaching could be two massive back-to-back weekend workouts followed by three or four light days. Or it could be an entire week staying high in a hut and packing in long days with a couple of interval workouts that might necessitate a full week of recovery.

Specificity and Cross-Training

By specificity, we mean training in ways that look like the event being trained for. After all, elite-level swimmers principally swim for training, champion cyclists ride, top runners run, and world-class skiers (snow dependent) ski. There is a good reason for this. The better the athlete, the more event specific the training must be to see appreciable gains.

That being said, beginner endurance athletes and those with long lapses in their training history can make initial gains in fitness by doing almost any prolonged endurance activity. In the lexicon of our times, this nonspecific training is referred to as cross-training.

As your fitness improves, your gains in fitness will become more elusive unless you shift to activities directly related to your intended activity. For example, at this stage in his career, Kílian won't see any benefit to his ascent speed by swimming laps or paddling a kayak (but these may be beneficial recovery workouts). He must train in ways that mimic the demands of his intended events.

As an uphill athlete (even a beginner) seeking to improve your endurance, you should give priority to weight-bearing exercise. Cycling is a great general exercise. However, bikes are just too efficient and this makes them less effective training tools from the time and specificity standpoint. The sitting position on the bike means that you do not have to support your full body weight, which greatly reduces the energy cost of the exercise and the muscle mass used to propel yourself. The bike also limits the range of motion, eliminating the coordination, balance, and variability of the footing required while covering uneven terrain. Cycling can be great for recovery workouts and when rehabilitating from injuries. Kílian used to use cycling in a high gear as muscular endurance training. But it formed a very small part of his training volume and now has been dropped.

Swimming is another great exercise that has little carryover to our mountain sports but is an excellent recovery tool. The prone position in swimming means the heart doesn't work as hard to pump the blood. The water also keeps the body cool, leaving more blood available for the working muscles. If this is beginning to sound like running and hiking should be emphasized in your basic preparation time, then you are getting the picture.

What are the implications for the nonelite-level athlete? Any exercise, regardless of modality or intensity, will benefit an unfit person. But the benefits of cross-training diminish pretty fast once you are at the competitive recreational level. If you can only handle running less than twenty-five miles (forty kilometers) or six hours per week, then you will see benefits from adding other modes of exercise like hiking, cycling, rowing, stair machine, or even swimming. If, however, you are comfortable with a much higher training volume and want to maximize performance gains, then your additional training energy needs to be devoted to running. The sports covered in this book are all foot borne and require adaptations that will only occur from foot-borne training.

Individuality

"If you give ten different athletes the same workout, you will see ten different responses."

– Renato Canova

The individual nature of each athlete's response to training has made many a coach's hair turn gray. This aspect is often either overlooked or misunderstood in the application of training methods. Factors that influence individuality are:

- Lifetime training history. Were you inactive during much of your life until recently becoming interested in endurance sports? Or were you part of a running or cross-country ski team through adolescence? People with years of endurance training, especially in childhood through adolescence, will have retained many of the structural adaptations made during those years even if they have been relatively inactive recently. Adaptations to training come much slower after the teens and twenties and will require much more work to make happen after middle age.

- Recent training history. Have you been hitting the gym religiously three days a week for a CrossFit burn for the past two years? Or have you been logging six to ten hours a week of running and hiking in the mountains? Or have you been sedentary the past ten years due to work and family constraints? All these will impact how you should approach your training.

- Life stressors. The variety of stress in your life from school, work, family, and relationships all will impact your ability to handle training loads.

- Fast- or slow-twitch muscles. Are your muscle-fiber types naturally FT or ST dominant? This, too, plays a role in how you respond to endurance training. See the sidebar below.

If we all responded like a machine, the same way to every training input regardless of the above factors, then training would be as simple as following a road map from point A to point B. But we are highly complex organisms and each of us has unique qualities we bring to this venture that result in an individualized, unique response. One of the most common mistakes made is to copy the training of someone else, especially when that person is very successful in his or her sport. The popular media loves to report the details of the final six weeks of workouts that led to so and so putting in a record-breaking performance. While this can be inspiring, it is all too easy for the readers/viewers to believe that if they too complete these magical workouts, they too will have extraordinary results. If these journalists really wanted to be helpful they would be telling us what those champions did for the past ten years that allowed them to not only handle those final workouts, but to benefit from them. It is the long-term, capacity-building training history that determines the effectiveness of the short-term utilization workouts.

Are You a Fast-Twitch or Slow-Twitch Athlete?

Without going through the pain or expense of a needle biopsy, there are some other ways to determine whether you are FT or ST dominant, including the following:

FT Dominant:
- Good sprint performance
- Good vertical leap
- Produce high levels of lactate during easy workouts
- Can't hold peak fitness for long

ST Dominant:
- Do not have a fast sprint
- Poor vertical leap
- Cannot produce much lactate at high intensities (low anaerobic capacity)
- Maintain peak form for longer
- Recover from long, hard aerobic training quickly
- Do not need as much fueling during long workouts

FT Needs
- More aerobic base (Z1–Z2) training to become less reliant on anaerobic system
- Should not use much long Z4 training; better with shorter repetitions (<2 min) to keep lactate low

ST Needs
- Frequent, small doses of speed to improve anaerobic capacity

Training Stimulus and Recovery: How They Are Related

NOTES FROM KÍLIAN

I was already doing many days of eight to ten hours of road cycling when I was twelve. My idea then was to do long days cycling, pushing a big gear because I wanted to be a strong climber. I started serious training when I was thirteen when I started training properly with a coach; that first year I trained 600 hours. I discovered that I like to train and suffer. We did many long hikes in the Pyrenees. I was building a lot of endurance when I was young. Starting that year, I did 80- kilometer (50-mile) runs; long trainings. I was very young for such long runs.

And then I kept going, adding about 10 percent more training hours a year. For the last eight years I have held my annual training volume between 1,000 and 1,300 hours. If you want to increase to this high number of training hours, you have to increase no more than 10 percent a year for several years.

I know some world-class skiers and mountaineers who train 600 hours a year and they are very good. For shorter-distance running and ski-mountaineering races, this is sufficient. For the really long races, the higher volumes are necessary.

From earlier discussions, you know that your body's initial reaction to the stress of training is to become weaker. After sufficient recovery you achieve a higher level of fitness than before the training bout. But just what do you do in this recovery period? Is it bed rest? Is it reduced volume or intensity? How long do you need to recover before the next workout?

These important considerations dictate that correct training is a balancing act. The writing of a training plan is the easy part. The tricky part is the successful implementation of that plan so that you arrive at your highest level of fitness at the correct time. This is where many athletes get it wrong and what we hope to help you avoid.

The most underestimated component of a training plan is the recovery. Some level of fatigue will be your nearly constant companion when training. Fatigue is your body's feedback to you about the training. Learning how to interpret that feedback and respond appropriately will be fundamental to successful training.

RECOVERY TIMES

Let's suppose that you are tired from the previous day's exertions. Given that it takes between eight and seventy-two hours to restore intramuscular glycogen, it is usually enough to just delay the next heavy training bout for a day or two. When fatigue is significant enough to prevent another similar or harder workout than Zone 1 or Recovery intensity, aerobic training must be done on the intervening days before the next similarly challenging workout will be effective.

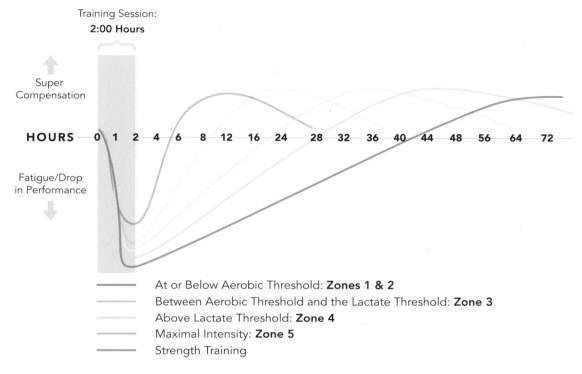

Training Session:
2:00 Hours

Super Compensation

HOURS — 0 1 2 4 6 8 12 16 24 28 32 36 40 44 48 56 64 72 —

Fatigue/Drop in Performance

—————— At or Below Aerobic Threshold: **Zones 1 & 2**
—————— Between Aerobic Threshold and the Lactate Threshold: **Zone 3**
—————— Above Lactate Threshold: **Zone 4**
—————— Maximal Intensity: **Zone 5**
—————— Strength Training

Fig. 3.4 Recovery and Adaptation Times

The vertical scale is purely qualitative, but the horizontal scale is in hours. While there is some interpersonal variability to these numbers, the originator of this scale collected data on hundreds of swimmers over many years to arrive at these values. It has been the authors' experience that these values hold quite well. Reproduced from *The Science of Winning* by Jan Olbrecht, courtesy of F&G Partners Publishing.

Endurance training has a dramatic effect on the amount of intramuscular energy stores, with better-trained athletes having as much as three times the intramuscular glycogen stores as the untrained person. That means that these recovery times between workouts are highly individualized. However, this is somewhat balanced out by the fact that the better trained will usually be training harder and for longer, so in the end, rough guidelines do present themselves.

High-intensity exercise and strength training require the longest recovery times of two to three full days before you'll be prepared to absorb a similar load. Low-intensity endurance workouts of two to three hours or less will normally be recovered from in eight to twenty-four hours. Long-duration (over two hours) training at even low intensity may require twenty-four to forty-eight hours for the restoration of glycogen stores. Refer to figure **3.4**. Eating during and within thirty to sixty minutes of finishing these long workouts will greatly reduce the time needed for recovery, sometimes by days.

In the Mountains, Durability Equals Speed

Mike Foote

When I first started running 100-mile ultramarathons in 2009, my primary goal was to be fast. However, after a decade of racing and adventuring in the mountains, I've realized that durability, not speed, should be the North Star of my training.

The events that appeal most to me, steep and slow 100-mile mountain runs like UTMB or the Hardrock 100, are races of attrition. People get injured, people slow down, and people DNF. Although it is contrary to think about it this way, the people who finish first aren't necessarily the fastest; they are the ones who are the least broken and who slow down less overall. I grew more attracted to this mindset rather than one of pure speed. Instead of striving for speed, I limit slowing down. To achieve that, I cultivate durability. And for years, this desire for durability has informed how I train.

In 2015, alongside a couple of close friends, I ran from my front doorstep in Missoula, Montana, to Banff, Canada, crossing the region known as the Crown of the Continent. Over three weeks we covered 600 miles of mostly off-trail ridgelines, traversing thirteen mountain ranges in the effort. Day in and day out we soldiered north through technical terrain, chossy climbs, and heinous bushwhacks. Throughout the expedition, I was pushed to my limit, but I never questioned my ability to finish, and I didn't have a single injury flare up. Looking back, I don't think I would have realized that dream if speed was all I cared about. My durability got me through.

The bad news is that there are no shortcuts to durability. The good news is that working toward making both your body and mind more resilient to the stresses of training and racing—and dare I say life—is a fun and engaging process.

A few key components of my training that have increased my durability are training volume, strength work, and prioritized self-care.

I'm a firm believer that having a high-volume training load will set you up well for being able to handle the workload of big races. The downside is that it can take time to build the capacity for such big goals. But it's worth it for having that well to dig from twenty-two hours into a twenty-four-hour push.

Also, I believe in the positive benefits of strength training. Going to the gym, even once a week, can have a huge impact on your ability to stay injury free and keep moving forward.

Finally, I focus on all the ancillary work that supports the training. I prioritize massage, foam rolling, yoga, and more in order to keep my body "put together." Also—spoiler alert—I've learned that diet and sleep are important as well. Shocking, I know.

Looking back on the last ten years of training for and racing ultras, I don't think I'm any faster at running a mile. But I seem to be running 100 miles in the mountains quicker than when I began. And that's good enough for me. ∎

Mike Foote is an aspiring efficient mountain traveler who has stood on the podium at many of the biggest ultramarathons in the world. He is also a member of the US Ski Mountaineering Team. In 2018 Mike, coached by Scott Johnston, climbed and skied 61,200 feet in twenty-four hours, setting a new world record in the process.

Mike Foote refueling at the Chapman Aid Station, about 80 miles into the 2017 Hardrock 100. Mike placed second behind Kílian Jornet in that race. Photo: Steven Gnam

NOTES FROM KÍLIAN

I have never needed to think too much about special recovery techniques because I can recharge quickly. I know that muscular fatigue from hard efforts like steep uphill intervals and the recovery from long aerobic training require different kinds of recovery.

Fatigue caused by hard muscular endurance work can take seventy-two hours to recover from. If I do something like a fast race or a day in the mountains with a lot of vertical, and destroy the muscles, that will take me two days to recover from. I can keep going the next day but I will have heavy legs and I go more slowly on those days.

Quality of rest is also very important. Staying at home, working around the house, sitting in the office—this is not proper resting. Rest means doing nothing or doing everything very slowly.

Aerobic fatigue is different. I can do things for a long duration, but I find that to determine the right amount of recovery I have to listen to how my body feels. If I feel the training will not do anything for me, that it will not improve me, I stop and take a rest day. If every day is like that for you, maybe you are not well trained enough for the level you are pushing. And some days you might feel like you are doing the workout just to do it; at that point it might be important to rest.

If you do not feel a progressive increase in energy, strength, and overall fitness from week to week, you are either training too hard, not allowing enough time for recovery, or your active recovery sessions are too intense. There are always a few "blah" days here and there, but if the general trend for a week is down, not up, you need to address the situation. The first step of acknowledging the fatigue is usually the toughest one.

Far too many times, we have had athletes ask us training questions after they have become injured or overtrained. And invariably, when we explain these concepts, their response is, "Oh, I guess I was definitely overtraining or underrecovering." By the time they ask, "Now what do I do?" it is often too late for all but the most drastic measures.

ENHANCING RECOVERY

Certain steps can and should be taken to speed up the recovery process.

For athletes who are pushing the limits of training that their bodies can absorb, recovery strategies become an integral part of the overall plan. For those who are time limited rather than energy limited in the amount of training they can fit in during a given week, recovery can still be a useful tool, but may not be so essential.

Luke Nelson, a little haggard after running the 2014 The Rut 50K on Lone Peak, Big Sky, Montana. The 2014 race drew the top mountain, ultra, and trail runners from around the world as it served as the final race in the Sky Running series. Photo: Steven Gnam

Christian Varesco loosens up with a run in view of the Pale di San Martino range clearing after a summer storm. Dolomites, Italy. Photo: Federico Modica

The following is a list, in order of importance, of some of the most common methods used to enhance recovery.

Diet

This is the most important component for recovery.

Food is fuel. And you need to eat with an eye toward recovery. What does this mean? Realize that heavy and prolonged exercise has a depleting effect on your nutritional stores, especially glycogen. The sooner you can begin to get the caloric building blocks into your system, the sooner they can start to repair the damage and depletion done by the training bout. While research indicates that there are some variations in effective post-exercise feeding strategies, some general guidelines seem to arise.

Consume 100–200 calories in the first thirty minutes after exercise of over an hour. Have these calories in a form that does not upset your stomach (you may need to experiment). Eat these in a ratio of 3:1 or 4:1 carbohydrates to protein. It is during this post-exercise window that the muscles can replenish their glycogen stores quickly. Miss this window, and recovery can be delayed by up to days depending on the workout/race.

Sleep

We all have a general sense of how a good night's sleep or lack thereof affects our energy and outlook the next day. There is solid science to back up your seat-of-the-pants feeling.

Quality sleep is vital for the recovery process. A lot of important stuff happens during REM (rapid eye movement) sleep that aids your body in repairing damage inflicted by training. Much of that rebuilding comes about as a result of various hormones released during sleep. REM sleep is a critical phase of sleep that is not definitively understood, but we do know that it occurs in several blocks of 90 to 120 minutes throughout the night and it involves a state of very deep relaxation that aids the recovery process. Two of the best stimulators for the release of your body's natural human growth hormone, known as somatotropin or HGH, are REM sleep and vigorous exercise. HGH is one of the body's primary tools for adapting to higher training loads. Enhancing its production is an easy and smart way to develop better strength and endurance.

Anything that gets in the way of REM sleep is going to have a serious impact on your recovery. Ever spend a fitful, sleepless night? How recovered did you feel the next morning when it was time to tackle a big day? But getting even fifteen minutes of deep sleep during a nap can have an amazingly refreshing effect.

Massage

Stiff and tight muscles are often the most obvious sign that you have been working your body hard. Endurance activities involve many thousands of repetitions of the same or very similar movements. This repetition often results in acute inflammation of these muscles, which you perceive as stiffness and soreness.

Prior to the 2015 Mont-Blanc Marathon, Kílian Jornet receives a painful massage from his physiotherapist, Arnaud Tortel. Chamonix, France. Photo: Jordi Saragossa

Kílian Jornet using his Compex electronic muscle-stimulator machine to help his legs recover between training days during a high-volume training week. Chamonix, France. Photo: Jordi Saragossa

The inflammation actually stimulates some of the adaptations to the training, but it can be too much of a good thing. Massage by a skilled practitioner increases the blood circulation in tired muscles. Improved circulation speeds the replenishment of vital nutrients, reduces this muscular inflammation, and accelerates recovery. This is the reason professional cyclists use massage after heavy training and between stages on multiday races. It works! A recent study by Dr. Mark Tarnopolsky of McMaster University showed that as little as ten minutes of deep-tissue massage had a dramatic effect on speeding recovery.

Self-Massage

Since most of us can't access or afford a daily massage, it's nice to know that self-massage can be equally as effective. Numerous tools for self-massage have been developed, and we've tried many but have come to rely on balls. They are small and easy to travel with. They allow you to get more directed pressure on small or larger areas than a foam roller can. Our favorites are the MobilityWOD 80mm ball and the Roll Model balls. The book *The Roll Model* by Jill Miller is a masterpiece on how to use the ball-rolling techniques to speed recovery and treat chronic musculoskeletal problems. We won't go deeply into this practice, but we highly recommend the book.

Basically the ball rolling produces a shearing effect on the muscle fibers, which reduces adhesions and loosens stiff muscles better than anything we have used outside of the hands of an expert sports-massage therapist. You control the pressure and the positioning so that you target just the area you need to. For some

Athletes letting off some steam during the Vertical Kilometer Crepa Neigra race in Canazei, Val di Fassa, Sass Pordoi, Italy. Photo: Federico Modica

people, the pressure of the ball will be too intense and a foam roller will be a better initial tool. Once you are able to apply full weight to the foam roller, it will be time to think about progressing to the balls. Using these self-massage techniques right before bedtime will help you relax and prepare you for sounder sleep.

Electro-stim machines can be very effective recovery tools because they act a bit like massage when used in the recovery setting.

Reducing Life Stressors

Using relaxation techniques, such as meditation, can be an aid to recovery by reducing ancillary stress. Your body responds to stress, in large measure, with the same reactions regardless of whether that stress is a result of work or of training. If you have a stressful life, then it may be that one of the best training strategies for you is finding ways of reducing that life stress so you can handle more training stress.

Recovery Workouts

Calling these *workouts* is a bit of a misnomer; they should not be viewed in the same way as normal training. While certain ones can have a maintenance effect on aerobic qualities, their main use is to speed the recovery process. While it may

Laura Orgué playing in Arches National Park, Utah. Photo: Martina Valmassoi

seem counterintuitive that more exercise will do anything other than deplete your already-taxed reserves, these very-low-intensity sessions can have a powerful restorative effect. Coaches have known this for decades; the scientists are still trying to figure out why.

Keep in mind the following when using recovery workouts:

- The intensity must feel very easy. More discussion about this is found in "Understanding the Language of Intensity" on page 79.

- They are most commonly used by athletes who are stacking workouts as closely together as possible, often twice a day, but can be helpful after an especially tough workout.

- Alternate modes of exercise, such as cycling, paddling, and especially swimming, will give needed relief to overused legs.

- Even a brisk walk can be a good recovery workout if you are really tired or feeling a little sick. Light exercise almost always beats being sedentary for aiding recovery.

Jeff Browning (no. 2), starting the 2013 San Diego 100, in which he placed first with a time of 16:59:24. California. Photo: Jeff Johnson

The Everest Marathon: My Wild Introduction to Ultrarunning

Anna Frost

There I was on the ground, only three kilometers from the finish of the 2009 Everest Marathon. I was crying, barely able to breathe, covered in dust and blood, and nursing a massively swollen ankle from earlier in the race. And now a yak had head-butted me. *A yak.*

I'd been in Nepal for eight weeks, and the yaks had never bothered me. But this one just didn't like me. It turned around and rammed into me, splitting all my knuckles open and knocking me to the ground. I was lucky that it hit my hand first, because otherwise it might have broken a rib.

The yak herder trotted over, picked me up, and pushed me along the trail. "Come on, come on, keep running, keep running!" he urged. I continued toward the finish, still crying.

Up until about a week before the marathon, the training had been going well. This was my first big non-European international race as a sponsored runner, and I'd arrived early to acclimatize. I also wanted to explore the area. I hired a porter to carry my bag from teahouse to teahouse so I could run the long way to the next village—up and over a 5,000-meter pass and back down through another valley. My porter would tell me before I left which hut he would be at, and I'd meet him there. It was an amazing way of being liberated to go longer and lighter.

Each time I reached a high pass, I felt really small. There you are at 5,000 meters, and it's still 3,000 more meters up to the tops of the highest mountains around you. It makes you realize how insignificant you are, and it reminds you to be grateful for Mother Nature.

In addition to these point-to-point runs, I was also doing my typical mountain-running training. Two or three days each week, I would stay at the same teahouse and do hill repeats. I'd find a steep trail and do anywhere from 30-second to 5- or 8-minute intervals. As I got more and more acclimatized, I was able to push harder and longer at those intervals.

More than once while on a run I was invited into a stranger's kitchen for a cup of hot coffee or tea and *momos*, little rice-flour dumplings with vegetables inside. I wasn't permitted to pay for the goodies, probably because I was so skinny at that point I looked like I needed some fleshing out. But it's also the ethos of the place: the people are happy and generous, so willing to give anything they can, even when they don't have much themselves.

After six weeks of exploring, training, and acclimatizing on my own, it was time to meet up with the rest of the Everest marathoners for our group hike to Base Camp. During the trek, I got really sick with the Khumbu cough; between the altitude and the hacking, I could hardly sleep. The closer we got to the start line, the worse I felt.

Race morning was no exception, but I had to do it. Off we went, and about 10 kilometers in, I twisted my ankle, practically touching the whole side of my shin to the ground. It swelled up immediately. I popped some painkillers and anti-inflammatory meds, shoved some snow in my sock, and kept running until my ankle got numb. The only other way out of there would have been on a donkey, and I had no interest in finding and riding a donkey.

Even with my cough and my stiff, puffy ankle, I was having a great race. I was leading the Westerners, and there were just two Nepalese guys far, far ahead of me—so far ahead I wasn't worried about their position. I just wanted to finish.

At a turnaround point beside a nunnery at about five kilometers to go, the nuns all came running out when they saw me and put white ceremonial scarves—ribbons of blessing—around my neck. They were really inspired to see a woman racing.

Anna Frost trains near Qaanaaq, Greenland. Photo: Kelvin Trautman

My yak encounter came just two kilometers later, which led to the herder encouraging me onward, toward Namche Bazaar. I made it, and I don't think I've ever been more thrilled to finish a race. I consider it my first ultra; yes, it was a marathon, but it was an ultra to get there and get through it—and get through the following day.

I woke up the next morning in a lot of pain. My ankle was enormous, and it was black all the way up my leg. My cuts from when the yak hit me were bright red and full of pus, because the dust up there is teeming with bacteria and disintegrated yak and horse poop. I'd developed conjunctivitis in my eyes as well, also thanks to the dust. I had some tea tree oil, so I rubbed that in my eyes, on my hand, and on my ankle. Then, using two sticks I found in the forest for support, I hobbled and wobbled my way down to the airport in Lukla for my flight back to Kathmandu.

It took me twelve hours to cover those 17.7 kilometers—the last leg of my first ultra.

Despite all the discomfort and unexpected twists and turns, I fell in love with the Himalaya. This good, bad, amazing, and fulfilling experience has inspired me to return year after year—three times to Nepal and now three times to Bhutan as well. I like to be reminded of the generosity and compassion of the people and that you don't need as much as you think. That less is more. It's true in life, and it's especially true in a race, when all you really need is the drive to keep putting one foot in front of the other toward the finish, even if one foot is swollen and there's a cantankerous yak in your path. ▪

Anna 'Frosty' Frost is a New Zealander with many passions, including two that intertwine beautifully: running and traveling. She has been doing both since 2004, exploring and discovering the world and herself through the highs and lows of the mountains and life. After nearly a decade spent traveling internationally and racing constantly—and mostly successfully—across all distances and types of terrain, she hit physical bottom. But she has come back with new life in recent years, having learned that running is just running. It is what she does, not who she is.

CHAPTER FOUR

Monitoring Your Training

It should be self-evident that the higher your goals, the harder you will have to work to achieve them. In doing this hard work, you will be pushing perilously close to the boundary of physical and mental stress you are capable of handling before something goes wrong. Most athletes look for some method of monitoring and analyzing their training load and/or the fatigue arising from that load. While a few rare individuals seem to manage using only their intuition and can get by with no monitoring tools, most of us will benefit greatly from learning to use one or more tools.

High is a relative term. An intolerably high training load for a beginner won't even be a maintenance load for a world-class athlete. There is no one-size-fits-all training prescription. *This is why we've created a book that teaches you the theory and practice of training rather than doling out a set prescription that may or may not fit your needs.* Thoughtful application of sound training principles accompanied by attentive monitoring always results in the best outcome.

First and foremost, adhere to the principle of gradualness in the progression of your training load. Except for rare instances of premeditated overreaching, give yourself a chance to absorb the previous load and build progressively. Our bodies do not like drastic changes.

Take an active interest in understanding the effects that your training is having on your body. This involves learning to listen to and interpret the subtle signals your body is sending. Listen carefully while they are still being whispered and before they become shouted alarms.

Ways to Monitor for Recovery

It is only natural that when you are exploring the limits of what your body can handle, you may occasionally overstep. Short-term tiredness goes with the

Rémi Loubet on an after-work run down Néron Ridge to Grenoble, France.
Photo: Ulysse Lefebvre

territory. Normally fatigue is short term because you recognize it early and deal with it by reducing the training load for a day or so, which is almost always sufficient to restore your body's homeostasis and get you back on track again. Pay attention to this short-term fatigue and don't let it become chronic, or you risk sliding into the realm of overtraining.

Don't train compulsively. If you are motivated enough to be reading this book, in all likelihood when you lack the motivation to train it is because your body is telling you to back off in the only way it can. Days on which you lack motivation to train are a clear warning sign.

Just because the training plan calls for a hard workout does not mean that you will be ready to execute it effectively or, more importantly, benefit from it. Fatigue has a determining effect on your preparedness to train. Accurately assessing your state of fatigue is critical to effective training. Here's a quick look at some simple ways you can monitor your recovery.

Fatigue

Endurance athletes must learn to embrace fatigue. We train to increase our resistance to it, and we race to see how well we can tolerate the pain and discomfort of it. Fatigue, in one form or another, is the stimulus that makes you fitter and it is by necessity the nearly constant companion of endurance athletes. Staying on the good side of the fatigue curve is one of the most important factors in successful training. Increase the training load faster than your body can adapt to it, and fatigue can very quickly go from being your friend to your worst enemy. Knowing fatigue in all its guises and how to control it so it does not control you is a learning process. Some athletes never figure it out and wonder why they come up short on the big day. But most of us will benefit from applying a little structure and a few rules to help us learn from studying fatigue and how it affects our individual body.

NOTES FROM KÍLIAN

Listen to your body. Sometimes it will say you can do it and you can push; other times you realize you need to stop before the prescribed time is over and say the training is enough for your body on that day. You must know how far you can go before feeling overtrained. The early years of training are best spent learning about your body and when you can push, and when not to push.

You want to discover your system, and we each need to learn to recognize these feelings in our own bodies. Sometimes you may become tired and not feel good after a lot of training days; that's okay because it's all part of learning about yourself. Make a note; remember (and study) what you did that led to that feeling. And move forward.

Caleb Ambrose relieves some fatigue at the twenty-mile mark during the thirty-four-mile circumnavigation of Mount St. Helens by the Loowit Trail, Washington. Photo: Steven Gnam

Understanding fatigue in its various guises is important if you want to manage it productively. We can categorize fatigue into three general groups. These types of fatigue often overlap and interact with one another, but for simplicity's sake we'll look at them individually.

1. Calcium Accumulation: When calcium ions accumulate in the muscle cells, muscle contractions are inhibited. The calcium pump that moves these ions back into the intercellular space fails to keep up with the build-up and very soon the muscle loses its ability to contract. This effect is most noticeable in short-duration, high-strength contractions. Think of the fatigue you experience when doing pull-ups. The duration of the event resulting in this sort of fatigue is usually under fifteen seconds. Recovery from this is on the scale of a few minutes. Typically, this type of fatigue is self-limiting, as your ability to contract those muscles power-fully will naturally end that type of movement; you cannot manage one more pull-up. However, if you drive yourself into this state of fatigue many times in a workout (as with several sets to failure of pull-ups), the follow-ing forms of fatigue can be induced and recovery can take days.

2. Metabolic: On a short time scale, there are products of metabolism that accumulate in the muscles that inhibit the synthesis of ATP. Lactate is the most well known, but the increased acidity from the accumulation of hydrogen ions is another one. This reduction in ATP production manifests as a reduction in muscle power and a consequent slowing. Think about the fatigue you experience when sprinting up a hill for sixty seconds at near-maximum effort. This fatigue is often associated with a burning feeling in the muscles. Recovery from it is on the scale of a few minutes. On a longer time scale, the glycogen stores available to power the metabolic process of ATP production can become depleted and muscle power drops as a consequence. Think of the classic "bonk" during multi-hour events that often is accompanied by mental confusion and a lack of coordination. Recovery from this is on the scale of a few hours to a few days.

3. Neurologic: The electrical signals transmitted from the brain's motor cortex, along the motor nerves to the muscles, require neurotransmitter chemicals at each synapse to relay the signal along its way to the muscle. When these chemicals become depleted through prolonged high firing rates, the electrical impulse becomes weakened and muscle power drops. Repeated or longer-duration, exhausting efforts of the first two types in this list can result in this form of fatigue. Normal recovery from this is on a scale of a few hours to several days.

THE CENTRAL GOVERNOR

A credible theory about the limits of human performance was proposed by the grandfather of exercise science, A.V. Hill, in the early twentieth century. Hill's VO_2 max theory has been modified and strengthened over the years. In Section One we mentioned this other highly credible theory about fatigue and the limits of human performance: Dr. Tim Noakes believes that the brain has a built-in self-preservation instinct that limits how far out of our homeostasis we can get before alarm bells begin to sound. Interestingly, while the causes for each of the foregoing types of fatigue are different, the result is the same: The brain reduces the muscle power output until homeostasis is restored. Noakes and many others have provided ample evidence to make this the most robust theory of fatigue to date. What does this mean for you? Noakes proposes that frequently pushing the body out of its comfort zone (away from its homeostasis) makes the governor more comfortable in allowing ever-increasing divergence from homeostasis before it begins to shut things down. You do this when you train. And it seems very likely that fatigue in all forms depends upon this, as yet, poorly understood relationship between the muscles and the brain.

Ryan Sandes rolls it out in the dormitory of Lac Blanc Refuge, Chamonix, France.
Photo: Kelvin Trautman

The Fatigue Matrix

The next step after grasping the causes of fatigue is to look at how the responses manifest so that you can recognize them. Recognizing the causes and results then leads to action: what you can do to mitigate the fatigue in order to speed your recovery. The suggestions we provide below are based on our accumulated experience and study. First, consider that we can group fatigue symptoms into two rough types: **Group A: Muscular (and nervous system)** and **Group B: Energy.**

As with most of the other simple models provided in the book, this one is not 100-percent accurate. The causes of fatigue overlap and are somewhat interdependent. You may have symptoms of all the following. Keeping these general categories in mind can help you decide on the best course of action.

Group A: Muscular

Are your muscles sore, or do they feel dead, heavy, and flat? In the first instance of soreness, this is caused by micro-tears in the muscles. In the second case, dead legs, the neurological fatigue mentioned above or glycogen depletion are the primary culprits.

Dirt, grit, blisters, sunburn, and sweat pustules are nothing compared to the relief and satisfaction Jenn Shelton finds after completing her long-term goal of running all 210 miles of the John Muir Trail. It took her four days to traverse the backbone of the Sierra Nevada from the high point of Mount Whitney (14,505 ft) to Yosemite Valley, California. Photo: Ken Etzel

Sore Muscles

Did you increase the intensity of your strength workout? Did you do some faster or longer downhill running? These are the kinds of things that might leave your muscles sore to the touch and make descending a set of stairs painful. The common term for this is delayed onset muscle soreness (DOMS). It usually peaks forty-eight hours after the workout. Mostly you just have to tough it out and do light aerobic exercise during the DOMS period. Here are the recommended do's and don'ts to deal with this condition.

Do:
Light aerobic recovery workouts
Swim, or at least lightly kick in the pool
E-stim on the recovery setting
Light massage
Ibuprofen after twelve hours post-workout
Ice bath after twelve hours post-workout
Frequent light stretching to reduce muscle stiffness
Get extra sleep

Eat extra protein, especially before bed
Self-maintenance rolling with roller or ball

Don't do:
Speed, power, or strength work
High-intensity aerobic interval work
Overstretch

Dead, Heavy, or Flat-Feeling Leg Muscles

This condition is usually caused by increasing training load too much in too short of a time. Have you increased the distance, vertical, or intensity of your training in the past ten days? Do you notice a lack of spring in your running stride? Do your legs feel extra fatigued when you're just climbing a set of stairs? Do your legs ache at night in bed? Has your performance or pace dropped off and do your workouts seem to take more effort? All these are big red flags and if ignored, can lead to a state of overtraining (covered in detail in a few pages). This is a complex type of fatigue that is probably a combination of Group B: Energy (glycogen depletion) and neurological fatigue. If your legs are not refreshed after a couple of very light days, then you need even more of the following.

Do:
Extensive use of the pool for swimming/light kicking exercise
Self-maintenance rolling with roller or ball (may need twice daily)
Deep-tissue massage
Compression garments
Elevate legs above heart
Increase post-workout carb intake

Ferritin

Ferritin is a very important protein in your blood that is responsible for storing and transporting iron across the cell membrane into the hemoglobin molecule. Elemental iron can't cross that barrier without being attached to ferritin. Since iron binds with oxygen in the hemoglobin, when ferritin levels are low, the oxygen-carrying capacity of your blood will be reduced. For endurance athletes, this results in a performance decline. The normal ranges of acceptable ferritin levels do not consider the demands of athletes, so can't be relied upon. The standard for "low" ferritin reading is 12ng/ml. For endurance athletes, a ferritin level below 50ng/ml will result in some reduced endurance performance. Levels below 30ng/ml will show as dramatically reduced performance and chronic fatigue. It is worth checking ferritin levels with a simple blood test if you have been experiencing these symptoms. It is often overlooked by physicians who are not used to working with athletes.

Light recovery-effort aerobic cross-training: cycling, rowing

Increase quality and quantity of sleep

Don't do:

Extensive aerobic workouts, especially with much vertical

Intensive workouts such as Zones 3–5 interval sessions

Muscular endurance workouts

Anaerobic endurance workouts like extended hill sprints

Drink much alcohol

Group B: Energy

If you are reading this book, in all likelihood you love to train. You don't need someone pushing you out the door to do your workouts. In fact, you probably need someone to hold you back from time to time. Your sport most likely helps define you, and when you feel lethargic and unmotivated, this can create emotional stress. But when you feel unmotivated and have low energy, you should take that as a warning sign. Your body is sending you a message and you may be suffering from this type of fatigue. Are you waking up tired in the morning? Even when sleeping more? Needing more sleep in the day? Are you feeling flat? Are you avoiding friends? Is work or family life more stressful? Then consider following this course of action for a few days to see if you feel some improvement.

Do:

Increase quality of your food

Increase quantity and quality of sleep

Make more social time with friends

Consider blood tests for cortisol, ferritin, testosterone, mononucleosis

Simple heart rate test; resting or stair test (see the following two pages)

Take a fish oil supplement

Stay off computer and/or similar devices one hour before bed

Easy and short Zone 1 aerobic workouts (can include a few short accelerations)

Don't do:

Intensive workouts such as muscular endurance or Zones 3–5 interval sessions

Consume alcohol

Add stress to your life, either physical or psychological

Perception

How you feel when you get ready to train or after a warm-up is the old standby and one we all use intuitively. Even if you do use one of the more concrete metrics listed on the following pages, you still need to do a reality check and confirm

Filippo Beccari going all out during a skimo competition in Italy. Photo: Federico Modica

that your body's sensations agree with the numbers. An important function of a warm-up is to assess your readiness to train. Be prepared to reduce or even cancel the workout based on how you feel.

Resting Heart Rate

An elevated resting heart rate suggests that your body's sympathetic nervous system is kicked into high gear, possibly as a result of overstimulation from a big training load. It can also be due to an infection or impending sickness, poor sleep, or some other stress in your life. But whatever the cause, you need to be watchful and monitor your response to training more closely over the next few days to see if your resting heart rate deviates even more or if it begins to return to a more normal level.

A simple morning heart rate test is worth trying out for yourself and seeing if you can connect cause and effect. Most athletes' results will be spotty with this resting heart rate method. There are other factors that affect the resting heart rate besides fatigue or illness. This is not to say that you should disregard an elevated morning pulse, but it should be weighed with other factors. Be sure to take the test at the same time and under similar conditions each day.

Step Test

This very simple test can be used to help gauge your recovery state/preparedness to train. It lightly stresses your nervous system and you simply note the results. Wearing your heart rate monitor, step up and down at a moderate pace onto a stair step. Do this for a minute or two at a fast enough pace to raise your heart rate about 50 to 70 beats/minute. The effort need not be very intense. Just enough to cause a reaction by the sympathetic nervous system. Note the maximum heart rate achieved and then sit down immediately and note your heart rate after one minute. The exact times you use and the stepping rate are not critical as long as you repeat them each test. By doing this test frequently as well as noting the quality of the corresponding training, you will soon see a correlation between the drop in heart rate and your recovery state.

Stair Test

This simple assessment consists of you walking or bounding (taking two steps at once) up a set of stairs that you climb daily and then checking how your legs feel at the top. You'll quickly begin to recognize the feeling that allows you to have a good workout and the feeling that tells you that you need more recovery.

NOTES FROM KÍLIAN

Besides tracking duration at each heart rate, I also track my vertical meters every day.

I note every workout I do on a spreadsheet with a short description of the training and a note about how I felt. I have recorded all my training this way since I was very young.

If a race goes really well, or if I did not feel fast, I like to go back and see what was before so I can try to understand it.

Use a Training Log to Monitor Training Load

Training effect indicates, in a qualitative way, how your body reacts and adapts to the various forms of training stimuli. *Training load* is a term used to describe, in a quasi-quantitative way, the type and amount of stress imposed by a single workout or period of training: the training load causes the training effect. They both depend on the type, the intensity, and the volume of work done in a training bout. The training load applied in a three-hour Zone 1 run may be roughly equivalent to the training load of a one-hour run containing five one-kilometer intervals done in Zone 4, but the training effect and adaptations will be quite different.

Quantify and Track

Training load is a function of the volume and the intensity of the work. Use a plan to guide you in what workouts to do when, and remember to use a log for recording your workouts. This history will allow you to plan better in the future. The more accurate and informative the recording, the more useful the information will be when you are next planning.

A training log can be as simple as a notebook or as sophisticated as an online logging and planning website. TrainingPeaks.com is the platform we use for our coaching, and the company's proprietary tracking metrics allow for remarkably accurate fitness and fatigue monitoring. Other online services like Strava, Movescount, Garmin Connect, and Polar Flow also offer training data logging and will all synch to TrainingPeaks, but as of this writing they lack its sophisticated tracking capabilities.

TIME

The simplest way to track training load is to keep track of training volume in either hours or distance. Logging miles or kilometers has been the standard metric for road runners for decades. Logging hours is the standard method for mountain athletes. As you know, in the mountains not all miles are created equally. Therefore, hours is a fairly good metric.

ELEVATION GAIN/LOSS

When combined with training time, vertical gain and loss accumulated in a workout or week or month can begin to give an even clearer picture of the training load for the foot-borne athlete. This is because for the mountain runner and ski mountaineer, it is the vertical component of the training that normally includes the intensity aspect of training. Even if the vertical training is done at a low intensity, the amount of muscle mass recruited is more than when training on less steep terrain. Increase vertical, and you increase the training load.

How Kílian Records His Training

For running, Kílian counts time, vertical meters, and distance. For skiing, he counts just the time and vertical meters. He also uses a simple scale to describe the technicality of the workout:

Tech 1: On-piste ski or good track/easy trail

Tech 2: Off-piste or rough track/medium trail

Tech 3: Off-piste or some scrambling/off-trail scrambling

Tech 4: Climbing

An unknown runner striving for an A-grade workout in the Lake District of England.
Photo: Jordi Saragossa

While there is no formula that can take into account steepness, footing, size of steps you may be forced to take over rocks, total climb, etc., it's enough to know that a 50-mile (80-kilometer) week with 6,000 feet (1,800 meters) of vertical gain and loss will have less load than a 40-mile (60-kilometer) week with 10,000 feet (3,000 meters). Your legs will let you know which they find more challenging. Record your vertical just as you would time and distance. It is necessary to progressively build the training load during the base-building period; in Section Four of the book ("How to Train") we'll show how much to increase this.

GRADING YOUR WORKOUTS

A useful and simple tool we often use for monitoring training progress is to give each workout a letter grade based on how you feel during the workout and record this value in your log. Using this grading method in conjunction with a recovery-monitoring test will give you some solid feedback.

A – means you felt like Superman and had plenty in reserve.
B – means it was a good workout. You completed the task with no problem.
C – means you did the workout but felt flat or off.
D – means you could not finish the planned workout or had to reduce it.
F – means you could not train that day due to fatigue or illness.

By grading each workout this way, you can make a quick scan of your training log over the previous few weeks and see trends or patterns. A good rule of thumb is that if you have more than two Cs in a row, or a C and a D within one week, you need to stop and assess what is going on. For some reason, you are not absorbing the training; the load is too high for your current fitness state or the recovery is insufficient.

Not every workout is going to be an A, but if your workouts keep earning poor grades, then your body is trying to tell you something. You may be getting sick and not have any symptoms yet. If you continue without changing something, the Cs will become Ds and begin to fill the pages of your log. At this point, you are no longer adapting to the training and are headed toward overtraining.

Returning to Training After a Break

Breaks can be planned or unplanned. Illness, injury, school, work, family, and friends can sometimes thwart your resolve to stick with your plan. Often the best strategy is to accept the minor setbacks with equanimity and try to learn something in hopes of not having to repeat them in the future.

Fatigue

This is perhaps the most common reason for unplanned disruptions in a training plan. See the preceding discussion about fatigue on page 25.

When beginning to train again after a fatigue-related break of more than two days, do not just jump back into training where you left off. It may well be that that load was too high and was responsible for your excessive fatigue. Instead, ease back into training with low-intensity workouts that are reduced in duration by 50 percent for a couple of days. This will give you a chance to assess your actual recovery state. If these go well, then increase to 75 percent for a day or so and reassess. Ramping back up too quickly can easily cause you to relapse and start the cycle over again.

Illness

Probably the second biggest reason that people get derailed from their plan, illness is one that usually carries with it the most potential for long-term damage. Many people attach a stigma of weakness to illness. Not wanting to admit to weakness, it's common for them to assume a state of denial about their illness. We have often heard, "Oh, I'm not sick. It's just a cold. I can train through it." This denial can result in that simple cold morphing into a sinus infection, upper-respiratory infection, or even pneumonia, all of which could take several weeks to fully recover from.

You have a cold because your body's natural defense mechanisms were not strong enough to keep this virus at bay. It is entirely likely that you are

Compulsion to Train

Letting a compulsion to train overpower the advice to not train when sick often results in the following pattern. See if this sounds familiar:

Day 1) Illness symptoms arise but you keep training normally for the first day.

Day 2) That night the symptoms worsen and so the next day you train lightly, thinking this will be enough to get over it.

Day 3) The symptoms are a bit worse so you take a day off.

Day 4) There is no change in the symptoms, but you get restless and go for a run.

Day 5) You are still not feeling great, but some friends are going skiing, so you go too.

Day 6) You are feeling a bit worse, so you take the day off. You're going to shake this thing.

Day 7) Your symptoms are a little better, and you're back to training. Hard workout. Yahoo!

Day 8) Feeling really sick now, you take the day off.

Day 9) You have a hard time getting out of bed.

Day 10) Chills and fever.

Day 11) Still weak.

Day 12) A little better. No training.

Day 13) Got to do something! But had to cut the workout short—no energy!

Day 14) Back in bed with bronchial infection. On antibiotics now.

You can see how easily two weeks can slip away while ineffectively trying to continue to train and ending up with an illness that will derail training for another ten days or so. What could have been brushed off in a week will now linger for the better part of a month. The result is that it will take a good deal of time to regain your previous strength.

sick because you are training too hard and/or not resting enough. While light-to-moderate training loads can boost natural immunity, heavy loads (high intensity and/or long duration) will suppress immunity, especially during the first hour immediately following the workout. Hence, the age-old parental admonition to change into dry clothes at the end of a hard workout and wear a hat in winter. Your body is especially vulnerable to infection during this window of time, and these extra precautions don't take much effort and really can pay off in keeping you healthy.

Our recommendation, after helping many athletes over many years, is that when the first signs of an illness show up, *stop training*. Your body and its limited

Previous page: Simon Duverney running the twenty-five-kilometer Hardergrat, a grassy ridge-crest trail that connects Interlaken with Brienz, Switzerland. Photo: Dan Patitucci

energy reserves are fully engaged in producing antibodies to fight the infection. Imposing an additional training load on a sick body will only further weaken your immune system and delay healing, as well as potentially open the door to additional infection. This simple but effective method guarantees that you'll be able to get back to effective training in the shortest amount of time.

AFTER THE ILLNESS

So what about after this cold or other minor illness? What is a good way to get back to regular training? You might still have some head congestion but your energy levels have improved. Even a common head cold is going to take two to three days to shake. Do not expect to jump right back to where you left off on that third or fourth day. Your aerobic system will have taken the biggest hit during your downtime. So, you need to return to training first with Zones 1–2 efforts.

To immediately engage in the same heavy training load you were doing before you got sick will usually be a letdown. Your perceived exertion will be higher as you are forced to rely on more anaerobic metabolism for energy. This will restrict the quality of the aerobic training you do during the first few days back. *We have found the simplest prescription for quickly regaining the flow in your training is to return to training with one day of easy training for every day you have been sick and away from training.* If you do this, you'll feel the improvement in aerobic capacity from day to day as it returns to normal. You can very gradually increase duration and intensity during these days. This method has worked well in many real-world applications. In most cases of minor illness, if you use this approach, within a week you will feel like your old self again.

Planned Breaks in Training

If you have the chance to anticipate an upcoming break in your schedule, it is possible to boost the training load for a short period, say a week, going into the business trip or family visit that's disrupting your training. Then, use that planned break as a recovery period, trying to get in just a few short, easy workouts. This sort of planned break following an overload period can be very beneficial to boost you to a higher level in the following days and weeks.

Try to incorporate this break into your plan a few weeks ahead of time so you can build into that hard week. This can remove the anxiety that often comes when missing training. You've planned for it, and you are using this break while visiting the parents or traveling for business as a chance to rebuild before tackling the next training block.

Reframing Adversity

Jared Campbell

In my early years training for the Hardrock 100, I would joke with friends that anything difficult or unusually demanding was "good training for Hardrock." A night run with a failed headlamp: good visual-acuity training. A long run after a stressful workweek without much sleep: endocrine system training. Running out of food and entering depletion mode: an opportunity to condition the body to tap into fat reserves. Lack of traction on icy or slippery trails: proprioception honing. Post-holing in knee-deep snow: resistance training.

Jared Campbell running down from the Grant-Swamp Pass during the early stages of the 2012 Hardrock 100. San Juan Mountains, Colorado. Photo: Fredrik Marmsater

To be a mountain athlete is to be comfortable with rapidly shifting situations. I don't mean just having the latest waterproof jacket or headlamp; I mean being able to mentally deal with the wild ride that often accompanies mountain projects, especially as they grow in time and scale. A seasoned mountain athlete becomes skilled at working through and gracefully absorbing any flavor of obstacle or challenge—logistical, equipment related, nutritional, climatic. To that end, I have found that a regimen of intentional "adversity training" can add a valuable tool to the mountain athlete's quiver—and even provide a mental reframing approach that has applicability beyond just sport.

In 2005, I shattered my calcaneus (heel bone) in a climbing accident. I was told that I'd never run again and that it was time to take up a different sport. Six screws and one plate later I was on the mend and hell-bent on continuing my bipedal activities. The post-surgery time frame represented a fantastic opportunity for both mountain crutching and upper-body strength training. Turns out I loved my forearm crutches, and I went on to summit many of my favorite peaks. I even "crutched" a half marathon.

Six years later, I spent the winter of 2011 to 2012 training for my first Barkley Marathons, a wild 130-plus-mile footrace in eastern Tennessee with arduous routefinding, notoriously bad weather, 60,000 feet of vertical ascent, and a seemingly endless list of things that could go wrong. Since the race's inception in 1986, only ten people had successfully completed it, a finishing rate of less than 2 percent. At the time, I had enough experience to confidently construct a suitable physical training protocol. What I really needed was to be mentally ready.

Training in January and February in the Wasatch Mountains for a footrace was problematic, as more intelligent people were on skis. Given what I knew about Barkley, I wanted to be completely comfortable operating in the worst conditions. I intentionally sought out the nastiest weather. If a storm was forecast to hit in the morning and clear in the evening, I would run in the morning. Given the infamous bushwhacking of the Barkley, I would eschew trails and vector up the most direct lines. If I found myself groveling through scrub oak, or scratching through manzanita bushes, I became thrilled with the opportunity I had been given for proper Barkley simulation.

I finished the Barkley in 2012 and went back to also finish in 2014 and 2016, becoming the race's first and only three-time finisher.

I have spent years consciously reframing normally bad situations into positive ones, an alternative response protocol that has enabled me to finish many of the toughest ultramarathon and mountain objectives. More importantly, however, it has positively influenced my perspective on nonrunning aspects of life as well. When confronted with dramatic or stressful life events, I find I am able to remain calm and measured. In every challenge there is something to be learned and a way to be a better person for it. In athletics as well as in life, find the silver lining and keep moving forward. ∎

Jared Campbell *is a Utah-based adventure athlete who is drawn to combining and applying multiple skills to accomplish seemingly impossible projects, from high-alpine linkups to multi-modality routes in the desert. In his teens and twenties, a healthy obsession with rock climbing took him across the globe. This led to bigger mountain linkups and, eventually, ultrarunning. He has completed more than thirty 100-plus-mile ultramarathons; he is the youngest ten-time finisher of the Hardrock 100 and the only three-time finisher of the Barkley Marathons.*

Overtraining Syndrome (OTS)

Athletes who try to extract their maximum potential will be in a delicate balancing act, precariously close to the physiological edge between supreme fitness and utter physical collapse. The higher the level of the athlete, the narrower that edge will become, and the harder it is to balance there. Increasing fitness comes only as the result of increasing the training stress on the body. The elusive goal of every elite athlete is to find the proper balance between training and recovery. Not enough training stress and you will fail to achieve your potential for this training cycle, perhaps by a few percentage points. On the other hand, too much stress and you risk falling off the overtraining cliff. Doing so can mean that you will fall short of your potential by a huge margin. Balancing training loads with the additional stressors of life, such as family obligations, school, or a demanding job, all complicate the job of maintaining this critical balance. Ignore these normal life stresses at your peril.

Overtraining is a medical issue. In its simplest form, it manifests as an injury. But an insidious and demoralizing potential effect of overdoing structured endurance training is the failure of the body to adapt to the training stimuli. When in an overtrained state, you become less fit even though you are training at the same or higher level than before. In most endurance sports, overtraining is responsible for more failed athletic goals and it shortens more careers than any other factor besides injury. Some athletes struggle with it with several years of stagnation before throwing in the towel.

Endurance athletes find themselves at the highest risk for overtraining due to the high energy demands involved in their daily training regimen. These can exceed 6,000 kcal/day during very heavy training. Unfortunately, most athletes don't intuitively recognize overtraining. In many cases, it takes so long for the athlete to acknowledge overtraining that by the time it is properly diagnosed, it is usually too late for anything but the most extreme measures.

NOTES FROM KÍLIAN

In 2007 I overtrained. I did a big winter with thirty races and then I started running right away. The first indication was that I was not recovering at all. I was super tired. Since I felt bad for a few weeks, I did a blood test to see if I had an iron deficiency. Sure enough, I had super-low iron levels. So I rested completely for two full weeks. After that I started training again very, very easily. I think I caught it early, so I did not need to take much time off, which was good.

Over- Versus Undertrained

It is far better to be slightly undertrained than to be even a little overtrained. This is an important training axiom to keep in mind. If you are undertrained and well rested, you can always draw a bit deeper from the willpower well in competition. However, if you are overtrained and tired, no amount of willpower can conjure strength and endurance from an empty well.

Motivation Versus Compulsion

Everyone involved in high-level athletics is driven to excel. Most endurance athletes fall squarely into the type A personality camp. These people typically adhere to the "more is better" training philosophy. After all, as a general rule, more endurance training *is* better. Willpower, perseverance, or drive—whatever you want to call the fire that burns hot inside your soul—is, without a doubt, the most important attribute you have as an endurance athlete. It can also be your worst enemy when it clouds your judgment and becomes a merciless taskmaster.

Overtraining and Lack of Recovery

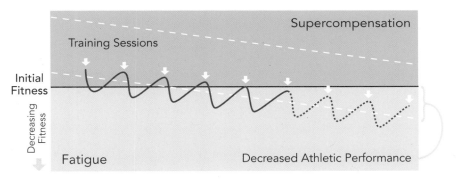

Fig. 4.1 Overtraining
Repeated training sessions without sufficient recovery time can easily lead to a long-term decline in fitness. This condition can take months to recover from if not recognized and corrected early.

Overtraining is not merely getting stiff and sore from a hard workout or needing a couple of extra days to recover from a particularly demanding race. In the exercise science world, that sort of short-term fatigue is called overreaching and is a normal part of the training cycle. When chronic overreaching develops into overtraining, a physiological bridge has been crossed that can be difficult to recross unless the athlete takes drastic action.

A Lesson Learned the Hard Way: Training Isn't Competition

Marc Pinsach Rubirola

I have been training for ski-mountaineering and trail-running races since I was sixteen years old. Now I'm twenty-nine, and I have the background to analyze both the right and wrong decisions I have made about my training programs along the way.

One of the biggest issues with my training was that for a long time I didn't carry it out according to my personal needs and limitations. During these years, I had the opportunity to share training, races, and travels with Kílian Jornet. We are friends, and lived together while we raced and trained with the national team, and we grew both as athletes and people alongside each other. It was a pleasure and a great motivation to learn many things with him.

However, there was also a problem: I wasn't taking my time to grow up, to put some space between him and me, to find my own way in training. Consequently, my performance didn't increase.

Everybody knows that Kílian is a talent with exceptional physical gifts and technique, as well as unparalleled psychological abilities for training and racing. But his way to be fit was dangerous for someone like me, and sometimes I followed his example in my training programs. Kílian was always one or two steps above me, and his influence normally helped me to improve my performance level. But it also led to my being overtrained.

Learning to accept this performance gap—these differences between my body and Kílian's body—took time, some seasons off, and no small amount of psychological struggle. It nearly drove me into a burnout situation.

One of the things I thought I needed to do was to train more every year: more hours, more kilometers, more vertical meters. Until I was twenty-three, this

worked, and my performance grew according to the increase in training load. At that time, I was training 700 hours/year and doing 190,000 vertical meters/season in ski mountaineering. When I tried to increase the load to 850 training hours/year and 220,000 vertical meters/season, I ended up overtrained for four seasons.

It didn't help that my endurance pace during long training was too fast (Zone 2 and above), especially when I trained with other athletes. This pace caused me too much fatigue, so that by the time competition season started, my body was already under excessive strain. I accumulated even more fatigue by doing a lot of long intervals at aerobic pace—for example, three ten-to-fifteen-minute intervals at Zones 3–4. This meant I was spending too great a proportion of those training sessions at a fast pace, while at the same time failing to target competition pace. You are always up to Zone 4 in ski mountaineering or skyrunning races, usually racing for one-and-a-half to two hours.

These mistakes were rooted in psychological and emotional processes. My team (trainers, doctors, physiotherapists, sponsors, friends) alerted me to the risks of following this kind of training, and I understood. Nevertheless, I didn't pay them much attention because I had internalized the idea that in order to be in the top tier, I needed to train more and more—that "no pain, no gain" was the only way to get the best results.

The 2018 European Championships in the Vertical Race were held in Sicily on Mount Etna on a very foggy day. You couldn't see the other competitors and you didn't know if you needed to push to catch someone or to push to not be caught. The conditions reminded everyone that the best way to race was to concentrate on your body, mind, and technique. Italy. Photo: Jesus DYañez

I also needed to feel fit, fast, and strong in each workout session and throughout the whole year. I didn't know how to rest and stay home without physical activity, and I strove for good marks and constant improvement in every training session. I treated each session like a race; I was always needing to prove to myself that I was strong and fit.

Maybe you can get good results in the short term this way, but my psychological and emotional configuration ultimately led to bad results, demotivation, and a lot of frustration and tiredness. In the end, I discovered that all of these wrong decisions were related to low self-esteem—an inability to trust in my personal way to get ready for race season.

It took time to restructure my mental approach and be competitive again. I had to accept that you can't increase training more than 10 percent between two consecutive seasons. I started being more gradual with my training, working my way back to the top slowly and over a period of years. I determined that my body can't train more than 700 hours/year and 200,000 vertical meters/season in ski mountaineering, and I now do the bulk of my training in Zones 1–2, at a very easy pace—the one I feel I could hold for hours without fatigue. And when I train with other people, I go my own pace, even if I end up running alone, with the group some meters in front of me. Training isn't competition day!

When it comes to intervals, I do repetitions at maximum speed for thirty seconds to three minutes. The most important aspect in this kind of training is that the speed is always maximum; if you can't do it at your maximum, it's better to go home and recover in order to be ready for a new session.

You shouldn't train like your favorite athlete or your friends, because there aren't two identical people, and workouts don't produce the same effect in two different bodies. The most important thing is to find what your body needs regardless of what the other people around you are doing. I had to learn to control my emotions in order to be self-confident in doing my own training. I began to focus on myself in isolation, to bring to my body what it—and only it—needs to stimulate an increase in performance.

I now understand that in endurance sports, it takes a lot of time for the body to reach peak physiological development and, consequently, be primed for competition. During training sessions, you build what you will be in the future on race day. ∎

Marc Pinsach Rubirola was born near the Pyrenees in Catalonia in 1989. When he was eighteen, he moved to Font Romeu in the French Pyrenees to study sports science and dedicate himself more fully to ski mountaineering and trail running. He now competes in around thirty races each year. Among his achievements are a skimo world championship title in the espoirs (under twenty-three) category (2011); fourth place in the Pierra Menta (2018) and the Patrouille des Glaciers (2010); third place in the Mezzalama Trophy (2011); a top-five finish at the 2015 World Championships; and many top-ten finishes in World Cup events.

A bird's-eye view of a competitor during the Vertical Kilometer Crepa Neigra race, Val di Fassa, Italy. Photo: Federico Modica

Early Signs and the Common Response

Overtraining is not your garden-variety fatigue that all endurance athletes learn to live with. When you step over this threshold, you are entering a medical condition that is poorly understood, multifaceted, and very difficult to diagnose except by those who have experience with it. Your family doctor is likely to call you a hypochondriac if you present the typical symptoms of overtraining. Even a moderately overtrained endurance athlete is still the picture of health and energy compared to the typical patient. Only in the latest stages of OTS will you present typical illness symptoms that are treatable with medical care.

OTS represents a breakdown of your body's natural adaptation processes. The endocrine and nervous system no longer behave as you have come to expect them to. What was once a light training load, because your body could adapt to it, even in a short-term fatigue state, is now an intolerable and destructive stress. You have to completely recalibrate your concept of *hard* and *easy*. Most of us are unprepared for this dramatic shift and unwilling to accept that we can go so quickly from feeling like an athlete to feeling like an invalid.

Rod Bien runs the ʻOhana Trail near his hometown of Kailua on the island of Oʻahu in Hawaiʻi.
Photo: Liz Barney

The first and most common sign of the early stages of overtraining is repeated shortcomings in performance accompanied by a feeling of flatness or low energy. The coach's or athlete's typical assumption is that this performance decrease is caused by a lack of fitness. After all, you were feeling *so* good just a couple of days before that it can't possibly be overtraining.

The common response when performance drops, especially by self-coached athletes, is to immediately add more training of some sort. The thought being that the training program lacks some key ingredient, and if they just add more of this or that, their lost fitness will return. After they increase their training with no improvement—and usually a further decrease in performance—they continue to seek solutions that involve more training. Thus begins a dangerous downward spiral that can ultimately lead to more than just physical problems. You have invested a huge amount of time, energy, and resources in your physical preparation. In many ways, your sport and your performance in it may define your persona. When you keep coming up short in training and races and suffer with constant deep fatigue, it *will* have dramatic and costly effects on your motivation and confidence.

Overtraining is more easily recognizable if you are doing training on measured courses or using measured paces and see your times drop off. It's much harder to recognize in mountain sports where the track is different every day. This is one reason that we advise having benchmark workouts you can do to check for progress or regression in your program.

Symptoms

The earliest effects of overtraining impact the sympathetic nervous system. It starts with the immediate effect of raising the heart rate for submaximum levels of exertion compared to your normal heart rates. You just don't have your normal pep and vigor and feel flat in training. The levels of the stress hormone cortisol begin to stay elevated between training sessions (this takes a trip to the doctor to determine).

If nothing is done to mitigate the early overtraining, it can progress to a much more debilitating type involving the parasympathetic nervous system. When the parasympathetic nervous system gets involved, there are more negative hormonal effects and a *lowering* of the heart rate for all effort levels compared to normal rates.

When this occurs, watch for one or a number of these unpleasant symptoms:

- Persistent, deep fatigue

- Prolonged elevated cortisol levels (requires a blood test)

- Lowered testosterone levels (requires a blood test)

- Decreased heart rate variability (requires a special HR monitor or EKG)

- Irritability

- Depression

- Weight loss

- Amenorrhea (absence of menstruation)

- Insomnia

- Lowered libido

- Loss of enthusiasm and motivation

The profound state of deep neurological fatigue reached at this point necessitates, at the minimum, several weeks of complete rest, and only then a gradual reintroduction of easy exercise. Sounds grim, right? It is a condition to be avoided at all costs. The best way to avoid this condition is to monitor your response to training by using the methods described earlier in this chapter. The cost of overtraining and underrecovering is so much worse than undertraining, it is far better to err on the conservative side.

Overuse Injury as Indicator of Overtraining

If a muscle is exposed to a new training load on a routine and consistent basis before adequate recovery and adaptation from the previous training session has occurred, at the very least, no fitness gains will be seen. More likely, however, is that the cumulative effect of this premature stress will cause small injuries that will weaken the muscle or tendon. The muscle/brain connection will then self-inhibit the ability to contract the muscle in an attempt to protect that muscle from further damage. A dedicated athlete can easily overcome this pain and suffering and manage to maintain the overuse, but soon a minor tear will turn into a major inflammatory cycle, leading to overt injury and scarring. Chronic tendonitis or worse—full tendon or muscle rupture—can occur.

While these injuries are not necessarily an indication of overtraining as discussed above, they do point out that the adaptation we seek through training is not occurring. This lack of adaptation can be a good indicator that you are on a collision course with overtraining if some remedial steps are not begun.

Take these warning signs for what they are: your body's red flags to get your attention that things are amiss. Rather than get caught up in numbers and times, etc., pay attention to the bigger picture of your body's responses to the training.

Many endurance athletes get a little overtrained at one time or another and hopefully only once. The dramatic wasting effects of overtraining need to be treated with respect when training loads become high.

Periodization

The concept of periodizing sports training into discrete blocks with distinct training aims first arose in the former USSR and gained widespread recognition in the West largely from the writings of Soviet sports scientists. It has been proposed and, in many cases, verified that athletes may achieve better results when their training is organized in a way that focuses attention on only a few physical qualities at a time. Note the earlier distinction between Capacity and Utilization Training methods, which is a form of periodization.

Not everyone uses a periodized training plan. Some very successful athletes adhere to a simpler structure of maintaining all of their athletic qualities all the time by including all different types of training in all phases of their yearly plan. To use this method with the best chances of success requires considerable self-awareness and an extensive training history. Those who fit that description probably don't need this book anyway, so we are going to lay out a basic periodized plan to help guide the rest. Like all training theory, it is not cast in stone and is open to wide interpretation and application based on the individual.

The general idea of periodization is to train for a goal many months away during a *macrocycle*. This can be an annual or seasonal cycle. Once the length of the macrocycle is set, then it is divided into several *mesocycles*. The mesocycles are where the distinct training targets occur. Each mesocycle will stand upon the preceding ones and support the following ones, so their organization is critical to the overall periodization structure. The mesocycles, which last a few weeks to a few months, are themselves divided into *microcycles*, typically seven days in length. Within the microcycle, the daily training prescriptions are used to influence the development of the qualities deemed appropriate for the mesocycle.

As the athlete progresses through the macrocycle and builds the capacity in the qualities that make up the event, it is important that those qualities previously built are not allowed to diminish to any great extent. Thankfully, it takes much less training stimulus to maintain a capacity than it did to first build it.

Transition Period

This period is meant to prepare the athlete for training either after a break following a major event or full competition season or when the athlete is new to regimented training. Depending on the length of the break that has occurred, the fatigue (mental and physical) carried over from the season/event, and the athletic maturity (in this sport) of the individual, this period may be as short as two weeks for an old hand coming off a very successful season, or as long as eight weeks for the newcomer or very worn-down veteran.

Base Period

This period is where the most crucial work of training is accomplished. It is where the athlete focuses on increasing the work capacity of each of the individual fundamental qualities that are needed for his or her event. This is where the base of training is developed. You need this foundation to be rock-solid if you hope to construct a skyscraper of fitness on top of it. During this period your fitness will be increasing, but this will be masked by a low level of fatigue. You'll be carrying this slight fatigue load from day to day as an essential part of the necessary training adaptation process. Because of this, you should not expect your best performance results in training or competitions during this period.

Precompetition Period

This is where the sexy training gets added into the base training. It is training that in most aspects mirrors the specific demands of the event you are preparing for. It combines most, if not all, of those fundamental qualities you just spent months developing. Its length is measured in weeks rather than the months of the Base Period. If you've done your base building well, this creates a fitness level that you have never reached before. Capacity maintenance and recovery workouts fit between more demanding Utilization Training sessions. Fatigue levels are still going to be high, but with better recovery before and after the most important workouts to allow them to be more effective. Examples of workouts in this period might be:

- If preparation for a VK: 8x3 min uphill in Zone 4 with 4-min easy walk-down recovery.

- If preparation for a 100-mile race: back-to-back eight-to-ten-hour days in Zones 1 and 2, three to four weeks out.

Competition Period

You've built up an impressive bank account of work capacity over the preceding several months. Now comes the time to start spending that money. Whether this period involves competitions or just personal achievements that push your limits, the principles will be the same.

This period is a delicate balancing act of wild spending sprees (competitions wherein you are utilizing all the capacity you have) followed by recovery—and hopefully interspersed with some capacity-rebuilding blocks during protracted inter-event periods to allow you to restock that bank account a bit. Depending on the number of races/events you are planning on and the stress imposed by them, you may very well not have much time to do extensive training once the race season is upon you. If you have a long, busy racing season, it can be helpful to set aside a training block during the race season where there are at least two weeks between shorter races and four to six weeks between ultradistance events to allow for the necessary recovery and subsequent rebuilding of the fitness base.

Recall that building fitness requires an extended period of chronically fatiguing yourself in order to get the adaptive stimulus needed to produce meaningful results. Undertaking such a program during the competition period, unless you find yourself with a few weeks between comps, will have little positive effect and potentially bad effects on your results. Blocks of two to three weeks between races can allow you to return to some maintenance-level base training, but remember that you'll be heavily fatigued after your last race and need time to recover from that. When you factor in that you'll also need some tapering time before your next race, your three weeks between races may allow only ten days of capacity-maintenance training.

The Life Cycle of an Ultrarunner

Krissy Moehl

I walked in the door from yet another long, cold, wet run—one of many over a particularly long, cold, and dreary Pacific Northwest winter. I was an emotional wreck after weeks of solo miles in depressing weather, my body often verging on hypothermia by the time I tried to unlock my front door. It was early February, just one month before I was set to race the 100-mile distance in the 2018 UTMB Gaoligong. I could tell that if I continued the training plan I'd originally mapped out, I wasn't going to make it to the finish line.

A 100-mile race takes more than training mileage to finish. It takes a deeper level of psych and motivation, which the dreary winter had sucked right out of me.

I am not a patient person by nature, but I am a patient runner, and the more I pay attention, the more I can apply the lessons I've learned through running to life. In this instance, I did what I'd instruct any of my coaching clients to do: I backed off. I cut my load from eighty to ninety miles a week to thirty, and I focused instead on strength training and flexibility. I cooked healing foods. I snuggled up with my pup on the couch. I laughed at the rain pounding on my window.

I knew balance was what I needed to regain my psych, but it wasn't an easy sell. While it's one thing to tell a client to rein it in, it's an entirely different conversation when it comes to myself. There is a confidence that comes with running. To build that same confidence and trust while sitting on the couch takes prior experience of pushing too hard and then failing on race day, and prior experience of resting and then having the best race of your life.

I didn't have that degree of understanding or patience fifteen years ago, when my then-husband and I traveled to France for our honeymoon and raced the first edition of the Ultra-Trail du Mont-Blanc. In 2003, only a few years into my trail-running career, I was full of curiosity and drive to see what was physically possible.

That summer, France experienced a massive heat wave. I was expecting similar sweltering conditions on race day, but the week before UTMB, a storm swept in with polar-opposite weather: sideways rain and frigid temperatures. Completely unprepared, I had to borrow clothes along the course from strangers; I layered in cotton shirts just because it was a layer. My IT band gave out around mile sixty, so I walked the final thirty-plus miles—all with my jacket cinched so that only my eyes, nose, and mouth were exposed. I even walked across the finish line. I won, but it was essentially by default. The second-place woman came in eight hours later, and the majority of the field—men and women—had stopped at either the 50K or 100K finish lines.

That race, which took a lot of grit and determination to finish, provided a first glimpse of how different the 100-mile experience is from any of the distances that fall under it. Fifteen years and many hundred-milers later, I'm intimately familiar with both the distance and the timeline for recovery—which has lengthened as I've gotten older. It's tough knowing that these big efforts will take me away from doing what I love—running—for two months while my body recuperates.

During those four weeks of pared-down training in advance of the 2018 UTMB Gaoligong, I regained my excitement for the race. My footwear sponsor had taken care of all the travel logistics, and they'd agreed to pay for my boyfriend, DJ, to join me as

Krissy Moehl at sunrise using a headlamp while trail running the Hardergrat, Switzerland. Photo: Dan Patitucci

my crew. In my twenties, just running a race was a big deal. With the 2003 UTMB, the driving question was whether I could actually run 100 miles. Now eighteen years into the sport, I don't know how many more of these international ultras I will do, and I mine each one for meaning. It meant a lot to me to share this experience with DJ, to have him see this important part of my life that is so different from what he sees at home.

We arrived in Beijing a couple of days before the race so I could promote my book, which is also published in Chinese. All the people I spoke with on the tour raved about the Tengchong region, where UTMB Gaoligong

is held. They described the food as spicier, the terrain as mountainous and beautiful and lush. They were right.

The magnitude of the event nearly dwarfed the scenery and the fiery food, however. There were smoke bombs and laser lights and announcers and loud music, and I don't think I've ever been in so many selfies in a twenty-four-hour period.

Once the race got under way, it seemed my training in the foothills near my home had prepared me well. The Gaoligong Mountains aren't huge—the highest we got was 9,000 feet—but the climbing and descending kept coming, ultimately delivering 27,500 feet of elevation gain and equal loss on an erratic elevation profile. The constant change in terrain wore me down mentally, but even in those low moments, my desire to run strong continued to fire. My strategy of pulling back in training had worked. I may not have as much curiosity and psych as I used to, but I now have the smarts and the wisdom to know how to rekindle my drive. It was incredibly rewarding to be in the race and feel the many years of learning pay off.

I was the first woman by more than two hours, tenth overall. Michel Poletti, the husband of the couple who started UTMB, handed me my trophy. He'd walked some of those final thirty miles of the inaugural UTMB with me, and now I'd won the first-ever UTMB International event. In that moment, it hit me how long I've stuck with this pursuit of ultrarunning. It's been eighteen years, fifteen since I first slogged my way around Mont Blanc. Running is the constant thread through my life. It has seen me through moves, relationships, and decades.

I'm a runner, but I'm not the same runner I was when I stubbornly walked across that finish line in Chamonix. I'm a runner who tries to stay present, despite also being a planner by nature. I'm a runner who'd rather run than recover from race after race. I'm a runner who is always learning the lessons that long distances have to offer—and trying my best to apply them to life.

I'm a runner who seeks meaning beyond the distance. ∎

Krissy Moehl *ran her first trail ultra at age twenty-two. In her eighteen-year career, she has run more than 100 races. She has sixty female wins and two outright wins. She grew up in the sport and continues to build her life as an ultramarathon runner, coach, motivational speaker, and race director. She recently added author to her quiver of titles: her book* Running Your First Ultra *was published in December 2015. Krissy is an ambassador for Patagonia, Vasque Footwear, Pro-Tec Athletics, Ultimate Direction, and Lily Trotters. Follow her online at www.krissymoehl.com, and find her on Instagram: @krissymoehl.*

CHAPTER FIVE

The Application Process: Where Theory Meets Reality

In this chapter we move from intellectual underpinnings to the practical application of training theory. This will take you one step closer to and better prepare you for making your own plan.

One thing should be abundantly clear after reading the earlier sections of this book: Top endurance athletes have maximized their aerobic capacity. This means that their AeT is pushed right up close to their LT. Remember the Ten Percent Test? The LT, in turn, is pushed right up near the maximum heart rate. The following two graphs are made from the lactate tests of one athlete. Figure 5.1 comes after a five-month base training season that included a high percentage of Zone 3 and Zone 4 training with very little time spent in Zone 1 or Zone 2. Figure 5.2 is after a five-month base training season using the method described in this book.

For every event covered in this book—from the speediest Vertical Kilometer, to a 100-mile run, to a multiday ski tour—the biggest limitation to performance will come from your aerobic metabolism. Hence we will focus most of our attention there. All other training will be acting in a supplemental and supportive role to enhance that aerobic development.

So how do you develop this essential quality for yourself? Using the models and principles previously introduced, we're now going to explain the various methods available to maximize your aerobic metabolic output.

Kimberly Strom running in the Khumbu Valley, with Ama Dablam behind, Nepal. Photo: Dan Patitucci

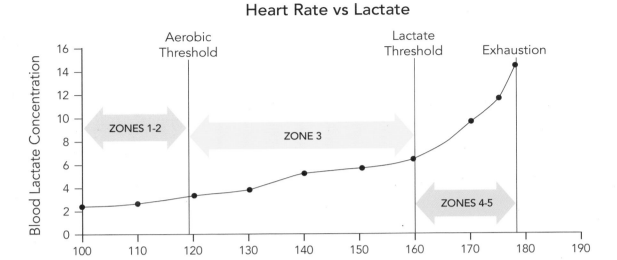

Fig. 5.1 Heart Rate Versus Lactate in Low-Aerobic-Capacity Athlete

Here we see the results of a blood lactate test for an athlete with low aerobic capacity. It shows the AeT (the top of Zone 2) occurs at a heart rate of around 120 bpm, which corresponds to a running pace of about 10 min/mile (6:12 min/km). The top of Zone 3, or the LT, occurs at a heart rate of 160 bpm, corresponding to a pace of 8:20 min/mile (5:10 min/km). With this forty-beat spread between thresholds, this athlete has Aerobic Deficiency Syndrome and needs to do considerable aerobic base work.

Testing

Establishing your own body's metabolic response to exercise is important if you want the best plan. And since we are talking application now, testing is the logical place to start.

Aerobic Threshold Testing

Determining your AeT establishes the most critical metabolic reference point you can know and serves as the foundation from which to build your training plan. We recommend that you know this intensity. Several methods exist and we'll discuss them in order of ease of implementation.

1) MAF Method: The Maximum Aerobic Function is a simple method developed by Dr. Phil Maffetone in the early 1980s that has gained considerable acceptance in the ultrarunning world. It is a simple formula: subtract your age from 180 if you've been training consistently for two years without significant setbacks. Maffetone suggests the following modifiers based on your training history:

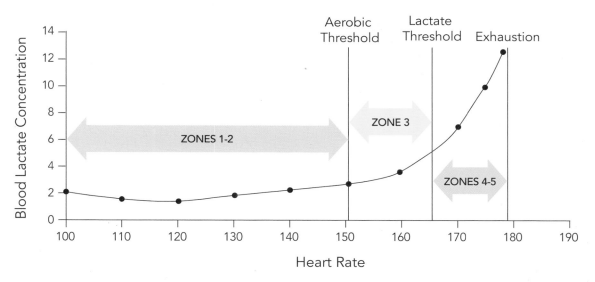

Fig. 5.2 Heart Rate Versus Lactate in a Well-Trained Athlete

Above we see the results of a blood lactate test for the same athlete after a season of proper training. The graph shows the large increase in aerobic capacity. Notice that the AeT has moved up to 150 bpm and corresponds to a pace of 8:15 min/mile (5:09 min/km) and the LT has bumped to 165 bpm and a pace of 7:30 min/mile (4:40 min/km). In this condition this same athlete can now sustain a pace for several hours that he previously struggled to manage for even one hour. Remember the vacuum analogy? This is what a powerful vacuum looks like.

- If you're recovering from an injury or long layoff or get sick more than two to three times per year, subtract an additional five.

- If you've been training for more than two years and showing regular progress, then add five.

In our experience, this formula does tend to err on the side of being conservative; it tends to set your AeT heart rate limit a bit low, which makes it a safe method, especially for newcomers and the less fit. Its biggest problem is that it can't account for increases in your AeT heart rate. Our experience shows that people who are new to this type of aerobic base training program will see a progressive increase in their AeT pace and the corresponding heart rate. With the MAF formula, you are stuck with a heart rate derived from a chronological model.

2) Ventilatory Marker: In hundreds of field tests in moderate-to-well-trained endurance athletes, we have seen a good correlation between the heart rate that can be maintained while breathing only through the nose or while carrying on a conversation with the blood lactate level of 2mMol/L (the commonly accepted

Day 30 ... or maybe 32 ... of Der Lange Weg (The Long Trail). David Wallmann, in the distance, and Philipp Reiter ski into the first light of day. France. Photo: Mark Smiley

measure of AeT). The caveat here is that this works only for those with good aerobic training backgrounds. For those who have no history of aerobic endurance training, or those who have a training background heavily biased toward high-intensity, short-duration work, or people with no history of regular exercise, these ventilation markers fail to correlate with blood lactates. If that describes you, then use the MAF method or read on.

3) Lactate step test. This test can be administered using a treadmill set to a 5 percent gradient or outside on a moderate hill. Start with a fifteen-minute warm-up to enable the aerobic system to come fully online. The test itself consists of a series of three-minute stages at increasing speeds that are just enough to elicit a bump in heart rate of about ten beats per minute. It is important to get the heart rate to stabilize as soon as possible at each new stage and hold it as steady as possible. At the end of each stage, a small blood sample is taken and measured using a portable lactate analyzer to determine the lactate concentration present in the blood. The test needs to be started at what might appear to be an unnecessarily low heart rate—probably walking—and very gradually increasing it ten beats per stage so that you slowly sneak up on the AeT. The heart rate of the AeT is reached when the lactate level reaches or exceeds 2mMol/L, or the first stage where the lactate number increases by 1mMol/L. If using a hill, simply walk back down between stages.

This test is also easy to administer to yourself or with a friend; for less than the cost of lab tests, you and a friend can buy your own lactate meter and do these tests whenever you want. Here is a great little meter we use: http://www.lactate.com/lactateplus.html.

4) Gas exchange test. This test is done in a lab on expensive equipment run by technicians. These tests can range from $150–$350 but are the gold standard for determining your metabolic response to exercise. They can determine your AeT, LT in terms of heart rate and pace (albeit on a treadmill), and, if taken to failure, your VO_2 max. Going to failure is unnecessary for the purpose of finding the two thresholds. Many labs will supply an easy-to-read graph of fat versus carb usage at various intensities. The lab tech should be able to explain the ramifications of these test results. The most valuable and actionable information from the test will be to see at what heart rate you reach your AeT and where it lies in comparison to your LT. If the AeT is more than 10 percent below the LT in terms of heart rate, then you can still make considerable gains in raising the AeT.

Caveat: Many labs and fitness facilities hawking physiological testing are unfamiliar with the AeT test or even the concept of AeT and will want to administer a VO_2 max test and along the way tell you where your LT occurs. This relates back to the sidebar about VO_2 max earlier in the Physiology Section. The problem with using this type of test for determining your AeT is that the VO_2 max test protocols often use short-intensity stages. This will have you zooming quickly through your aerobic zone because they are in a rush to get you to redline and measure VO_2 max—their goal—before you tire. They move through the aerobic zone so fast that your metabolism never stabilizes. To determine the aerobic response to exercise intensity, you need at least three-minute exercise stages.

Lactate (or Anaerobic) Threshold Testing

Unlike the AeT test, this one is fairly straightforward. It involves a maximum sustained uphill effort of thirty to sixty minutes' duration. A treadmill can suffice as a second choice. The less well trained should use thirty minutes of sustained effort, otherwise muscle fatigue will limit your ability to sustain a hard effort.

Start with a good warm-up of at least fifteen to twenty minutes. Do not test this when you have tired legs. Reduce training load for a few days beforehand to get the most indicative results. Finish the warm-up with two to three minutes of Zone 3 running or skiing. Start your recording HR monitor as you begin your test. Try to quickly settle into a pace that is maximum but sustainable for the full test. If you are attentive to your effort and heart rate, you will notice that your heart rate will settle in a very narrow range that feels comfortably hard. If you speed up even by two to three beats per minute, you will be forced to slow again

Luke Nelson embracing discomfort while diving into the difficult later stages of threshold testing.
Photo: Greg Snyder

very soon. Try to find this sweet spot and hold that intensity for the full test. At the end, your average heart rate will indicate your LT intensity (top of Zone 3). Well-conditioned athletes will be able to sustain this output for up to an hour. But less-fit individuals will fatigue, which is why we recommend the thirty-minute test length for them.

Aerobic Base Development: Volume Is the Key

You will never maximize your endurance without first maximizing your basic aerobic capacity (AeT).

While genetic gifts play the dominant role in preselecting who is going to be good at power and speed sports, perseverance and the ability to suffer are the hallmarks of the successful endurance athlete. No wonder endurance sports appeal to the type A personalities for whom more equates to better. A question we often get is, "Just how much is enough?" That is an impossible one to answer. What might not even count as much of a warm-up for Kílian, something he would do before breakfast on a recovery day, might overload others. It all depends on your capacity for this type of work.

Jeff Browning after a winter aerobic-capacity run on the Green Canyon trails in Logan, Utah.
Photo: Fredrik Marmsater

Putting Some Numbers to It

Figuring out your optimal training load is a highly individualized determination. We give some guidelines in the Programming Section of this book, but the best advice is to start small and work up rather than to bite off more than you can handle. When launching into a new season of training with a new plan, you'll be excited and hopefully well rested. Just as in a race, it is all too easy to go out too hard in the short term only to find that you overextended yourself in the first few weeks. This can be demoralizing and will require you to rethink your plan. It is much easier to adjust the training load upward after you determine that it is too light than it is to crumple, dejected or injured, from doing too much too soon. It is hard to progress if you have to move backward.

How can you tell you are doing the right volume of aerobic training? Here's a simple test:

> *When it comes to basic aerobic training (Zones 1 and 2): If you can't do the same workout you did yesterday again today, and tomorrow and the day after for days on end, then you are doing too much. You are doing too much volume or too much intensity for your current regimen to be considered an aerobic base-building program. Caveat: If the top of your Zone 2 is within 10 percent of the top of your Zone 3, you will need to be more sparing with the Zone 2 training. For you, the first sentence in this paragraph would include only Zone 1.*

World-class endurance athletes spend a prodigious amount of time training for their events. At the highest levels it is truly a full-time job, allowing for only enough time and energy to recover between workouts. Most of us won't have that luxury, but to put things in perspective let's look at the training of a nationally competitive mountain runner and skimo racer with a full-time job and family. These are weekly averages for a twelve-month period including a three-week break from training:

- Average hours training time per week: 12.5 hours. With three weeks over 40 hours, and 11 weeks over 23 hours. Annual total = 650 hours.

- Average elevation gain and loss per week: 9,843 feet (3,028 meters). With six weeks over 20,000 feet (6,154 meters), and 17 weeks over 15,000 feet (4,600 meters). Annual total = 512,000 feet (157,538 meters).

- Average running distance per week: 55 miles (90 kilometers). With seven weeks over 100 miles (160 kilometers), and 25 weeks over 75 miles (120 kilometers). Annual total = 2,860 miles (4,576 kilometers).

At the top end, Kílian trains in the range of 1,300 hours per year and over 1.5 million vertical feet. Keep this in mind when you read of his amazing feats of

Chad Sayers ascending the southwest ridge of Mount Shkhara, Caucasus Mountains, Republic of Georgia. Photo: Jason Thompson

speed and endurance. You are seeing what Dr. K. Anders Ericsson, the psychologist and world expert on excellence, calls the iceberg illusion: the end product of a preparation process measured in years. Whether or not Kílian has some special genetic gifts is immaterial. What matters is that he has, since childhood, created a structure in his life where he could devote himself fully to training.

The point we want to make with these figures is not to intimidate you or to suggest that you must train at this level to succeed. *Base your expectations on the reality that your results will be directly proportional to the time you spend in preparation.* A trio of forty-five-minute stair machine workouts a week will not allow you to reach your ultimate potential. But this may be a perfectly reasonable starting place for you, given your personal constraints. The important thing is to start from the right point, and then progress, adapt, and in the process, learn some valuable lessons.

So, why not just do what the pros do? Because you will not have the work capacity of a pro and will likely end up overtrained and/or injured if you merely copy a world class–level training program. The human body has an amazing capability of adapting to imposed loads if it is allowed sufficient time for the adaptation to occur. There is no secret or magic. It is just a work ethic and building a lifestyle around that work ethic.

Getting Started

When you first embark on a program of aerobic development that has as much as 90 percent of endurance training done at or below your personal AeT, it often provokes some questions and comments. While an elite runner is not running slowly when he is in his low-intensity zones, the sad reality is that for many athletes, their Zones 1–2 training will be at an excruciatingly slow pace that seems like it cannot possibly have any beneficial training effect at all. If you find yourself in this situation, welcome to the club: the Aerobic Deficiency Syndrome (ADS) Club (see ADS discussion on page 46). The reason your AeT pace is so slow is that your aerobic capacity is low. In other words, your aerobic metabolism can crank out only enough ATP to support what may be a disappointingly slow pace. The only way to increase your speed at an aerobic level of intensity is to increase your aerobic capacity, which means you must train at and below your AeT.

If you have ADS, it is going to be possible for you to, initially, do almost all of your aerobic training at or very close to your AeT or top of Zone 2. The reason for this is that the pace will be slow enough to not tax your muscles. The problem that most people will have is going slow enough. They have become used to training at a pace usually well above their AeT. The common mistake of trying to constantly push the endurance limit up by training right at the LT is almost an epidemic in the endurance training world. Getting used to slowing down to an aerobic pace is going to take a lot of discipline for most people. But there is no shortcut and without this, the whole aerobic training house will be built on a very shaky foundation.

Remember from our previous examples that *low intensity* does not mean *slow* in well-conditioned athletes. Those who have spent the time to maximally develop their aerobic capacity can maintain prolonged high speeds at their AeT.

So, the first step is to get that aerobic base built as well as you can manage, given your time constraints, both in terms of your annual plan and your daily schedule. Just remember: when in doubt, go long and easy.

There is no prescription suitable for everyone. Some athletes with a very high aerobic capacity will be able to run 100 miles a week at a 7-minute-per-mile pace (4:20 per km). Others will get out of breath on the slightest uphill grade, be forced to walk to maintain an aerobic pace, and will struggle with 20 miles a week.

By maintaining a steady diet of this training for months on end, the components of your aerobic system will become much more powerful. You can recheck your aerobic development every two weeks or so by doing your own AeT time trial. Since this will be relatively easy, you can just toss it into a regular workout. Simply note your time at the same heart rate over one of your regular courses so you can compare it in a few weeks. If training is being done correctly, you will see encouraging drops.

Just remember that when you close the AeT-to-LT gap to within 10 percent, you'll need to reduce the amount of Zone 2 training and do more Recovery and Zone 1 workouts. Do not feel that if you are not running right at your aerobic limit, you are not getting the aerobic benefits. Now you are ready to introduce some Zone 3 and Zone 4 training.

Endurance Training Methods

Finding the balance between long duration, low- to moderate-intensity training and short-duration, higher-intensity training is one of the things that makes coaching and training more art than science. While we've explained some useful general guidelines, the balance of this mix depends upon the event begin trained for (specificity) and the individual being trained (individuality). Shorter events need more high-intensity training. More seasoned athletes need more high-intensity training.

Two distinct methods exist for improving endurance: continuous and intermittent (interval) training. We'll delve into each in this section.

Continuous Training for Improving Basic Aerobic Capacity

By continuous, we mean a steady-state exercise lasting for a minimum of thirty minutes and up to several hours. This is how you'll be accumulating all those hours in Zone 1 and Zone 2 that need to make up about 80 to 90 percent of your total annual training volume. Don't let the term *basic* in the title above mislead you into thinking this stuff is basic and you can skip right past it. That is not the kind of *basic* we are referring to. We are using the term here to mean a base of support for any other training to come on top of. Without this base, the rest of the training will never be as effective. Even a thirty-minute morning jog can be beneficial for maintenance. Keep in mind the role *continuity* plays: These low-intensity, continuous workouts need to be done often and regularly to have their intended effect.

WARM-UP

This seemingly simple task is so misunderstood and misapplied that we feel the need to lay out some prescriptive terms and guidelines to be followed in the warm-up process. The warm-up serves the purpose of preparing the muscles to do the workout in their optimal state. As a general rule, the higher the intensity

(continued on page 166)

Next page: Alyson Dimmitt Gnam doing some continuous training beneath Mount Assiniboine on the British Columbia/Alberta border, Canada. Photo: Steven Gnam

Tracing My Own Lines

Luke Nelson

Jared and I were about thirty-five hours into our Nolan's 14 Fastest Known Time (FKT) attempt, and I was intent on quitting. I couldn't imagine all the ground we still had left to cover after what we'd already done.

Earlier in the day, when we were standing on the fifth or sixth summit, I asked Jared to point out the last mountain we would summit. "You see that mountain on the horizon?" he said. "It's past that." My mind exploded—I could barely see the peak clear out on the horizon, and the one we'd end on was even farther away.

There are fourteen fourteeners in the Sawatch Range in Colorado, and for Nolan's 14 you start at one end and pick your own route through the range, summiting each of the peaks. It's about 100 miles with 46,000 feet of ascent. In September 2017, Jared Campbell and I set out to break the existing record for this do-it-yourself traverse.

I've always been drawn to moving efficiently in the mountains. I didn't come to running from a running background. I started mountain running about ten years ago, and before that I traveled through the mountains by other means: I kayaked, climbed, backcountry skied, and snowboarded. Movement in the mountains has always been the most intriguing part of endurance to me.

For several years my main focus was trail racing, but there were always these secondary mountain projects calling to me. They remained secondary because I had to taper for a race or recover from a race. I'd do them between races or would use them as long training runs. Then I made one a primary focus: in August 2014, Jared and I set the FKT for the 12,000-foot peaks in Idaho. We climbed all nine of them in a single push. The previous FKT was thirty-eight hours, and we cut that down to twenty-eight hours.

I began to feel more of a desire to channel my race-type efforts into FKTs and moving on my own in the mountains. This time of soul-searching came down to a pivotal discussion with my coach, Scott Johnston. "Look, you have to make a decision between doing these amazing adventures and racing, because you can't do both," he said. "It's just too much to do well."

Pulling back from racing is a hard thing to do as a professional mountain runner, because that's where the community comes together, and that's how your fellow racers and your sponsors gauge your ability. To march to your own drummer is tough. At first I was really nervous, because I didn't know what my sponsors' reaction would be, but the companies I work with have been extremely supportive.

I made projects like the Idaho linkup the theme of my summer in 2017. Jared and I did a multiday crossing of what was the Bears Ears National Monument, about 140 self-supported miles in three days, and then we followed that up with an FKT of all the 13,000-foot peaks in Utah in a single push. There are nineteen of them, and we did all of those in thirty-three hours. Jared and I dream big—sometimes too big.

I love that you can have a loose date range for an independent objective. You can wait for things to align perfectly—whether that's training, weather, or conditions—and get after it when everything is ideal. With Nolan's, the date range was August to mid-September. As soon as it looked like the monsoon season was coming to an end and the weather window was opening up, we nailed down a date, did our final prep, and went for it.

Out there on Nolan's, when I decided I was going to quit more than a full day in, Jared played some brilliant mental chess to get my mind going again in the right direction. We spent hours moving forward, Jared listening to me insist I would drop when we reached my dad, who was crewing.

At last we made it to my dad. Jared took off his shoes. Then he started eating some food. Five minutes ticked by.

"Hey, man, let's keep going," I said. I understood that even though I wasn't mentally prepared for the task, physically I was. It doesn't matter whether or not you can imagine how far you still have to go; all you have to do is keep putting one foot in front of the other.

We rallied and got it done. We didn't break the record, but we have the second-fastest time in 53:29.

While trail racing is super fun, and races are great places to gather with the community, I see far more potential to do very interesting things moving independently in the mountains as opposed to just going to a race. At a race you are tied to a course. You are limited by someone else's imagination—by what they think is difficult. One of the biggest catalysts to my transition away from racing was that I was looking to draw my own lines in the mountains, to follow a little different path than most.

Nolan's is the most difficult thing I've ever done. The sleep deprivation, the altitude, the off-trail travel—all of those things combined in 100 miles was pretty amazing. It goes to show that most of us can do more than we think we're capable of. That's a recipe for an incredible adventure: when it exceeds what's considered possible. ∎

Luke Nelson *has spent his life wandering the mountains. After climbing, kayaking, and snowboarding throughout his youth, he discovered running just over a decade ago as a way to move through the high country. He has dozens of podium finishes in mountain running races and ski mountaineering races, including winning a US Ski Mountaineering National Championship. Overall, what he enjoys most is moving quickly and efficiently through the mountains.*

Luke Nelson is all smiles after completing a two-day traverse of the Boulder-White Clouds Range. Ketchum, Idaho. Photo: Steven Gnam

of the workout or race, the longer the warm-up. For workouts in Zones 1 and 2, a perfectly good warm-up can be accomplished by easing into the pace of the workout for ten minutes. However, if you are doing high-intensity training, we suggest following a warm-up routine outlined below. On days when you are tired, allow a longer time for the warm-up to assess how you are feeling and if any adjustments need to be made to the day's planned workout.

Stage 1: Your body will have likely been in a fairly sedentary state before beginning the warm-up. As such, the parasympathetic portion of the autonomic nervous system will have been dominating. This is the portion of your nervous system that drives the resting and digesting functions. This part of the warm-up serves a purpose of getting the sympathetic nervous system activated. This dilates the capillaries in the skin and muscles and adjusts blood pressure accordingly so that the working muscles can get their full complement of blood and oxygen. Raising the body temperature is a key part of the warm-up. This is best accomplished with light aerobic exercise. Notice when you begin to break a sweat. That is an indication of the capillary dilation and elevated temperature. Expect this to take at least ten minutes. This period also serves the purpose of getting the aerobic system fully online.

Stage 2: Limbering callisthenic movements and dynamic stretching done at a gradually increasing pace and effort will begin to activate some of the stretch reflexes in the joints and prepare your muscles for higher loads. You should not feel any strain during this portion of your workout. This stage can last from five to ten minutes. If you are moving into an interval session, finish this phase of the warm-up with two to three minutes in Zone 3 using the training mode of the main workout (running or skiing).

COOL-DOWN

The purpose of the cool-down is to gradually return your body's systems to homeostasis, reduce the core temperature, metabolize some of the waste products, and relax psychologically from the focus of the workout. The higher the intensity of the workout (or race), the longer the cool-down should be. A long, low-intensity workout may not require any cool-down other than a couple of minutes' walking at the end. After a high-intensity workout or race, a typical cool-down should be twenty to thirty minutes of the Recovery Zone or Zone 1.

RECOVERY WORKOUTS

The importance of these very low-intensity workouts cannot be overstated. As your AeT improves, your Zone 2 workouts will impose higher neuromuscular loads and need to be spaced further apart. These lowest-intensity recovery workouts will begin to fill a bigger and bigger part of your training volume. You

Example Warm-Up Routines

- Easy aerobic running or skiing in Z1 until you sweat. Maybe 10 to 15 minutes.
- If a low-intensity workout is planned, move directly into that.
- If a high-intensity workout is planned, move to the next steps.
- For running, do the following exercises with gradually increasing intensity:
  10 air squats, no rest, then …
  10 leg swings for each leg, no rest, then …
  10 trunk rotations for each side, no rest, then …
  High-knee running in place for 20 seconds, no rest, then …
  Bouncing on your toes for 20 seconds, no rest, then ….
  2 to 3 minutes in Z3–Z4 uphill.
- For skimo, do the following:
  3 min uphill skiing in Z3, no rest, then …
  2x10 sec uphill skiing in Z5 with 2-min recovery between.

will need more modulation of the training load. This light aerobic work has a dramatic restorative effect on a tired body.

The jury is out on the *why*, but almost all endurance coaches have seen the value of prescribing these mellow workouts. Author Scott Johnston has coached very well-trained cross-country skiers who thrived on long recovery workouts. Several Western coaches of Kenyan runners have remarked about the Kenyans' dependence on very long, "stumblingly slow"–paced recovery runs as key elements of their training.

Most people will find thirty minutes to an hour a useful amount per workout. It may only be a twenty-minute brisk walk before bed. Whatever the underlying reasons, this very low-intensity training should not be dismissed as too easy to be doing anything worthwhile. At the very least it is preparing your body for the rigors of the upcoming workout by speeding the recovery process. If done properly, you should feel better at the end of this workout than when you started. And you should also feel much better the following day than you would have had you foregone this workout.

When you get in the practice of doing effective and consistent recovery workouts, you will notice that the next day's workout will almost always feel great. If it doesn't, then you either needed more recovery work or an easier pace. This is also the place to add in cross-training like biking and swimming, especially if your legs are feeling beat-up.

KEEP IT SIMPLE

Heart rate and ventilation will be your best guides here. It may mean slowing and even walking the steeper uphills to maintain the intensity at the desired level. Don't

Athletes in the Lagorai Cima d'Asta Ski Mountaineering Race. Photo: Federico Modica

worry that your heart rate drops on the downhills. Just let it drop. If you are running, don't thrash yourself on every downhill in a vain attempt to keep your heart rate in the zone. The downhills provide a valuable strengthening effect in mountain sports, so don't discount them just because your heart rate is low. We recommend counting your full time—both up and down the hills—for hilly workouts.

PICK-UPS

A very effective, and fun, workout is to include short pick-ups (speedy segments) into long Zone 1 and Zone 2 workouts. These pick-ups will range from eight to ten seconds in the earliest stages, and last up to fifteen seconds in the later stages. We could argue over why these work so well as a training stimulus, but suffice it to say that this strategy has nearly universal acceptance among endurance sports. Begin adding these after a few weeks of aerobic base training.

You may find that it suits you to do your pick-ups early in the workout when you are freshest and do them in a structured repetition style, or to toss them into the workout throughout as the terrain and feeling motivates you.

By doing these early in the workout, you'll be fresher and faster, developing more of a speed- and strength-training effect. By doing them late in a workout, you'll be asking your legs to push fast when fatigued and will get more of an endurance effect.

The volume of the pick-ups during an individual workout should initially be limited to no more than six to eight, and the speed should be only a fun, fast pace—never a full sprint. Do at least two minutes of easy running between reps. We have found that a single workout per week of these is plenty. If done consistently in the base aerobic phase, these will do a good job of preparing you for the harder work to come.

HIGHER-INTENSITY CONTINUOUS WORKOUTS

These workouts serve a valuable purpose in training the mixed metabolic processes above your AeT and around your LT in Zone 3. As mentioned in the discussion of intensity zones, this training has a powerful effect on improving endurance and can be seductive. Don't fall into the trap of letting most of your distance runs morph into the following types.

Tempo

Tempo workouts involve continuous fun, fast efforts (Zone 3). They are usually from twenty to sixty minutes in length. Their intensity can span the full breadth of Zone 3 (between the AeT and LT). Remember that if you have done a good job of increasing your aerobic capacity, then your AeT will be within 10 percent of your LT. This will translate into a narrow Zone 3 heart rate range; often fewer than fifteen beats. The goal should be to hold as steady an effort/heart rate as possible for the entire time. Resist the temptation to turn these workouts into hard efforts or personal time trials. That is not the purpose and, in fact, going too hard will defeat the purpose, which (once again) is to hold a steady effort/heart rate. Use a ten- to twenty-minute Zone 1 segment before and after the workout to warm up and cool down.

Also, well-conditioned athletes can benefit from adding a Zone 3 tempo segment (twenty to thirty minutes) in the middle of a long Zone 1/2 workout.

Progressive Distance

Progressive distance workouts have a similar effect as tempo workouts but with the added stress of doing the faster running at the end of a long workout. Start very slowly with a warm-up and gradually increase the pace or effort/heart rate during the workout. The main section of these workouts where you are operating just below and above your LT can last for ten to thirty minutes and will greatly enhance endurance due to your prefatigued state. These workouts can be done for as short as sixty minutes but become much more effective when extended beyond ninety minutes and even up to two hours.

Example progressive distance workout: Start with forty minutes in Zone 1. Then move to thirty minutes in Zone 2. By now you should have a sense of whether this is a good day to push harder or if it would be smart to back off and finish the workout in Zone 1, saving the hard work for a day when you feel better. If you do feel good, add on twenty minutes in Zone 3. If still feeling strong, increase the effort for a final five minutes in Zone 4.

To get the full benefit, you will want to have one or two days of recovery workouts after these higher-intensity continuous workouts. One workout like this each ten to fourteen days after the early Base Period will be a sufficient stimulus even for the well trained.

SUMMARY

- Gauges of whether your aerobic intensity is appropriate include: Are you recovering overnight so that you can do the same workout again day after day? Can you carry on a conversation while doing these workouts? Can you breathe through your nose while doing these workouts? Is your blood lactate level staying below 2mMol/L while doing these workouts? Is your AeT pace increasing on a biweekly to monthly basis?

- Be patient. Do this unglamorous work well, and you will be greatly rewarded later. Rush through this period, try to take shortcuts, or interject much long, high-intensity work during this time, and you will be shortchanging your long-term chances before you even get into the racing season.

- Include pick-ups in one distance workout each week to begin to build some specific-strength endurance before moving on to more demanding high-intensity aerobic interval training.

- After at least six to eight weeks of base training, you may find it useful to start adding in higher-intensity continuous workouts once every ten or so days.

High-Intensity Interval Training for Maximizing Endurance

"It is an important but unresolved question: Which type of training is most effective for building endurance? 1) To maintain an intensity level representing 90 percent of the maximum oxygen uptake for forty minutes. Or 2) To tax 100 percent of the oxygen uptake capacity [author's note: Zone 4] for sixteen minutes."

– Per-Olof Åstrand, *Textbook of Work Physiology*, 1970

A new study by Stephan Seiler may have settled this question. In it, well-trained endurance athletes used four by four minutes, four by eight minutes, and four by sixteen minutes with a two-minute rest interval training protocols. The four-by-eight-minute method showed significantly better gains in endurance than the others. Interestingly, the length of the work period turned out to select for

Philipp Reiter at his aerobic intensity while running in Yosemite National Park, California.
Photo: Jordi Saragossa

the intensity. Going as hard as one could sustain for the duration and number of repetitions resulted in the four-minute periods being done at the top of Zones 4–5. The eight-minute periods were done in Zone 4, and the sixteen-minute periods in Zone 3.

While true for the well-trained and elite-level athletes, less well-trained athletes with lower muscular endurance will not be able to sustain the high speeds/intensities for the full duration of these work periods or the full workout. For this reason we suggest the inclusion of Zone 3 intervals and Muscular Endurance training for most athletes as preparation for these Zone 4 workouts.

A LITTLE HISTORY – THE WHAT

Interval training has been around for over a hundred years in various forms, but we owe the popular, modern variation of it to one man. In the late 1930s German track coach Woldemar Gerschler coined the term *interval training* when describing his method of intermittent training where high-intensity work bouts were separated by intervals of rest. His theory was that it was during these intervals of rest that the most important changes to the heart muscle occurred that resulted in an increase in stroke volume. Today, the word *interval* is normally used to describe the work bouts rather than the rest periods. The changes to the heart's stroke volume that Gerschler saw are the

reason that Zone 4 intervals are often referred to as VO_2 max training. Recall that stroke volume is the main limiter to VO_2 max.

Gerschler and his fellow researchers proposed that by breaking the competition distance down into short segments, repeating several of these relatively short bouts of high-intensity work separated by rest intervals, the athlete could accomplish a larger volume of high-intensity training, with its cardiovascular benefits, than could be obtained from a continuous bout of exercise of similar duration. Doing so resulted in unique adaptations, and this gave birth to structured intermittent training methods.

The basic principle of interval training is that you go fast, then recover, then repeat. Gerschler stipulated a very strict procedure for the application of his interval methods, but in the intervening years many variations of how many repetitions, the duration of the repetition, the intensity of the repetition, the length of the recovery interval, and whether active or passive rest have been used. Hundreds of studies have been done on interval training to determine what works best. The ultimate answer is … it depends. Recall Per-Olaf Åastrand's quote at the beginning of this section.

It depends on:

- What training effect is desired

- What training background the athlete has

- When during the training cycle the interval training occurs

Interval training is an important component of the overall endurance training program. It will yield the best long-term results when imposed on a solid aerobic base (a high AeT) and done in conjunction with a high proportion of purely aerobic training. But most importantly, it should not be considered a shortcut to fitness, nor a stand-alone method of training.

THE HOW

"I think of my high-intensity training as falling into a few different, simple types: VO_2 max / Z4, muscular endurance / Z3, and strength like hill sprints (see below)."

– Kílian Jornet

We can make a rough division of the use of intervals into aerobic intervals and anaerobic intervals.

- Aerobic intervals are meant to maximally stress the capacity of the aerobic system (both carbohydrate and fat fueled). The effect is decided by the intensity of the work periods that are done in Zones 3 and 4.

Previous page: Jenn Shelton runs hard past the Whitney group on the way to Mount Russell (14,094 feet) in the Sierra Nevada Mountains, California. Photo: Ken Etzel

Go hard, rest, repeat. Alyson Dimmitt Gnam catching her breath on top of a ridge in the Lewis Range, Glacier National Park, Montana. Photo: Steven Gnam

- Anaerobic intervals serve to maximally develop the anaerobic capacity and specific strength. The intensity must be very high: Zone 5. To be effective, you need to be recruiting the highest-power (FT) muscle fibers. These fibers fatigue quickly and need a long recovery. You need to be well rested and take long rest intervals between the individual work bouts. Don't do these with tired legs. They are used sparingly for the events covered in this book.

Many people mistakenly feel that these should be exhausting workouts where you drive yourself to nearly complete system failure. To be sure, this is very *hard* training and it will be tiring. But if you are reaching far beyond your current capacity for this sort of work, you may push yourself so far into fatigue that you need extra recovery time or even days off. Doing this too often can mean a loss of continuity of training.

Before we get into the details of discussing workout makeup, we're going to review the basics of interval training. We'll start with the aerobic intervals since, for most endurance athletes, these will predominate the interval volume.

Skimo training on the Passo del Tonale, Trentino, Italy. Photo: Federico Modica

AEROBIC INTERVALS

These have a powerful effect on improving aerobic endurance and can be separated into two realms: Zone 3 intervals, often called threshold intervals, and Zone 4 intervals, referred to as VO_2 max or aerobic power intervals. Both should be done using sport-specific methods.

Threshold Intervals (Zone 3)

The purpose of doing these intervals is to raise the LT speed and to increase the duration that it can be maintained. They range from twenty to sixty minutes of hard work, depending on the development stage of the athlete. These have a strong muscular endurance training effect.

If you are new to this training method, start with short-duration repetitions, such as three to six minutes. Use short, active recoveries in the ratio of 3:1 or 4:1 work to rest. Experienced endurance athletes may work up to 3x20 or even 2x30 minutes for one of these sessions.

Since this is a fun sort of hard and feels like training, some athletes inadvertently include some in almost every session. As we hope you understand by now: there is not one workout or one intensity that can optimally achieve what the combined effect of several different intensity doses and durations can achieve. While threshold interval workouts are an important component of the training repertoire, they make up a small percentage of the overall volume on a yearly basis for the most successful endurance athletes.

Aerobic Power Intervals (Zone 4)

Aerobic power (often called VO_2 max) intervals are conducted at intensities greater than LT; usually at near 95 percent of max heart rate. Total volume of the work bouts can range from fifteen to thirty minutes. These workouts maximally utilize the capacities of all the systems involved in endurance. The effectiveness of these workouts is very reliant on the athlete's muscular endurance, which is why, in the Planning Section we recommend using a period of special muscular endurance work and Zone 3 training to build sufficient muscular endurance to make these Zone 4 intervals more effective. If your leg muscles become tired and you are forced to slow down, causing the heart rate to fall below the Zone 4 range, you are no longer getting the intended benefits of Zone 4. This is why, for best effect, these workouts need to be done when you are rested. The less fit you are, the shorter the work periods should be. Muscular endurance will be discussed in more depth in the Strength Section.

When you are comfortable with Zone 3, meaning you can manage around 10 percent of the total weekly time in Zone 3, begin to add Zone 4. Do this by replacing some of the Zone 3 time with Zone 4 time. Replace two minutes of Zone 3 with one minute of Zone 4. If you struggle to recover and handle this shift, reduce the volume of Zone 4.

30/30s

These are a good way to introduce Z4 intensity into your interval routine and add in a bit of speed to what may become some fairly slow but hard uphill efforts. You'll need a good warm-up that culminates in three to four minutes at Z3. Then you'll be ready to roll right into the 30/30 sets.

Thirty seconds is not very long to run or ski hard, so you'll need to control your pace so that you don't start out too fast and then are forced to slow dramatically after the fifth one. The best way to do this is to build your effort and heart rate to where you are hitting Z4 by the middle of the second 30/30 repetition. Then slow for thirty seconds—but only enough to allow your heart rate to drop five to seven beats. Repeat this until you feel the power and speed drop or until you notice that you can't get your heart rate into Z4. As your endurance improves, you'll be able to increase the volume of this workout.

We like to start athletes with 2x6 min of 30/30s with a couple of minutes easy between the sets so they can get the feel of the pace and effort. Next session, go to 2x8 min, then 2x10 min, until you are doing 2x15 min, then go for one twenty-minute session. Thirty minutes total time in one bout is a good goal but tough to achieve. These are especially useful for skimo, where speed and turnover need to be trained along with endurance.

When at this stage in your training progression, do the Zone 3 and Zone 4 workouts on separate days and allow at least seventy-two hours between them.

Work periods range from thirty seconds up to eight minutes, with a work-to-rest ratio of 1:1 up to two minutes. Two minutes is adequate for longer work periods. Rest intervals should be active and not full rest so that the aerobic system stays revved up.

MUSCULAR ENDURANCE

Muscular endurance is a special form of strength training used to increase the endurance of the faster-twitch/higher-power muscle fibers that are responsible for the limits of endurance performance. This type of training is done by imposing extraordinary loads on the muscles, which causes local muscle fatigue in the specific locomotion muscle groups rather than a global fatigue. You can do this by either using steep hills and/or by adding weight to your body, or by doing special gym workouts discussed later. This method can be employed throughout the Base Period. Since it is a form of strength training, this method is covered in the Strength Section on page 198.

ANAEROBIC INTERVALS

You may ask why athletes involved in the sports we cover in this book need to concern themselves with increasing what seems like a quality that only sprinters need. After all, haven't we spent the last hundred-odd pages emphasizing the importance of the aerobic system? Anaerobic-capacity training in the methods described below are actually a form of very specific strength training. It turns out that improving this type of sport-specific strength also improves *economy*. Improved economy means lowered energy cost at any given speed. This can have major performance implications over multihour events. Anaerobic intervals will make up only a tiny but important fraction of any endurance athlete's overall training.

Increasing anaerobic capacity is a slow process because the amount of work that an athlete can handle in this realm is quite small compared to the daily and sometimes twice-daily aerobic workouts. This has led many coaches to observe that "Sprinters are born and distance runners are made." Translation? Almost everyone will respond positively to endurance training, whereas speed and power is largely a genetic gift. Therefore, responses to this training will vary greatly. It used to be thought that raising the anaerobic capacity was impossible, but more recent long-term observations indicate that it can be raised with judicious training over several years. We're not going to turn you into the next Usain Bolt with this training, but the work will improve your uphill speed in a way that complements the endurance training.

Training to increase anaerobic capacity uses the same basic format as an aerobic interval session: go hard, rest, repeat. But in this case you will take a longer

Kílian Jornet, clipped into a fixed line, negotiates a ridge on day four of the 2017 Pierra Menta. Kílian went on to take second place that year. France. Photo: Jocelyn Chavy

recovery between repetitions. The distinction from aerobic interval training is that these exercises are not meant to train endurance, so it is important that the anaerobic system is fully (or very nearly) restored so that each repetition can be executed at the same maximum intensity. This requires very short work periods of eight to fifteen seconds, separated by long recovery times of at least one to two minutes if the intensity of the reps is in the correct intensity range. A rest-to-work ratio of at least 4:1 or 5:1 and up to 10:1 is used. If the rests are too short, the workout will shift to training endurance because the high-power muscles you are trying to train, which have poor endurance, will not recover and will drop out of the recruitment pool. Then the more endurance- trained motor units take over. The result will be slower reps and less anaerobic-capacity/ strength improvement.

Hill Sprints/Hill Bounding and Downhill Speed
A very effective anaerobic-capacity leg-power workout we like to use is Hill Sprints or Hill Bounding once a week during the Base Period. These are repetitions of very short duration (eight to ten seconds) with complete recovery (one to two minutes). The training effect in the early workouts will be mainly

Fig. 5.3 Hill Bounding

Hill Bounding is like Hill Sprints except you are taking long bounding strides with a maximum-effort explosive push on each stride and maximal time in the air.

neurological as your brain learns how to sprint. In our experience, most endurance athletes struggle with these workouts. The first several of these workouts may not even make you tired, so they don't feel like training and you'll wonder, *Why am I doing this?* The rest periods feel way too long, so endurance athletes want to shorten them. If you are not getting tired with these, it's because you are mainly using your slow-twitch motor units and they are so well endurance trained that they do not get tired in eight to ten seconds. *If it feels ineffective, then that's a sign that you need it even more.* As your brain learns to recruit more fast-twitch fibers, you will become more powerful. This will translate to longer stride lengths and improved economy.

Learning to run and ski downhill fast is like learning any skill: it takes practice. Both these skills take a lot of leg strength and agility. A good way to approach their development is to insert short (one to two minutes) high-speed downhill repetitions into some of your weekly easy-distance workouts. Increase the number and duration of these reps over the course of weeks.

Hill Bounding is done with a bounding stride where you exaggerate the length of the stride and spend more time in the air with both feet off the ground, and with a lower-tempo leg turnover than the hill sprint running. This can be done with poles by skiers and without by runners.

Anton Krupicka runs a rocky ridge in the Tetons, Wyoming. Photo: Fredrik Marmsater

Hill Sprint/Bounding Guidelines:

Use a 30-percent-grade hill or steep stairs. Steeper is generally better for building strength and power, but hills over 50 percent can be hard to maintain traction on. Stairs work best when you get very steep (if you can find steep and long stairs). Skip stair steps to create a bounding workout. Follow the long warm-up procedure outlined on the following page to avoid injury. If you are inexperienced with this type of sprint training, ease into this program by starting the workouts at 80–85 percent of maximum effort and slowly increasing the output during the repetitions for the first two to three workouts. Injury is a real risk when using this program.

Special considerations: The grade of hill/stairs in percent is a ratio of the change in vertical distance divided by the change in horizontal distance. A 30-percent (about seventeen degrees) grade rises three feet or three meters for every ten feet or ten meters of horizontal run. Long sets of stairs that will take you ten to twelve seconds to sprint up can be hard to find. The typical fire escape stairs in commercial buildings are usually in the range of thirty to forty degrees, making them an ideal gradient except that they have landings spaced about ten feet (three meters) apart. Regardless, they are fine to use if nothing else is available.

HILL SPRINT/BOUNDING WORKOUT

Warm-Up

This is very important!

1. Twenty minutes of running warm-up with a gradually increasing pace, finishing with two to three minutes at a Z3 effort. Break a sweat during this run. This gets your muscles warmed up and the aerobic system going.

2. Ten minutes of dynamic stretching: bouncing on toes, lunges, legs swings, and ballistic toe touches. This activates the stretch reflex in the tendons to let them know they are about to get a workout.

3. 2x20 or 30 sec medium-to-hard effort hill run or bound. These wake up the anaerobic energy system and the associated fast-twitch muscle fibers you need to do this sort of work. One to two minutes' slow walk downhill between these.

4. 2x20 sec skipping uphill. This gently introduces the dynamic and ballistic loading that you will be working next. One to two minutes of slow downhill walking between these.

Workout

Once you feel well warmed up and have no pain, you are ready to begin the main work.

1. Execute 6–8x10 sec of maximum power bounding with a long stride or running sprints. Take a two-minute easy downhill walk as recovery between sprints and a three-minute rest between sets when and if you increase the number of repetitions beyond eight.

2. Twenty minutes' easy jog cool down.

Workout Progression

1. You will progress by adding more repetitions to the workout. Do not increase the length of the repetitions beyond ten seconds.

2. If you are new to this form of training, be cautious. As mentioned above, this is a potentially injury-causing workout. Start with using 90–95 percent of maximum force. Only add force after you have handled two to three of these workouts with no problem.

3. Add no more than two repetitions per week to the total volume.

Note: One of the biggest problems endurance athletes have doing Hill Sprint and Bounding workouts is exactly what makes this particular training good for endurance athletes: they hate resting. This training requires a radical shift in thinking. The extended rests are a vital part of the training effect. There is a good reason why sprinters may only run a total of a couple hundred meters in a workout and spend most of their time stretching and resting on the grass. It's not that they are lazy. It's that intensity is king in these workouts.

ANAEROBIC ENDURANCE

This may seem like a misnomer. How can a power output that is sustainable for only a minute, at most, be considered endurance? For most endurance athletes, this training will make up only a tiny fraction of the yearly volume. As you will read on the next page, Kílian does only two to three of these workouts. Nonetheless, it can still play a role for any event that has surges, or where maximum outputs are required. This type of training is often misunderstood and consequently misused.

This stuff's very hard. It hurts. It requires a great deal of willpower. This is maximum training at its absolute maximum. You have to drive yourself to exhaustion to get the benefits. It has to be used judiciously. Most endurance athletes have a very low capacity for this type of work. It may take only two to three of these workouts spaced seven to ten days apart to reach the highest levels of anaerobic endurance needed for the events covered in this book. Fast-twitch athletes or born sprinters can do much more and will see bigger gains. But that is a tiny fraction of mountain athletes. This is definitely *not* a type of training that should be included in all phases of training. Less well-trained individuals should use it with caution only in preparation for important short races like the VK. The benefits are small and the risks are high.

Two of the popular interval methods for this type of training are:

- Maximal work bouts of two minutes with a work-to-rest ratio of about 2:1, repeated four to six times or until exhaustion. These will build very high levels of lactate, and the theory goes that many beneficial aerobic and anaerobic adaptations occur from this sort of workout. Due to the short recovery periods, fatigue may prematurely halt this workout, limiting the volume of training and hence its effectiveness.

- A second type involves going the maximum speed for twenty to thirty seconds with a recovery of two to three minutes, repeated eight to twelve times. These intervals allow a higher speed, and with their longer recovery, may allow a greater volume to be completed in a session. As you read, this is Kílian's preferred method.

NOTES FROM KÍLIAN

Before every race season, I do two to three shorter-interval sessions for my maximum speed. These intervals are short and I go as fast as I can on a slight hill. These are bouts of twenty, for a maximum thirty seconds. I will do ten rounds, then rest for a bit, then do another ten rounds. Maybe a third round if I still feel a lot of bounce in my legs and heart. This usually happens only in the second or third session. This helps me have that extra gear for a really short, hard effort in a race (like in a good fight with a strong competitor).

Unlike the aerobic interval methods explained earlier, the point of anaerobic intervals is to produce as much lactate as possible and to maintain that high level for as long as possible. The workouts are exhausting and require significant recovery time along with a healthy dose of aerobic regeneration work afterward.

In the Planning Section we will demonstrate how to incorporate these workouts into your own training plan.

Kílian Jornet doing a hill-sprint workout in Norway. Photo: Jordi Saragossa

Mike Foote Sets New World Record for Uphill Vertical Skied in Twenty-Four Hours

Laura Larson

Mike Foote cranked up his final lap—his sixtieth—with fifteen friends in tow. It was nearing 9 a.m. on March 18, almost a full day after he first started skinning up and skiing down the 1,020-foot Ed's Run at Whitefish Mountain Resort in Montana. During the previous lap, he'd eclipsed the world record for vertical ascended and descended in twenty-four hours on ski-mountaineering gear. This last push was a celebration.

"It was really emotional and really special, and I was surrounded by people that I love," he says. "It was an amazing thing." It was also his second-fastest lap of a very long day.

Foote reached the bottom with seven minutes to spare, having gained a mind-bending 61,200 vertical feet since 9 a.m. the previous day. "I could have, in theory, climbed for five more minutes and then descended again, but I chose [not to]. It felt like a very clean thing. I did a final full lap, and I was really happy being done."

The Missoula-based ultrarunner and skimo racer had been training toward this esoteric goal for several months. Austrian Ekkehard Dörschlag had set the bar at 60,000 feet on the dot in 2009, during a twenty-four-hour event at a ski resort in Austria, and once Foote stumbled across his achievement, the desire to surpass it took hold. He had been on the hunt for the skimo equivalent of a mountainous 100-miler, and here it was: an effort perfectly suited to a guy who shines in steep, technical, long-duration trail races like the Hardrock 100 and UTMB. He was going to chase some vert.

Foote began collaborating with Uphill Athlete Master Coach Scott Johnston in December 2017, and together, the two came up with a program that would have Foote—already a high-level athlete—doing the bulk of his workouts at event pace. They calculated this to be around 2,800 to 3,000 feet per hour, which would give him the necessary buffer for transitions and descending.

"By defining the pace that he needed to maintain, that gave us a target to use. That formed the basis for the whole training strategy. It really wasn't that complicated," explains Johnston. "Mike has an incredibly high work capacity, so he managed to put in some phenomenal weeks of vertical. Some of the numbers are staggering."

Over the three months leading up to mid-March, Foote averaged 29,233 vertical feet per week and racked up a staggering 42,360 feet, 50,526 feet, and 50,942 feet during his three biggest weeks. Most weeks saw him training over twenty hours, with a peak of twenty-four hours.

"My workouts were less about intensity and more about long, slow efficiency—really holding that zone and that effort for very long periods of time and seeing how that felt," says Foote. "Skiing allows me to do higher volume in [terms of] time, because there's no impact, so my body can handle it better."

Before the record attempt, the two biggest days Foote had ever had on skis—both around 20,000 feet—were back-to-back, just a few weeks out from the event. The block went amazingly well. "I felt like I could have done it then," he says. But then a switch flipped, and his body rebelled. "I cratered afterward, and the next week I felt horrible. I had to travel that weekend, and I missed a lot of sleep and didn't really recover. Then I was in the hole."

Mike Foote halfway through the 600-mile Crown Traverse from his doorstep in Missoula, Montana, to Banff, Alberta, Canada. Photo: Steven Gnam

That hole cast a pall over Foote's initial laps on March 17, leaving him wondering if he had he overdone it in training. "I was feeling pretty junky for the first two to three hours," he admits. "I went into this very negative spot of feeling like I might let everybody down and I wasn't going to be able to do this thing I'd put so much time into and made so many sacrifices for. I was mentally in a tough spot."

A lot of it turned out to be no more than jangly nerves. Once his body eased into the activity, he fell into a comfortable rhythm. "I was just trying to stay super consistent," Foote says. "I wasn't really looking at my watch or anything, I was just trying to ski by feel."

That methodical approach carried over to the descents, which he used for recovery while still prioritizing speed. "It was important for me to not take the downhill for granted. I definitely pushed every single descent to find that balance between going down really, really fast but at the same time not trashing myself," he says.

Ever mindful of time, he streamlined the transition process by setting his base-area crew up with an additional pair of Dynafit skis and several pairs of skins. When he'd get to the bottom, he'd click out of one pair of skis and click right into another pair, prerigged with skins.

As he churned out lap after lap, Foote fueled steadily, consuming everything from gels and Coke to real food like soup broth, PB&Js, sweet potato muffins, and sticky rice balls with bacon. "I was able to eat about 400 calories an hour, which is just a ton," he says. "I also went through two-thirds of a quart of maple syrup, which I'm really proud of."

By the twelve-hour mark, he'd already racked up 33,500 feet. Plus some fans. The North Face tent stationed in the middle of the run during the day proved to be a draw, attracting numerous skiers curious to see what was going on. (Foote is a TNF Athlete; the company fashioned a custom skimo suit for him for this effort.) At the bottom, these skiers became spectators and cheerleaders, giving Foote a much-needed energy boost and creating a fun, supportive atmosphere.

The weather was perfect during the day: forty degrees and sunny. But when the temperature dropped into the twenties that night, the sloppy daytime mashed potatoes froze up, rendering the surface conditions extremely tricky. "I was doing a lot of sliding backward on my skins," Foote recalls. "I had to really yard on my poles and straps just to push myself up the hill." (A few days out, he still has numbness in his left hand from that overreliance on his straps.)

To make matters even more challenging, he battled a downslope wind for six-plus hours that night, and his quads and feet were killing him on the icy, chattery skis down.

"I was literally yelling out loud on the descents when I would hit a chunky section. I've never experienced anything like that," he says. His feet were battered from being stuck in the same sweaty ski boots for the full twenty-four hours—a decision he regrets. "When I finally took my boots off, it was not a pretty sight."

During the night, his 3,000-foot lead on the record eroded to 1,000 feet—a mere twenty minutes. He knew he needed to dig deep. "I was thankful for the pacers, because they were keeping me honest, but I was still going pretty slow." Among those pacers was fellow ultrarunner Luke Nelson, who stuck with Foote for six hours. "Luke cracked the whip on me in a big way and was an awesome, awesome support out there," he says.

By morning, Foote had maintained his gap on the record, and he finished strong, surrounded by that gaggle of pals. He was reawakened to the power of simply moving forward, of putting one foot in front of the other. "You'll come out the other end. I always forget that, and then I'm reminded during something like a 100-mile mountain race or this effort," he says. "It's a really unique experience to feel so close to giving up, so close to quitting, and then to be able to focus on the movement—on relentless forward progress, and then suddenly your body and your mind come back around."

Absolutely integral to his success was his crew of twenty-odd friends, including his girlfriend, as well as a string of other unexpected helpers along the way. These included people like the groomers who, unbidden, started coming by to put down fresh paths of soft corduroy for him during the night, making those teeth-chattering descents a little less brutal.

"No way could I have done this alone," Foote insists. "It's a reminder that to reach your best moments, it's important to have support." Along with pacers and folks wrangling gear at the transitions, he had people walking beside him handing him food and others taking care of all the documentation necessary for a world-record attempt—photos, lap times, everything to ensure the twenty-four hours would hold up under scrutiny.

"It was a full-on team effort." ∎

Laura Larson *is a writer and editor whose career has taken her from outdoor publishing to celebrity gossip and back to outdoor publishing. She splits her time between proofreading how-to and where-to guides for* Mountaineers Books, *writing for* Uphill Athlete, *and trying to keep up with her dog on the local trails. He deserves a lot of the credit for her two 50-mile and six 50K finishes since 2015.*

Mike Foote in the daylight hours of his record-setting attempt for human-powered vertical ascent and descent on skis: 61,170 feet in 24 hours. Whitefish, Montana. Photo: Steven Gnam

SECTION THREE

Strength and the Uphill Athlete

CHAPTER SIX

Strength Training for the Uphill Athlete

*Athletes strength train to improve performance in their event and for injury preven-
tion, not to become stronger in the gym. This is especially true for endurance athletes.*

A lot of studies have tried to answer the question of how strong an endurance athlete
needs to be. Two seemingly contradictory findings emerge from most of the studies:

- Endurance sports typically utilize up to only about 25 percent of an athlete's
  maximum single-repetition strength, but do so for up to many thousands of
  repetitions.

- Nonetheless, increasing max strength does seem to have a positive effect on
  endurance.

While few studies of this type have been directed at mountain endurance
athletes, it is safe to make the following assumption: Strength plays a big role in
mountain sports where an athlete has to lift his or her body up and lower it down
over potentially many thousands of meters.

While it makes intuitive sense that a certain minimal level of strength is required
for endurance sports, if the second bullet point above were to be taken to its ultimate conclusion, Olympic weightlifters should be the fastest marathoners. Clearly
this is not the case. Why?

Strength is largely a *neurologic* quality, whereas endurance is largely a *metabolic*
quality. Restating this: Strength depends on the brain's ability to recruit the greatest number of muscle fibers for a task. Endurance depends on the rate of metabolic

Previous page: Strength is a crucial contributor to an athlete's speed. Here, a team races across
the exposed ridge of Mont Coin, with Mont Blanc looming in the background, during the 2010
Pierra Menta skimo race. France. Photo: Jocelyn Chavy

Opposite: Forrest Coots earning his turns in the remote Cerro Castillo zone of Patagonia, Chile,
while on a sixteen-day ski trip exploring the area. Photo: Jason Thompson

Katie French and Alyson Dimmitt Gnam put their strength to use dropping into a creek bed while circumnavigating Mount St. Helens, Washington. Photo: Steven Gnam

turnover of ATP molecules. We use the modifier *largely* above because these two qualities overlap and are interdependent in endurance sports.

Among similarly performing endurance athletes, the stronger ones tend to have better performance. This means that among all marathon runners with finishing times between say 2:10 and 2:15, you could list their running time and certain strength test results and see a strong correlation between performance and strength. Just being able to deadlift more does not guarantee that you will be a faster runner. But if you can deadlift more than those with a similar running speed, chances are very good that you will also run faster than those people. More importantly, sport-specific strength correlates better than general strength when it comes to predicting performance. Studies have shown that sport-specific strength exercises like standing broad jump, the single-legged hop, and even the thirty-meter sprint are decent predictors of 5K running race times when comparing runners with similar times. These exercises are much more running specific than a general leg strength exercise like the deadlift.

So, how much strength is sufficient? The answer: No one really knows.

General Versus Specific Strength

Before going too deep into any discussion of strength training, we need to define some terms and concepts.

General strength is nonsport specific, meaning that it may bear little or even no similarity to the movement, speed, or range of motion made in the sport for which you are training. For an athlete, general strength provides a base for the more sport-specific strength training that follows and it makes the athlete less injury prone.

Specific strength is sport specific, meaning that it mimics quite closely (exactly, in some cases) the demands of the sport. This type of strength training has a direct bearing on the athlete's performance in that sport.

General Strength

Ski mountaineering, skimo, and mountain running are all locomotive sports involving single-legged propulsion. Effective movements in all of these rely on good hip stabilization in order for the prime-mover muscles to do their job best. So, even general-strength training for these sports should place heavy emphasis on single-legged strength exercises.

Most of the popular gym-based strength exercises fall under the "general" category when training for sports.

So, why bother with general-strength training at all? While there certainly are mountain athletes who avoid general-strength training altogether, you'd be wise to consider your own needs rather than blindly following what others do. If you are deficient in general strength, it could well benefit you to engage in a simple strength training program. It can make the sport-specific strength training (which relates directly to performance) more effective.

Keep the statement at the beginning of this chapter in mind as you develop a strength training program to improve performance in your sport. In the end, you don't care how much you bench press or deadlift, right? You mainly care how fast you ski, run, or climb, right? Nonetheless it is easy to get swept up in the "gym strong" mentality and overdo the general strength. Spending too much time and effort on general strength can not only detract from more beneficial specific training time, but it is possible to become too strong with the bulky muscles that come with that excess strength.

Let's use one of the most popular general strength movements, the back squat, as an example of what we are talking about. The back squat is a popular general-strength movement for many sports because it engages some of the biggest prime-mover muscles in the hips and legs as well as the core. Improving this strength up to a point can translate to better sports performance. But where is that point? Again, no one really knows.

In strength, speed, and power sports like sprinting, the field events of throwing and jumping, or American football, increasing squat strength will correlate quite closely with improved performance. For endurance sports where we propel

Diego Pazos winning the Mont-Blanc 80K in Chamonix in 2015. France. Photo: Martina Valmassoi

ourselves with one leg at a time, an exercise like the squat will fit only into the general category.

Even though we can't make categorical recommendations regarding how much general strength you need, we can make some suggestions. If you are a mountain endurance athlete who can't do a half squat with your own body weight carried on your shoulders, you could probably gain performance and durability with added strength. But it is doubtful that being able to squat twice your body weight will add anything to your performance, and may in fact detract from it. Your performance would no doubt benefit more from spending the additional hours doing specific-strength exercises, rather than trying to increase your squat strength by twenty pounds.

Similarly, the pull-up is a very good upper-body general-strength exercise, and if you are a skimo racer who can't do a single pull-up, you would probably see gains by improving this general strength.

However, no athlete, especially the amateur with job, school, and family obligations, has unlimited time or energy to devote to training. You need to examine the strength demands of your sport before diving into a bench press program when your goal is improving your VK time.

Specific Strength

These workouts should model the ranges of motion and speeds of your event quite closely. Why? The brain's muscle-recruitment patterns are a learned skill. Doing very heavy and slow movement in a semispecific-strength exercise like a single box step is a great way to build general strength in those muscles, but at some point in your progression you need to transfer that box-step strength into a specific exercise like Hill Sprints. The speed of muscle contraction is much faster, and those motor neurons need to be trained to produce the sport-specific movement pattern and contraction speed, and not just slow strength. This is the justification offered by endurance athletes who predominately use specific-strength methods.

A simple exercise that meets the needs of the mountain sports being covered in this book is sprinting or bounding uphill. Both the speed and gradient add the resistance and result in the desired strength-training effect using the sport-specific movement patterns for all these sports under consideration.

Economy and Muscular Endurance

While exceptional levels of strength are not required (and may even be detrimental) for athletes participating in an endurance sport, *sufficient*, and especially

Anne Gilbert Chase training at The Mountain Project in Bozeman, Montana.
Photo: Jason Thompson

sufficient specific strength do contribute to better movement economy. How? Increasing strength allows for longer strides with less effort. It takes a smaller percentage of an athlete's maximum strength to propel him- or herself farther in one stride. Especially for ultrarunners, the decrease of stride length during races is one of the most powerful predictors of race results. Muscular endurance training can greatly improve the ability to ward off the sort of late-race neuro-muscular fatigue brought on by pounding down hills. We will dig deeper into muscular endurance training later.

Speed and Strength

Speed of movement is directly related to strength in that movement. In general, the stronger you are, the easier it will be for you to overcome the resistance to your movement. For mountain sports, overcoming gravity when going uphill, or resisting it when going down, requires strength. So, gaining strength, especially specific strength, up to a point benefits you. But, too much can hurt if it adds mass and lowers the strength-to-weight ratio. The quality we call muscular endurance is more important in successful training for all endurance events than pure strength. As we will show, there are many ways to develop it—from specific muscular endurance, circuit-style workouts, to uphill Zone 3 interval training, all the way to long runs on hilly terrain.

Muscular Endurance and Strength

The boundary between strength and endurance becomes blurred when we talk about a concept called muscular endurance (also called local muscular endurance and strength endurance). As the name implies, muscular endurance relates to the amount of strength that can be maintained over an event-specific length of time. Because of event specificity, this term takes on very different meanings for a 100K runner versus the VK runner.

The shorter the event, the larger the role played by muscular strength; the longer the event, the greater the importance of muscular endurance. But the governing concept in both cases is the same. The reason for the merging of strength with endurance is that to complete many repetitions (be that 100 reps at 50 percent of your maximum strength or 20,000 reps at 20 percent) depends both on the maximum strength and also the endurance (metabolic) qualities of the most powerful muscle fibers needed to complete the task. In chapter eight we will look more closely at ways to assess and improve muscular endurance.

Verónica Bravo running through the fog above Palma de Mallorca, Spain.
Photo: Martina Valmassoi

Summary

Some important points to keep in mind as you read ahead are:

- Athletes, and especially endurance athletes, use strength training as one of several tools. They do not get stronger just to be stronger. They get stronger to enhance their performance.

- Not all strength training is accomplished in the gym by lifting weights.

- Gaining strength without adding to overall body mass is critically important for endurance sports. After all, you have to carry those muscles around.

- Improving muscular endurance can have a very strong positive effect on improving performance and should be considered an important part of most training programs. By enhancing fatigue resistance, it maintains higher levels of running economy in long events.

Next page: Clare Gallagher chasing her why during a winter training run up to Chasm Lake, Colorado. Photo: Fredrik Marmsater

Don't Forget to Pack the *Why*

Clare Gallagher

Aside from the myriad preparations I do for an ultra-race, from the physical to the mental, I also bring my *why* to the start line. I'm never going to run a 50K, let alone a 100-miler, just for the hell of it. If anyone aloofly says that they run these just for kicks, they're lying.

We all need a *why*. Mine has evolved over the few years I've been in the sport. I ran my first 50-miler—in Thailand—only six months after my last collegiate track race, and then I tackled my first 100-miler less than two years after that. My *why* began as a mixed curiosity of, *Can I do this?* Plus, *I really want to run in the Golden Triangle*. Eventually it got to, *Why not try a 100-miler?* combined with, *Well, I have nothing else going for me right now*.

But the most common *why* to the many ultras I've run, aside from the fact that I'm a little sick in the head, is that I really love running long across mountainous terrain knowing that it will never get any easier. Sure, I can be more prepared, fitter, more experienced, and tapered before an ultra, but I've yet to finish a race and think, *Wow, what a delightful cruise that was!* It's always going to suck somehow. And I love it.

You'll sprain an ankle. Your hydration flask will explode and you'll lose all of your Coke on a devastatingly hot trail section. You'll chafe the skin off your inner thighs. You'll come to in a bathtub outside Auburn, California, at 3:00 a.m. while your mom bathes your raw pink body, and you're screaming because *something* is wrong with your leg and there's hardly any skin left in your butt crack. You'll feel tired and slow and fat and stupid and want to quit. You'll think the world is ending. You'll contemplate finding broken glass just so you can step on it to make the misery end once and for all.

You'll pee blood. You'll poop blood. You'll crap your pants and dig so many holes that you'll lose count. While flying downhill, you'll hit a sharp rock exactly on the blister on your big toe, causing it to sear so badly that you'll see black dots. You'll yell at your selfless friend who gave up her weekend to pace you. Then you'll cry, begging her for forgiveness. You'll threaten your boyfriend: *If you don't find me some ibuprofen...* You'll sob at evergreens, appalled that they are not helping you through this. You'll laugh with aspens, complimenting their breathtaking golden leaves.

You'll wonder if you've lost your mind.

You'll eat a jar of frosting and finish it with a liter of Coke. You'll fantasize about vegetable broth and salt pills. Your headlamp battery will die in the first mile of your first 100-miler. You'll fall face-first on a flat fire road, smashing your already-tweaked patella. You'll eat a pack of seaweed-flavored potato chips in your first ultra, cementing your addiction to the sport. You'll vomit. You'll DNF a race—heartbroken and physically broken.

Then, approximately thirty minutes to three weeks after the last agony-filled shitstorm, you find yourself sheepishly researching your next race. How are we so stupid?

Maybe within all of the sucking, all of the suffering, there's magic that we tap into during ultras.

I keep coming back for the moments of utter serenity, deep in a forest or high on an alpine trail, or even just grinding away on a godforsaken fire road. I live for the quietness. Where it's just me, a little human creature moving by her own steam somewhere on this beautiful planet. I patter along far enough that maybe, using a powerful telescope, an alien from another world could see the route I traveled across Earth that day. The alien doesn't have to know about the anguish ... that's mine to cherish. ∎

Clare Gallagher is a trail runner and a lunatic. She thought running track and cross-country at Princeton wasn't cool enough, so she moved to Thailand to teach English and run her first ultra. Subsequently, she gained ten pounds of fried rice and Thai sweets (not a joke). She's been significantly less injured since then (also not a joke). So please eat some ice cream.

CHAPTER SEVEN

General-Strength Assessment and Improvement

Endurance athletes can't afford to get stronger at the expense of added muscle mass. They've got to carry that muscle around with them and supply it with fuel and oxygen. The following information is designed with this in mind. You will not find any recipe for gaining muscle mass here.

For the lower body, the goal is first to ensure better single-leg, hip, and knee stabilization so that you can apply power more effectively through the major joints to propel yourself farther in each stride. Single-leg stability originates mostly in the hips, specifically in the gluteal muscle group. Without adequate strength in this important muscle group, it is common to see unhealthy knee and ankle alignment. At best, this will have a negative effect on movement economy, power output, and stride length, and at worst, this will set you up for overuse injury. If while standing on one leg, your knee makes a side-to-side movement during either knee flexion or extension, you may have some weakness that warrants remedial work best done with basic strength exercises.

Upper-body strength and its role in performance is often overlooked by runners and especially by skimo racers. The shoulders, arms, back, and chest all contribute directly to stride length in both skiing uphill and in running. If you do not think that the upper body and arm swing play a role in running or skimo, here's a simple experiment: Strap your arms to your sides and then try to run or ski quickly. Get it? Even in running, the arm swing transfers a great deal of energy to the legs.

Having a relaxed shoulder girdle that allows a fluid swinging motion of the arms will impart additional power to your legs and result in added stride length,

Laëtitia Roux of France, one of the most accomplished women in skimo, during a 2015 Pierra Menta victory with Mireia Miró. France. Photo: Jocelyn Chavy

An unknown runner, Mount Fuji, Japan. Photo: Martina Valmassoi

whether you're running or skiing. Very high strength levels are not important to runners, but the endurance to maintain that arm swing for hours *is* important. When your back and shoulders become tired, your arm swing will suffer—and so will your stride length.

In the following pages we'll show you some well-tested basic exercises and explain how to combine the ones you need into a workout, and then how to progress that workout over the course of weeks and months. Do not feel constrained to do only these exercises. They are by no means all-inclusive. Adding or substituting similar exercises will have similar positive results.

Assessment and Basic Exercise Programs for Legs and Hips

It will be informative to assess your basic strengths and weaknesses by testing yourself using a few simple exercises before launching into a strength-training program. Do this by moving through the exercises listed in the routine that follows this introduction. As you assess your strength, keep in mind that some athletes may be best served by doing unglamorous remedial strength work, just as some need to do the remedial, slow running to correct ADS, while others with good basic strength will be best served by using exercises further along the progression to specific strength.

While there are certainly other strength assessments that can be used, we are going to suggest some simple tests to assess knee stability. Weak hip muscles, specifically the gluteus medius, are the culprit in many running overuse injuries to the knee and lower leg. The aspect to monitor in all these exercises is the ability to keep the knee lined up over the toes when viewed from the front. You can face a mirror or you can simply look down to see if your knee moves side to side during these exercises. If your knee moves inward, toward the centerline of your body when you put weight on it, as your knee either bends or straightens, then you have an alignment issue that is very likely related to a hip stability/ strength deficiency.

In most cases this is easily fixed by simply improving the lateral hip muscles' strength by using the exercises described in the following pages. However, in some cases the services of a professional strength coach will be required. The simple assessments provided below are not a substitute for professional advice.

Air Squat Test (Easy)

This is the simplest assessment. Assume a normal squatting position: feet at shoulder width, toes pointed outward slightly, arms held out in front horizontally at shoulder height. Squat down to bring your butt between your heels as low as you can while keeping the spine in a neutral position (straight, not flexed or hyperextended). Watch your knees as you go down and come up out of the squat.

- Do your knees collapse in at all?

- Can you hold your knees outward so that they remain aligned vertically over your toes?

If you cannot maintain knee alignment over your toes, you can stop the test here and start with the Stage 1 strength program. If you can hold them in alignment with conscious effort, go to the next test.

Fig. 7.1 Squat Test

To perform this test, stand with feet shoulder width apart and toes angled outward slightly. Squat to where your thighs are parallel to the ground, and stand back up. Do your knees cave in toward your centerline? Or, do they track in line over your toes? The illustrations above show the difference between good form where the knee tracks over the toe and the poor form where the knee caves inward.

Ryan Sandes looks for more power during a route recon before attempting to break the FKT for the Drakensberg Grand Traverse in Northern Drakensberg, South Africa. Photo: Kelvin Trautman

Box Step Test (Medium)

Stand facing a box or step that is just below the height of your knees. Your toes should be no more than twelve inches (thirty centimeters) away from the box. Step up onto the box while watching for any inward collapse of your knee toward the midline of your body. And then step down from the box. Repeat this several times on each leg while observing how your knee tracks.

- How far toward your body's midline does each knee move?

- Do your hips move outward to the side as your knee collapses inward?

If either of your knees collapses to the inside by more than about one inch (2.5 centimeters) and/or your hips shift to the outside by a similar amount while stepping up onto the box, you can stop the test here and use the Stage 2 strength program. If you can hold knee alignment, go to the next test.

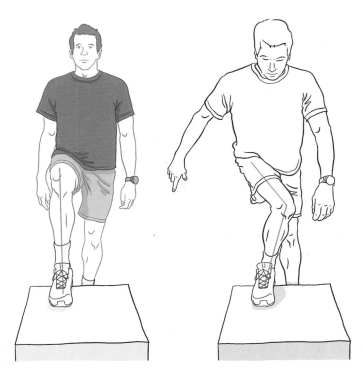

Fig. 7.2 Box Step Test
Stand about 12 inches (30 centimeters) in front of and facing a box or bench that is just below your knee height. Step up onto the box and note whether your knee moves inward or if it tracks closely over your toes as you step up.

Sit-to-Stand Test (Difficult)

Stand in front of and facing away from a hard-surface chair or preferably a bench that allows you to sit on it with your knees bent at ninety degrees and thighs parallel to the ground. Lower yourself to the sitting position on the bench or chair. Do not relax your leg muscles but immediately stand up by using only one leg. Do not hinge your upper body forward at the hips. Try to keep your torso fairly upright. Notice how your knee tracks over the toes of the foot you are standing on as you rise into a standing position. For many people, arising from a seated position using only one leg will be impossible due to strength. In that case, add a thick book or two to the chair or bench so that you can just barely rise on one leg, or try the box step test.

- How far toward your body's midline does each knee move?

- Do your hips move outward to the side as the knee collapses inward?

If either of your knees collapses inward by more than one inch (2.5 centimeters), use the Stage 3 strength program. If you can manage this difficult test with good knee tracking, move directly to the specific-strength program.

Fig. 7.3 Sit-to-Stand Test

Lower yourself to a sitting position on a bench or chair. Immediately raise yourself back to a standing position using only one leg. This is very challenging to perform at all, let alone with good knee control.

If after three weeks of the following strength programs, you do not see marked improvement in your knee tracking/control, consult with a good physiotherapist to determine if you have some underlying structural issue. When you have achieved the appropriate level of knee control, you can move to the next stage of the strength progression.

Stage 1 Leg and Hip Program

This group of exercises is designed to first teach your brain how to turn on the lateral gluteal muscle groups and then to build some strength in them. Initially use high reps with low resistance; four sets of twenty reps or until you fatigue. Take a one-minute rest between sets. Between sets of these leg exercises, insert a set of upper-body exercises that are described in the next section. Retest for knee alignment after a couple of weeks, and move on to Stage 2 when appropriate hip stability is gained.

Fig. 7.4 Squats with Knee Band
A good hip-strengthening exercise can be done by squatting with a rubber band placed just above the knees.

Fig. 7.5 Single-Leg Lateral Band
A more advanced hip-strengthening exercise is done by placing a rubber band around your knees (either above or below) and while balanced on one leg, extend the unweighted leg to the side and back at about a 45-degree angle.

Stage 2 Leg and Hip Program

Start these with just your body weight to learn the movements with correct form and control by doing three sets of fifteen reps on each leg, with one to two minutes' rest between sets. Progress by increasing reps each session to the point of fatigue. Between sets of these leg exercises, insert a set of upper-body exercises covered in the next section. When you can do three sets of thirty reps with perfect knee control and balance, move to Stage 3.

Fig. 7.6 Box Step-Up

Stand about one half of your stride length in front of a box or step that is just below knee height. Step up onto the box mainly using the front leg to pull you up with minimal assist from the rear leg. Maintain proper knee tracking over your toes throughout this exercise.

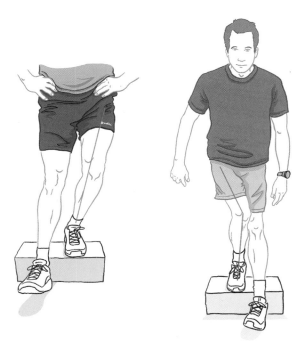

Fig. 7.7 Box Step-Down

The left figure shows the box step-down exercise with proper knee alignment. The right figure shows the weighted knee collapsing inward due to poor hip strength. If you cannot maintain good knee alignment when doing this exercise, use a lower box to step down from.

Fig. 7.8 Front Lunge

From a standing position, step forward onto a bent front knee. Push back and up to return to the standing position. Alternate legs for the required number of repetitions. As you gain strength you can add resistance by adding a weight vest, holding a barbell to your shoulders, or holding a dumbbell or kettlebell in front of your chest.

Dimitra Teocharis tests her strength at the Marmoleda Full Gas race on the Marmolada Glacier in the Val di Fassa, Italy. Photo: Federico Modica

Stage 3 Leg and Hip Program

Once you are proficient with Stage 2 exercises, progress by adding weight to the same exercises. Select enough resistance in the form of a weight vest, pack, or barbell on your shoulders so that you can just manage eight reps with perfect form. Do four sets of six reps using this weight. Between sets of the leg exercises, insert a set of upper-body exercises covered in the next section. Take a two-minute rest between sets of the same exercise.

Assessment and Basic Exercise Programs for Upper Body

While not particularly obvious for running and skiing, it can still prove very worthwhile for you to evaluate your personal upper-body strengths and weaknesses as well as perhaps improve them. As with the leg and hip exercises, this list is far from exhaustive and instead represents a bare minimum for those with little to no strength-training background.

Skimo Upper Body

Skimo is a quadrupedal sport: all four limbs are used for locomotion. In skimo's sister sport, cross-country skiing, the arms and upper body play a significant role in propulsion (up to 20 percent in diagonal stride classic technique, which mirrors skimo uphill skinning). Even though the upper body plays a smaller role in skimo due to less ski glide in the climbing sections of the course, there is probably still a 5–10 percent contribution to propulsion from the upper body and arms. Have you noticed how fatigued your arms become during a strenuous climb? This should be a clue as to their contribution (or lack thereof) to your skinning.

Increasing the strength and endurance of the poling muscles will lead to an improvement in uphill skinning endurance. We will look at the methods a skimo racer can utilize to improve these qualities and show how to incorporate workouts into your training plan a bit later in this section; suffice it to say that if you are not incorporating ski-specific upper-body training into your program, you are not doing everything you could to maximize performance.

Push-Up Assessment

With this single simple test, you can get a good handle on your overall upper-body strength. This is a good exercise for runners because it requires strength in the arms, shoulders, and core. Assume a plank position so that your hands and toes support all your weight, as if you were going to do a standard push-up. Keep your spine in a neutral position so that your hips don't sag or rise up into an inverted "V." Place your hands in a comfortable spot below your shoulders.

If you cannot hold this top position for five seconds without sagging or raising your hips, place your hands on a chair or bench top and assume the same push-up position. If you can now manage to hold this top position for five seconds, take a two-minute rest and then count how many push-ups you can do. If you can't hold this top position, then move your hands to a countertop (about one meter high) and try again to complete at least one inclined push-up from your toes. See the illustrations on page 218 for clarification. If you can manage to do only inclined push-ups, start with the Stage 1 Upper-Body Program.

If you can hold the normal push-up top position for more than five seconds, rest for two minutes and count the number of push-ups you can do without losing form. If you can do fewer than five proper push-ups, use the Stage 2 Upper-Body Program.

If you can do more than five push-ups with good form, use the Stage 3 Upper-Body Program.

Pull-Up Assessment for Skimo

The simple pull-up (palms facing away) or chin-up (palms facing you) is a good indicator of basic upper-body pulling strength. There are other ways to train ski-specific single-arm poling strength and endurance (to be discussed in the next chapter), but we'll use the pull-up for this general-strength assessment.

Using either a chin-up or pull-up grip, hang from a bar and pull yourself up until your chin is just above the bar. Start with slightly bent elbows and with your shoulder blades pulled down (retracted). Don't start in a fully extended hanging position.

Fig. 7.9 Lower Pull-Up Position

When hanging from a bar at the bottom of the pull-up position, try to hang with the shoulder blades retracted, as in the illustration above right, rather than loose and extended, as in the illustration above left, as this may cause injury to weak shoulders.

If you cannot hang in this bottom position with your shoulders retracted, use the Stage 1 Upper-Body Program.

If you can hang in this lower position, then try hanging with your chin above the bar. Use a stool or have a friend lift you to get to this top position. Hang for as long as you can in this position. If you can hang for two seconds or less, use Stage 1. If you can count to three seconds or more, use Stage 2.

If you can do between one and four pull-ups, use Stage 3.

If you can do five or more pull-ups, use the Specific Strength–Training Methods for skimo in chapter eight.

In our view, a well-equipped gym is a simple, clean space with basic free weights, simple boxes, bars, and rings. Aaron Bollschweiler working on upper-body strength. Momentum Climbing Gym, Sandy, Utah. Photo: Andrew Burr

Stage 1 Upper-Body Program

Runners: Use the appropriate level of incline from the push-up assessment that allows you to complete three sets of as many inclined push-ups as you can do with two to three minutes' rest between sets, during which you will add a leg exercise. When you can do more than eight push-ups in the third set, progress in this exercise by moving to a lower surface to use for your inclined push-ups, and repeat until you can once again do more than eight reps during the third set. Keep decreasing the incline angle while holding good plank form as you get stronger.

Skiers: Add either assisted pull-ups or a lat pull-down machine. Complete three sets of the maximum repetitions you can manage with two to three minutes' rest between sets. When you can do more than eight reps in the third set, increase the weight or reduce the assistance. See the exercise descriptions on the following page.

Inclined Push-Ups

Start with the level of incline that allows you to complete the prescribed set and reps, and progress as per the instructions above.

Fig. 7.10 Inclined Push-Up

If you are unable to do a proper push-up on the floor, then elevating your hands on stairs, or even a table, will help you get started in developing important upper-body and core strength.

Assisted Pull-Ups (Skimo)

Use a lat pull-down machine or a pull-up bar and an assist tool to remove some body weight, such as a rubber band or a stool to place a foot on. See illustration for how this exercise is to be performed. Find the weight or a level of assistance that you can barely manage for six repetitions. Use this weight for the prescribed sets and reps. After six workouts like this, try moving to Stage 2.

Fig. 7.11 Assisted Pull-Up

If you are unable to perform full body weight pull-ups, you can place a foot on a stool, or use a strong rubber band, for some assistance.

Stage 2 Upper-Body Program

Runners: Once you have mastered the incline push-up by moving to a low incline (such as the first stair tread or a low bench), you will have developed some strength in your arms, shoulders, and core. The next stage will introduce knee push-ups with your weight distributed between your hands, placed on the floor, and your knees. Complete three sets of as many knee push-ups as you can with two minutes' rest between sets, during which you will do a leg exercise. Once you can complete three sets of eight reps of knee push-ups, you should be ready to move on to regular push-ups. Do this by completing as many good-form standard push-ups as you can in each set. In each set, when you can no longer hold good form, switch to knee push-ups, completing the remaining reps up to eight in each set. If you can do more than three sets of eight reps of standard push-ups, move to Stage 3.

Skiers: Using a pull-up bar, get your chin above the bar using assistance. Remove the assistance and hold that top position as long as you can. Drop from the bar and rest for two minutes, during which you will do a leg exercise. Repeat this four times. When you can hold the top position for more than a count of five seconds in the fourth set, use the middle position with elbows bent at ninety degrees and repeat the same sequence.

Fig. 7.12 Knee Push-Up

Another good way to work up to full body-weight push-ups is to start from your knees. As you progress, you can begin the set on your toes and then drop to your knees when you lose proper form.

Fig. 7.13 Isometric Bar Hang (Skimo)

Hanging in a locked-off position partway through a pull-up movement is a great exercise for developing strong shoulders. The ability to exert force on your poles when skinning uphill can be a significant benefit for skimo racers.

Stage 3 Upper-Body Program

Runners: Now that you have sufficient strength to do a few good push-ups, develop more strength by making the push-ups more challenging. You'll always start this workout with at least one set of eight regular push-ups, followed by three sets with added resistance. Limit reps to four per set. Take two to three minutes' rest between sets, during which you will do leg exercises. The easiest way to increase the resistance is to elevate your feet on a stair, bench, chair, or exercise ball. Wearing a weight vest is another way to add resistance for stronger athletes.

Skiers: By now you are able to do at least one pull-up/chin-up. This routine will build strength quickly by increasing the load and by using the slow-lowering technique. Complete four sets of two to three repetitions with a three-to-five-second slow lower on the last repetition of each set. Add enough extra weight so that you can manage only two to three reps. When you can do five normal pull-ups/chin-ups, then progress to the Specific Strength–Training Methods section in chapter eight.

Fig. 7.14 Elevated Feet Push-Up

The above illustrations show variations on the standard push-up to make it more challenging.
Once you can manage fifteen push-ups, consider trying these instead.

Fig. 7.15 Weighted Push-Up
A weight vest or weight plate are the best ways to increase push-up strength.

Fig. 7.16 Pull-Up/Chin-Up
The pull-up is the king of upper-body general-strength exercises and engages virtually every muscle from your waist up.

Mountain running demands a strong core. Here, Dan Patitucci grabs some meters after a summer snowstorm painted the meadows white. In the background is the Jungfrau, Switzerland. Photo: Janine Patitucci

Core Strength

Core strength is another aspect of general strength that plays a critically support-ive role in locomotive sports like skimo and running. It serves this function by stabilizing the pelvis, spine, and shoulders so that the arms and legs can perform their propulsive functions most effectively. The stability of the pelvis is especially critical because it supports the bulk of the body weight, provides the anchoring for the legs, and provides the base of support for the spine. Many running inju-ries can be traced to weakness or imbalances of the core muscles, most of which attach to the pelvis. However, because of the general nature of core strength training, it is often overlooked by endurance athletes as unimportant. We caution against underestimating its usefulness. The core muscles are mainly made up of slow-twitch fibers. This imbues them naturally with a lot of endurance, but typi-cally not so much strength. So, increasing their strength even a little can make a big difference for most athletes.

In both running and skiing, an effective arm swing causes a slight counterro-tation of the shoulders relative to the hips, causing a little twist along the spine. If the core is not able to transfer this energy effectively from upper to lower body, you will be losing power.

Improving core strength is challenging because you first need to learn how to actively engage the deep muscle, transverse abdominis (TA), that is not used for locomotion but is the primary stabilizer of the pelvis. Because it doesn't move any major joints it is hard to isolate and engage, unlike the more obvious prime-mover muscles of the arms and legs. Learning to engage the transverse abdominis (see sidebar below) is not like learning to do a bicep curl or a squat; it's hard to tell if it is activated.

Don't get discouraged by slow progress. It's normal. If you are having trouble holding good form and find your back swaying like an old horse, or you can't hold the small of your back flat to the floor while doing leg lifts, you have poor pelvic stability caused by a weak core and can benefit from improving that strength.

How to Activate the Deep Core Muscles

This chapter's exercises require proper form to protect the spine and gain strength in the correct, deeper muscles. The TA is the deepest muscle in the core musculature and protects the spine and connects the upper and lower body. The TA wraps like a corset around your visceral organs. It ties together the pelvis and the lower six ribs in the front with the thoraco-lumbar fascia on your lower back to fully encircle the middle of your body. Unlike some of the more easily activated core muscles, like the rectus abdominis (seen in the six-pack) or the obliques, which flex the spine (like in a crunch) or twist the spine, the TA muscle is not used for movement. Its purpose is purely stabilization. When you engage the TA, it tightens against all its anchor points and provides stability to the lower spine and pelvis. But because this engagement does not result in noticeable movement, it can be hard to tell when you have activated the TA.

The easiest way to activate the transverse abdominis is by activating the pelvic floor muscle, which works simultaneously with the TA. To find the TA, lie supine on the floor with knees up and feet on the floor and place your fingers on the ilia, the front hip bones. Move the fingers inward one inch (25 centimeters) and downward one inch. Pull up through your pelvic floor, as if stopping the flow of urine, and feel the muscle under each hand engage. Once you're familiar with this feeling, isolate the TA from the pelvic floor by drawing your navel to your spine, or imagine zipping up a tight jacket. Once you learn to activate the TA you can practice this while sitting or standing. If you feel your spine flex (like doing a crunch), then you are trying too hard and causing the activation of the rectus abdominis or oblique muscles.

When you have that feeling of tightening this girdle muscle, you can move to doing a plank exercise. In the plank position with forearms resting on the floor, there is no spine flexion (crunch) and the TA serves a key role in preventing the sagging of the hips. This is an isometric exercise, so you will just hold the position until you begin to shake or lose form (feel your hips sag or rise up as compensation). To maintain engagement throughout the workout, you may need to start your plank from the knees rather than from the toes.

Tamara Lunger, Philipp Reiter, and David Wallmann nearing the summit of Rheinwaldhorn in Switzerland. Photo: Mark Smiley

Core Strength Assessment

To test yourself to see if you have adequate core strength, do this simple test, which will allow you to most effectively target this critical strength.

PLANK

This exercise tests the strength of the transverse abdominis, the most important core stabilizer muscle. If you are deficient in the test, you will use the Stage 1 and 2 exercises explained on page 231.

Get into the plank position as pictured with your weight on your toes and forearms, elbows directly under your shoulders, and a neutral spine (no sag or arching). Time yourself while holding this position as long as you can before losing perfect form. Stop as soon as your back sags or your spine is no longer straight. Choose the stage of exercise that corresponds to your assessment results.

Stage 1 – Less than thirty seconds

Stage 2 – Thirty seconds to one minute

Stage 3 – Longer than one minute

Fig. 7.17 Plank Variations

The top drawing shows good plank form. If you are unable to hold this position, then you can start from your knees. If you are stronger, you can add challenge by lifting alternate legs and holding till you begin to lose form. Adding a weight or weight vest is a great way for the stronger athletes to improve transverse abdominal strength.

WINDSHIELD WIPER

This exercise tests the strength of the obliques, which are used for transferring power from the arms to the legs. The name for this one suggests the action of your legs as they wipe across an imaginary windshield.

Lie on your back with your arms outstretched from your shoulders and your palms placed against the floor. Now flex your hips and raise your legs so that your feet are together with toes pointed at the ceiling. Slowly rotate your hips so that your feet lower to the floor to one side; keep your feet locked together with knees straight. You'll want to resist the rotation of your shoulders by pushing down hard with your hand on the side you are rotating toward. Just lightly touch the floor with the side of the lower foot before raising both feet back to the twelve o'clock position, then move them to the other side where the other foot will touch down. Return your feet to the twelve o'clock position for one repetition.

Do this slowly and with control and perfect form. If you cannot manage to keep your knees straight, or legs together, then bend your knees and do the same rotation while keeping your knees together and pointed at the ceiling when you are in the twelve o'clock position. Choose the stage of exercise that corresponds to your assessment results.

> Stage 1 – Zero reps with straight legs
> Stage 2 – Fewer than five reps to each side with straight legs
> Stage 3 – More than five reps to each side with straight legs

Fig. 7.18 Windshield Wiper

Lying with your hands outstretched to the sides at shoulder level and toes pointed to the ceiling, swing your feet to almost touch the floor on each side, mimicking the action of a windshield wiper. Keep your knees straight, legs together, and toes pointed up. Move with control. Counteract your body's tendency to rotate with your arms. When you can do ten repetitions to each side, add challenge to this exercise by wearing boots or ankle weights.

Previous page: Strength equals confidence when you need it most. Janine Patitucci trail running in the Italian Dolomites with the Cristallo in the background. Photo: Dan Patitucci

Core Strength Workouts

Strict form is critical so that you target the weakest muscles in the chain rather than relying on stronger muscles, which can compensate for the weaker ones' inability to provide stability. If you feel your form break down, such as sagging hips, shaking, and wobbling, then you've overloaded that set of motor units and provided an adequate training stimulus.

We typically use the Core Strength routine as the finish to our warm-up before moving into the Leg Strength routine.

Stage 1

If you find yourself really struggling with either or both of these exercises, you need to develop more core strength. There is a good chance that you are simply unable to activate these core muscles effectively. To learn how to do this, you need practice. If you can't do these simple exercises, you will not be able to effectively use those muscles in your sport.

Exercises

Plank from the knees. 6x15 sec hold or until loss of form. Rest one minute between sets.

Windshield wiper with bent knees. Six sets of max reps. Rest one minute between sets.

Stage 2

If you can manage close to a minute of plank hold time without losing form or can do a few reps of windshield wiper with straight legs, then you'll benefit from performing longer sets of these as you prepare for Stage 3.

Exercises

Plank. Six sets of max holds until you lose form. Rest two minutes between sets.

Windshield wiper. Six sets of max reps. Rest two minutes between sets.

Stage 3

At this level it will be necessary to get creative and find ways of adding resistance to the exercises. Select three or four exercises from the following pages. Feel free to find others that challenge the same muscles and movements. Use enough resistance so that you can manage no more than ten repetitions (total or per side) or thirty seconds of isometric hold before your form deteriorates from fatigue. Do no more than five sets of each exercise. Rest two minutes between sets.

Weighted Plank
Add a weight to rest on your butt. See page 227 for information on how to do this exercise.

Weighted Windshield Wiper
Add weight to your feet by using ankle weights or heavier shoes or boots and perform straight-leg windshield wiper.

Fig. 7.19 Marching Plank
Lift each limb in succession. Hold until you start to lose form and then lift the next limb.

Fig. 7.20 Kayaker

Seated on the floor with feet off the ground and using a heavy dumbbell, rotate to touch the weight to the floor on each side.

Fig. 7.21 Standing Trunk Rotation

With feet placed at shoulder width and holding a weight in front of you, rotate aggressively in each direction. It is the stopping and starting of the rotation motion that provides the strength effect. Use a heavy weight and swing fast.

Planning Your General-Strength Workouts Stages 1 Through 3

After completing the above assessments you should choose the appropriate stage at which to start for each of the leg, upper body, and core exercises.

1. Warm-up.

2. Core exercises. Complete the appropriate exercises for the stage you have determined.

3. Move to the main part of the workout (below) using the appropriate stage.

Stage 1 Workout

Four times through the following circuit with a two-minute rest between circuits:

- 1x20 reps: squats with knee band

- One set of the appropriate stage push-up exercise (include appropriate stage pull-up exercise for skimo)

- 1x20 reps: single-leg lateral band

- One set of the appropriate stage push-up exercise (include appropriate stage pull-up exercise for skimo)

Stage 2 Workout

Three times through the following circuit:

- 1x15 reps per leg of box step-ups

- One set of appropriate stage push-up exercise (include appropriate stage pull-up exercise for skimo)

- 1x15 reps per leg of box step-downs

- One set of appropriate stage push-up exercise (include appropriate stage pull-up exercise for skimo)

- 1x15 reps of front lunge

- Rest three minutes and repeat

Stage 3 Workout

Four times through the following circuit:

- 1x6 reps of box step-ups with weight

- One set of appropriate stage push-up exercise (include appropriate stage pull-up exercise for skimo)

- 1x6 reps of box step-downs with weight

- One set of appropriate stage push-up exercise (include appropriate stage pull-up exercise for skimo)

- 1x6 reps of front lunge with weight

- Rest three minutes and repeat

It Will Get Better

Anton Krupicka

One of the truisms of ultradistance events is that "it never always keeps getting worse." The idea behind this is that no matter how physically and mentally depleted you may feel, as long as you persevere—put your head down, grit your teeth, and keep the faith—eventually your body will rebound from the trough that it's in and you'll experience a resurgence of energy.

For those who have never gone through this, it's hard to believe and, indeed, illogical. It takes a degree of faith.

I had maybe my most profound experience with this quintessential low point followed by a high point in my very first mountain ultra: the 2006 Leadville 100. At mile 80, despite my pacer's best efforts to goad me along, I was reduced to walking on flat ground, even downhills, and was pretty quickly doing mental calculations as to how long it would take me to walk the rest of the race. My legs had simply given up on the running motion.

However, only five miles later, I experienced an inexplicable surge in energy unlike anything I had felt since the first half of the race. In the matter of a few minutes, I went from despair to charging to the finish, running every step of the last fifteen miles, even occasionally putting my pacer into a spot of bother. At the time, I had no explanation, and I almost couldn't believe that I was actually experiencing this illogical phenomenon that veteran runners had told me about before the race. Perhaps I just needed to smell the barn.

But there was one thing no one ever seemed to tell me: while an ebb in energy is almost guaranteed to happen at some point in the final quarter of these long efforts, the sneaky secret is the same thing can just as easily happen in the first quarter or third of a long race. And it doesn't have to ruin your race if you don't let it.

The very next year at Leadville, I was in great shape and leading the race 20 miles in when I gradually sunk into a perplexing funk. My energy and motivation plummeted, and though I already held a commanding lead, I entertained a few insidious thoughts about dropping. How was I supposed to run another eighty *miles* at high altitude when I already felt this terrible? Fortunately, by backing off the intensity slightly, pushing the seemingly insurmountable remaining distance out of my mind, and eating and drinking a little extra, I gradually rebounded.

When I began to climb the race's infamous Hope Pass at mile forty, I actually ran every step and went on to win the race in my personal best time, which remains the third-fastest time ever in the history of Leadville.

The point is, don't get rattled if you feel off—or even downright awful—early in a long outing. The body's peaks and valleys of energy are unpredictable and often hard to explain—especially when coming off of a long taper before a goal effort. But the thing to remember is that you are totally capable of rebounding and performing at your very best later on, no matter how improbable that may seem in the moment. Focus on pacing and staying present and positive. Don't project too far into the day and despair at how much farther you have to go—and be diligent with nutrition and hydration—and things will eventually come around. ■

Anton Krupicka ran his first marathon when he was twelve years old. He is a two-time winner of the Leadville Trail 100 and a veteran of mountain ultraracing around the world. He used to spend all of his time going uphill on just his feet, but for much of the past decade he has put an equal amount of energy into going uphill on skis, a rope, and a bike, depending on the season. He lives in Boulder, Colorado.

Anton Krupicka training in Boulder, Colorado.
Photo: Fredrik Marmsater

CHAPTER EIGHT

Specific Strength–Training Methods

By *specific* we mean methods that mimic in some ways the joint angles, forces, muscle-recruitment patterns, and muscle-contraction speeds as well as the metabolic demands of your sport. These specific methods are meant to convert whatever level of general strength you have into sport-specific strength.

In this chapter we will discuss methods of developing both more power and more muscular endurance. These methods can be used by anyone and they will have positive performance benefits. However, if you have deficiencies as discussed in the previous chapter on basic strength, we highly recommend you correct those deficiencies before using the following methods.

The biggest limitations to performance in these mountain sports comes from · the need to overcome the force of gravity in climbing up hills. On the uphill is where we see the greatest difference in speed between the elite and the amateur. If you can improve the power and/or muscular endurance of your uphill propulsion, your performance will benefit directly.

Strength

Uphill running and skiing performance can be improved by increasing the specific strength. High levels of this quality will allow higher levels of the all-important muscular endurance. One of the most sport-specific strength exercises for this is what we term Hill Sprints. There is a full description of Hill Sprints (for runners) or Hill Bounding (for skiers) in the Methodology Section on page 179. Adding poles will help simulate skiing uphill. Include Hill Sprints/Bounding starting in the early Base Period of training for any intermediate and higher-level athlete if basic

Kimberly Strom runs a steep ridgeline above Saas-Almagell, Switzerland. Photo: Dan Patitucci

strength is adequate as defined in the preceding chapter. If you have already developed a high level of uphill leg strength from previous training, you can consider moving straight to the ME workouts (below). Otherwise, it will benefit you to include a few weeks of this type of strength and power work. You can also add occasional Hill Sprint workouts throughout your full training plan to maintain this specific strength. However, if faced with a choice due to time constraints, shorten or omit Hill Sprints to allow more time for a muscular endurance building period.

Muscular Endurance

As we've stated earlier, high levels of strength are not important for the sports covered in this book. However, a particular strength-like quality called muscular endurance is very important. In fact, it is one of the major components in determining endurance performance. As a reminder: This quality is defined as the ability to do many repetitive movements with a *relatively* high percentage of the maximum strength. By *relatively* we mean that the more repetitions you are doing, the lower will be the percentage of your maximum strength. The immediate effect you should feel during these workouts is fatigue localized in the working muscles. While anyone can benefit from this method, the best results will be seen by those athletes with high strength and aerobic capacity. It is tempting to overuse muscular endurance training because the performance benefits are felt quickly and dramatically. When using muscular endurance workouts, it is critical that you do a high volume of basic aerobic training in Zone 1 for maintenance.

There are several ways of improving muscular endurance. We will show you workouts we have used with many types of athletes with universally positive results. As you read through these, notice that despite their very different methods, they share the one component that makes them cause local muscular fatigue: extra resistance. By artificially imposing greater muscular loads during training than will be encountered during the event, we can force local muscular endurance of the working muscles, as opposed to cardiovascular fitness, to be the limitation. In our examples, we do this by either adding weight or using a very steep hill.

DO YOU NEED MORE MUSCULAR ENDURANCE?

As mentioned earlier when discussing high-intensity training, Zone 3 and Zone 4 workouts have a powerful muscular endurance training stimulus. Recall that Kílian uses his long, steep uphill Zone 3 runs as muscular endurance training. The effectiveness of any high-intensity session is highly dependent on the athlete having adequate levels of muscular endurance. Kílian has very high levels of local muscular endurance. This allows him to sustain these high intensities for the full duration of the workout. However, many endurance athletes do not have

Oskar Irsara and Raffaella Rungger on perfect singletrack in the Italian Dolomites.
Photo: Dan Patitucci

sufficiently high levels of local muscular endurance. Do you feel yourself slowing in workouts, especially those under two hours when you should not be running out of glycogen stores? Do you feel the heavy, dead legs that lose their bounce in long workouts? Do you feel that low-level burning and acute fatigue in your legs during high-intensity training? Do the downhills beat your legs up? If so, you need to improve your muscular endurance.

The Frontier Fiber Model

The slowing you feel with that leg fatigue is caused by the muscle fibers that are allowing the high speed in the first place dropping out of the pool of recruited fibers. Remember, these are faster-twitch fibers than the ones used at slower speeds. Every increase in speed requires your brain to recruit more of these more powerful fibers. These can produce greater force, so are needed to sustain higher speeds. The problem is that by virtue of them having highest-power, they have less endurance. They are right at the frontier of your endurance at that speed. Every speed will have its *frontier fibers*: that last group (the highest power bunch) of fibers to be recruited by the brain for this speed. The frontier fibers needed to sustain a pace you can hold for three hours have very good endurance and will

not become fatigued until the run exceeds three hours. Whereas the group of frontier fibers needed to sustain the pace during a VK race or Zone 4 interval session have much more power, but much worse endurance, so can fatigue in a few minutes. As you go up the fiber power scale, your endurance drops to the point that the fastest FT fibers (used to sprint) will fatigue in seconds.

These frontier fibers' endurance is, to a very large extent, what limits you. One of the main reasons traditional endurance training methods have included Zones 3–4 workouts is to recruit these frontier fibers and cause them to develop more endurance. If they fatigue too quickly and drop out of the pool of recruited fibers, they are no longer getting the desired training effect. You can tell this is happening when not only do you slow but your heart rate drops despite the increased effort. Do you feel that your legs give out before your breathing during high-intensity workouts or races? If so, you are limited by the local endurance of the working muscles and should consider adding this type of training to your program.

Along with traditional Zone 3 and Zone 4 training, we'll describe workouts you can use to specifically target local muscular endurance. You risk too much of a good thing if you use these workouts too close together or too close to conventional Zone 3 and Zone 4 interval training. Chances are good you will feel these workouts in your legs for a few days. For that reason, if you are new to this form of training it's best to use these workouts in the Base Period as preparation before starting Zone 3 and Zone 4 aerobic interval work. They can also be alternated with Zone 3 and Zone 4 interval workouts. But be sure to keep these separated by 72 hours and maintain a high volume of Zone 1 aerobic base training during this time.

As with all training, especially higher intensity, there is no single rule that works for everyone regarding how much or how often to do these. But for someone just getting started with this type of training, one day per week will be plenty. Those who have more experience with high-intensity training or higher muscular endurance can often manage two workouts in a week before it will begin to negatively affect the volume of aerobic training. We recommend starting these workouts with little to no added resistance so that you can learn the movements and develop the strength and elasticity in the muscles and tendons to avoid injury. After that you will want to be very gradual in ramping up any loads.

While there are numerous ways to improve muscular endurance, many athletes have had many years of great experiences with the methods we describe. These workouts have an almost-immediate effect on uphill endurance. If you do not feel improvement in your hill climbing from week to week while doing these, there is a good chance that you are doing too much rather than not enough. You may not be getting sufficient recovery or easy aerobic training during this time.

Jeff Browning crushing the scree below Grant-Swamp Pass on a Hardrock 100 course recon. Silverton, Colorado. Photo: Steven Gnam

Swann Juillaguet races while secured to a fixed rope on day four of the 2017 edition of the Pierra Menta skimo race. Photo: Jocelyn Chavy

GYM-BASED MUSCULAR ENDURANCE (ME) WORKOUT

Not everyone who loves mountain sports has easy access to mountain terrain. Or maybe you're a runner who wants to increase muscular endurance during a dark, cold, and snowy winter. Author Scott Johnston first experimented with gym-based ME programs in 1991 when working with an elite cross-country skier leading into an Olympic year. Since then we have developed countless others for different athletes and different sports. We have learned a lot over the years through this experience. One of the most important lessons: Don't let the non-sport-specific nature of these workouts fool you. They have proven very effective at improving uphill and downhill running and skiing performance, especially for those without ready access to mountains.

GYM-BASED ME WORKOUT

Warm-up

A good warm-up is essential for this workout. You need to be sweating before you start the workout. Here is a warm-up we find effective:

Do 200 total reps of your choice of four or five different core exercises without stopping. Pick some that you like or find challenging. Try to do a minimum of 20 reps of each exercise before moving on, with no rest, to the next exercise. Then rev up your aerobic system. Fifteen minutes should do it. How you do this is not so important: bike, run, climb stairs, row, or do a mix. Importantly, finish with two to three minutes of moderately hard effort (Z3).

Gym-Based Exercises

Fig. 8.1 Box Step-Up

Stand about one half of your stride length in front of a box or step that is just below knee height. Step up onto the box mainly using the front leg to pull you up with minimal assist from the rear leg. Maintain proper knee tracking over your toes throughout this exercise.

Fig. 8.2 Front Lunge

From a standing position step forward about half your body length dynamically so that the front leg catches most of your weight. Keep the knee behind the toes of that front foot.

Fig. 8.3 Split Jump Squat

From a front lunge stance spring upward and switch feet before landing with the opposite foot forward. You can add resistance best with the use of a weight vest or weighted pack. Count reps on just one leg. Do ten reps on each leg.

Fig. 8.4 Squat Jump

From a squat position spring upward as explosively as you can. Swinging your arms powerfully will increase the load on your legs and help make this more dynamic. Land quietly, absorbing the load using your toes and knees.

Kilian Jornet doing steep (and technical) sprints above the Val Veny, Courmayeur, Italy. Photo: Sébastien Montaz-Rosset

Workout

- 6x10 reps each leg of box step. Rest one minute between sets. Ten reps with one leg before switching.

- 6x10 reps each leg front lunge. Rest one minute between sets. Ten reps with one leg before switching.

- 6x10 reps each leg split jump squat. Rest one minute between sets. Alternate front legs each jump.

- 6x10 reps squat jump. Rest one minute between sets.

Complete all six sets of each exercise, taking one minute of rest between sets. Take no more than two minutes' rest between exercises. The tempo of the exercise should be about one repetition per second.

Workout Progression

- First and second workout use body weight only.

- Third and fourth workout add 10 percent of body weight.

- Fifth workout do eight sets of each exercise and add 10 percent of body weight.

- Sixth and seventh workout do six sets, add 10 percent of body weight, and reduce rest to 30 seconds.

- Eighth workout do eight sets with 10 percent of body weight added and 30 seconds rest.

Continued longer-term progression:

- Ninth workout do six sets with 15 percent of body weight added, resting one minute.

- Tenth workout do six sets with 15 percent of body weight added, resting 45 seconds.

- Eleventh workout do six sets with 20 percent of body weight added, resting one minute.

- Twelfth workout do six sets with 20 percent of body weight added, resting 45 seconds.

Use a weight vest or a barbell on shoulders or hold dumbbells for added resistance.

The percentages of body weight listed above are suggestions. While these seem to work well for most athletes, you may need to use more or less depending on your basic strength. Start lighter and increase the weight only as you feel the effects of the previous workout. Make adjustments gradually and err on the conservative side. These workouts can be spaced out by as much as ten days, but if you go more than twelve days, repeat the previous workout rather than moving ahead to the next one. You do not need to go through the full eight workout progressions to get the benefits. Or you may find that you have time to add more workouts to see bigger gains during your off-season.

OUTDOOR ME WORKOUT

This workout resembles a conventional Zone 3/Zone 4 uphill interval workout. It works well for those with some big and steep hills nearby and without easy access to a gym or weights. We've used it with very good results for both skiers and runners. There are several ways to accomplish this training and a fair bit of latitude exists, so don't get too hung up on the details. Keep the big picture in mind: Make your legs be the limitation of your ability to sustain the work intensity. Make your legs tired! Preferably before your breathing shuts you down.

The biggest challenge for most people is finding a steep enough hill. Look for a hill that is in the range of 20 to 50 percent in gradient. The steeper the hill, the easier it is to feel that your legs are the limitation in your rate of climb, not your breathing or heart rate. Several methods exist to increase the muscular load on your legs: steepness, stride length, and added weight. Any and all can be used depending on what kind of terrain you have available and how strong your legs are to begin with. Let's discuss how you might incorporate these three factors:

- Steepness: This could mean running or hiking straight up the fall line at a gradient on excess of 20–50 percent. Most people will call a trail steep when it exceeds 20 percent, but for these workouts to be most effective, steeper is better. This is what Kílian is referring to when he talks about doing long, steep uphills in Zone 3 as a muscular endurance workout. Settle into a pace you can sustain for many minutes with a subtle, low-level "burn" in your legs.

- Stride length/bounding: Use a long, bounding stride. This adds a significantly high muscle load and cannot be sustained for long. This is what Kílian is referring to when he mentions doing two minutes of long strides followed by a short rest until his legs recover, then two minutes of short strides. If you are bounding aggressively, two minutes is a long time. Be advised that you may want to start with ten to twenty seconds of bounding, or until your legs are burning, followed by a recovery to get your legs back, then the short-stride/high-tempo running until your breathing and heart rate hamper you. Then repeat many times.

- Additional weight: If you don't have access to steep terrain, you can simulate the same by adding weight to a small pack and doing either of the above methods. Start by carrying no more than 10–15 percent of your body weight. Add more only after you have seen the effects of this amount.

One session of this workout each week to ten days is adequate during the Base Period; otherwise it can impact the overall volume of training negatively. It is important to maintain a high volume of Zones 1–2 training during this phase.

OUTDOOR ME WORKOUT

Warm-up

Running 15 minutes with gradually increasing intensity so that the last two to three minutes are in Zones 3–4.

Workout Progression

As with the gym-based version of the ME workout, be prepared to get sore and have tired legs for a couple of days. You should feel the hills on your normal aerobic workouts getting easier within only two to three workouts of this type.

Using the traditional Z3 uphill method:

Start this workout progression by running or hiking (which you choose depends on the steepness and your muscular endurance) up the hill for eight to ten minutes with that low-level leg burn. Repeat two times, taking a five-minute moving recovery between reps. If you need to walk back down between reps because you do not have a long enough hill, that's fine. This can build to a full 40 minutes of steady uphill grinding.

Using a weighted pack for the above method:
This can be particularly effective for ski mountaineers who will normally be carrying a heavy pack and moving more slowly upward. It can also be used by those who do not have access to steep hills. Don't discount the usefulness of the fire stairs in tall buildings for this type of workout.

If you use the bounding variation:
Start with 10x10 sec of bounding up a steep trail. Between the bounding parts, walk back down until your legs are recovered and then repeat. There is no one prescription. For the aerobically fit who recover fast, this workout might look like 15x15 sec bounding with about one minute of running or walking down recovery (depending on steepness) between repetitions. This workout could progress to 20x20 sec of bounding with two minutes of recovery running. For the less fit, start with something in the range of 10x10 with two minutes of active recovery.

As with the gym-based muscular endurance training, if you do not see performance improvements from week to week, you are probably doing too much and not allowing enough recovery.

Upper-Body Training for Skimo

A good way for more advanced skiers to boost their performance is to include special upper-body muscular endurance training into the Base Period. Because this training only minimally involves the legs, it's easy to add arms-only workouts even into a heavy off-season of running training. You may find that they even aid your legs' recovery. We present two straightforward methods of doing this training below, but variations on these are easy to imagine. With these workouts you will be able to feel very strongly the muscular endurance limitation that we hope you feel doing the leg muscular endurance work. The muscle mass you use for this single-poling is small enough that it will not tax your heart's ability to supply oxygen. The limit you feel will be quite obviously in your arms and shoulders.

ROLLER SKIING

Roller ski training will likely only appeal to a minority of readers who seek the best training methods; we include it here for the sake of completeness. Roller skis provide a good simulation of snow skiing. When used with good technique they will improve your weight transfer, enhance your glide on each stride, and train your muscles in a ski-specific way. One drawback is that most paved roads are not as steep as the terrain you will be skinning up. However, using your arms only, even on modest uphills, will have the desired upper-body muscular endurance training effect. You will need classic roller skis and carbide-tipped ski poles. Be forewarned: Roller skis require a significant learning period. They have no brakes, so downhills can be very dangerous.

Early Base Period roller ski upper-body ME workouts can be done on relatively flat terrain by simply using the same poling motion that you normally use when skinning. Adopt a slight crunch position (a C shape) in your upper body to give you more muscle involvement for the poling motion.

Beginner

Those with little Nordic skiing background may find even poling on the flats for more than a couple of minutes very fatiguing. If so, this should be a clue that you could see big gains in uphill speed with even a small amount of time devoted to this type of training.

Fig. 8.5 Roller Ski Arms Only

This exercise is a great way to specifically train the upper-body muscular endurance needed for skimo. Hold the upper body and feet still and work with just the arms. You can adjust the load by increasing the gradient of the hill.

Example Workout

Start with continuous single-poling for ten to fifteen minutes on the flats to get the feeling of this type of workout. After a few workouts, you may feel ready to increase the intensity. A good way to do that would be to do 5x1 min at a moderately hard effort on a very gradual uphill with a two-minute recovery. Progress to 3x10 min with five-minute recovery periods where you are still skiing but very easily again on the flats or a very gradual uphill. Select the grade to suit your upper-body strength.

Advanced

Those with more upper-body strength and endurance should do these same single-poling ME workouts but on steeper grades. Mix steep and short repetitions with longer, lower-angle reps.

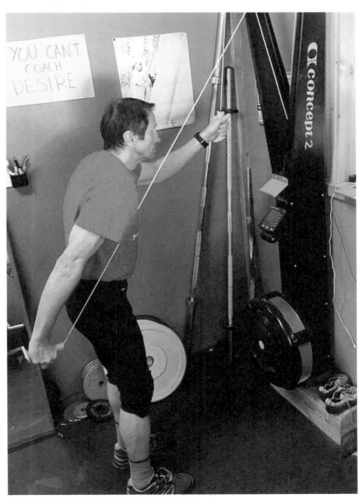

Author Scott Johnston uses a Concept 2 Ski Ergometer for a ski-specific upper-body muscular endurance workout in the Uphill Athlete World Headquarters gym. Photo: Seth Keena

These types of workouts can be included twice per week in the early Base Period as a second workout on days with leg-focused workouts. They can be continued on to snow and as a maintenance session or during breaks in the racing calendar.

SKI ERGOMETER

A common training tool for cross-country skiers is an ergometer, like a rowing machine, that uses ropes and resistance to simulate the poling action.

What follows is an example of a stand-alone upper-body ME workout progression that can be used as a second workout on days that involve a leg-oriented workout.

Progression:

- Week 1: 5 min easy single-poling finished off with 1 min at a moderate effort.

- Week 2: 5x2 min hard effort with 2 min active recovery like easy running/hiking on a treadmill.

- Week 3: 6x2 min with 2 min active recovery.

- Week 4: 7x2 min with 1:45 min active recovery.

- Week 5: 7x3 min with 2 min active recovery.

- Week 6: 8x3 min with 1:45 min active recovery.

- Week 7: 8x3 min with 1:30 min active recovery.

- Week 8: 8x3 min with 1 min active recovery.

Summary

Use the Base Period for developing strength and muscular endurance according to your needs as an athlete. If you are deficient in strength according to your assessments, then it may be that the first cycle of training you do using this book will include only general-strength training. As you train more and become stronger, it will benefit you to add Specific-Strength and ME training during the Base Period.

Luke Nelson, Chloë Lanthier, and Clare Gallagher running home in the Italian Dolomites.
Photo: Eliza Earle

SECTION FOUR
How to Train

CHAPTER NINE

Programming

"Training is not the work you do. It is the effect that work has on your body."

– Renato Canova

This is the part of the book where we get down to the business of helping you build an effective plan. Don't expect the next pages to lay out a detailed prescription. Because of the widely varying differences between athletes and the need for individuality, it is not possible to provide a one-size-fits-all training plan. If you've paid attention through the previous parts of this book, you will be able to use those general principles presented earlier while taking into consideration your own background, goals, and needs to craft your own customized plan, like a good coach would. This section of the book will explain how to implement the basic principles of training in a workable plan. Since the possible permutations of all the variables involved in creating an individual plan for all levels of athletes, for many different events with different seasonal goals, is nearly infinite, we will use example weeks and example workouts along with guidelines based on experience so that you can see how the pieces should fit together. We will not offer a cookbook recipe.

We know that one-size-fits-all training really does not fit anyone very well. We understand that highly motivated athletes and coaches looking for ways to maximize their potential have to look beyond the ordinary. See UphillAthlete.com for more in-depth information about training methods, including example weeks for the phases of different programs as well as example workouts and their proper implementation.

Previous page: Alex Earle puts in the early-morning miles above Le Tour, Chamonix, France. Photo: Eliza Earle

Opposite: Krissy Moehl running Handies Peak, San Juan Mountains, Colorado. Photo: Fredrik Marmsater

The classic Sellaronda Trail Run at Passo Sella, Trentino Alto Adige, Italy. Photo: Federico Modica

A well-coached but less-than-ideal training plan will give better results than the best plan in the world that is poorly administered. The successful administration of the plan is the main challenge when it comes to getting the most from your training. That is where the art of coaching takes over from the science of coaching. Why? There are few systems that we deal with on a daily basis that are as complex as the human organism. It is this amazing complexity that allows us to adapt to the stress of training in such impressive ways. It's also that complexity that makes implementing an effective plan a challenge. Which is the reason for the first 250 pages of this book.

A training plan presents training as a black-and-white affair. You either do this or you do that. However, a successful coach or successful athlete *must* operate in shades of gray on a daily basis. This gray territory is where the experience of a coach can help even the most seasoned athlete. And it is where the self-coached athlete needs to tread the most warily. That's why we spend so much time in the early pages of this book discussing how to monitor the effect that training is having on your body.

The writing of a plan, by necessity, uses a mechanistic view: Do workout A, receive benefits B. That mechanistic approach provides the guidance. But, on a daily basis you must subtly assess and interpret your preparedness to not only do the mechanistically prescribed workout, but also to apply those same skills in evaluating the benefit from it. We want you to have those assessment tools that enable you to make changes when they are needed. That is what the first half of this book was for: teaching you these tools and imparting some guidelines to help you in your application of the plan you are about to build for yourself. Keep in mind that the plan you write is merely a suggestion and not a blueprint. It will, of necessity, have to change as you proceed. Blind adherence to *any* training plan is an almost surefire route to inferior results, if not disaster.

Coaching yourself is difficult to do effectively. Professional athletes with years of experience use coaches not because they can afford to, but because they realize the importance of an objective observer to offer guidance when they are in doubt, and they know the value of having someone to bounce ideas off of.

Beginning the Plan

Keep your expectations in line with your commitment. Success at reaching your expectations breeds enthusiasm to continue, ensuring future success.

Be Realistic

Setting goals that are in line with both your training history and your available time is the first step. Biting off more than you can handle will, at best, lead to frustration, and may cause you more serious issues like injury and overtraining.

Have a Goal

Any goal is better than nothing. This can range from a simple, very personal, noncompetitive goal to the goal of winning a major competition. Not having any goal is like setting sail without a destination in mind. You don't need a map (training plan) if that is what you want to do. This book and the advice we offer is intended for those who seek to maximize their personal ability and want to use this book as their map. But first they need to know where they'd like to end up.

Deciding what it is you hope to accomplish when embarking upon a training program sounds so basic that it hardly bears mentioning. Surprisingly, however, failure to clearly establish this basic goal before beginning is what most often derails the best of intentions when it comes to achieving success.

Commitment

The best plan in the world will not be worth the paper it is written on if you don't do the work. For the sports we cover in this book, this means that you will be

Enrico Deflorian executes his plan while enjoying a beautiful sunset over the Latemar Group, Italy.
Photo: Federico Modica

spending hundreds of hours, probably alone, doing fairly repetitive, unglamorous work. You need to embrace the process or the end result will elude you.

To reach your maximum potential and to achieve ambitious goals will require sacrifice on top of the commitment to train. Commitment to the goal means not only doing the training itself but giving up things that conflict with or don't support the stated goal.

Outline for Planning

Where you start in your training is going to be based on your training history. You need to honestly evaluate where you are and how much time you can commit. Use the following reality test to help guide you in your selection of both training volume and race distances.

Make a tally of the average hours per week you have spent in the last year at work/school, sleeping, eating, traveling, and with family. The remaining hours are the hours you have available to train or participate in race events. Use this as a guide and a reality check regarding the absolute upper limit of how much time you have to train.

Ideally, you'll have one or two primary events ("A" priority) as your training focus. Including less important events ("B" or "C" priority) into the planning is not a problem. It can be much more difficult if you have several "A" priority events spread over a short time. We will explain how to plan for this, but only more experienced athletes will be able to pull this off. The most effective plan has your high-priority races or events spread out far enough from one another to allow adequate time for recovery and possibly training.

Once you know your target events, write them on a calendar and code them A, B, and C priority.

- A priority events are the biggies and what you will be building the overall plan toward. For them you will need a significant taper period leading in. They may require a significant recovery period afterward because they will maximally utilize whatever capacity you can bring to the starting line. If you have more than one of these in any training cycle, it will be important to have a base-building period between them that is at least several weeks long.

- B priority events are used as tune-ups and tests leading into the A event. If planned correctly and if your work capacity is high enough, these will not be major disturbances to the training plan. These might be shorter or less-demanding events where you can test fitness, strategy, equipment, fueling, tactics, and mental preparation. They should not be a big stretch beyond your current capacity, so they can be incorporated into the plan with only a slight drop in training load for a few days before and after. If they are so demanding that they disrupt the overall progression in training load, you are going to have problems preparing for the A event.

- C priority events are ones that you train right through, using them as just another workout. These need not be official competitions. They may be special test events you plan into the training schedule along the way to assess fitness. They should fit into the overall progression of your training plan; you should not have to adjust your plan for them. As your plans change, these can be inserted into the training plan later without disrupting the overall progression of training.

If you don't have a big goal but want to train effectively to build a base (increase your basic work capacity), then you can essentially do only base training. This is a strategy many people can benefit from because the biggest impediment to their performing better in the mountains is probably a lack of basic work capacity. For the events targeted in this book, nothing will get you further than improving this base. Athletes with a huge base, like Kílian, can perform well just off that base; this is what allows him to race so many times in a year.

Once you have this calendar set up and you know how many weeks you have to prepare for your goal, you can begin to lay out a very general plan. If you have never engaged in structured training, you will have to make a guess about where to start in terms of volume. No one can accurately predict your response to training without having some training history to serve as a benchmark. Those who don't have a training log to refer to will often only recall the most memorable/ bigger weeks and high points and not have a very accurate idea of the average week's training load. When in doubt, start easily, with a lower volume and overall training load than you think you can manage. With the excitement of starting a new training season with new goals, there is a tendency to jump into training too aggressively. Most of us tend to overestimate our ability to handle the work. After you have completed and logged a full training cycle of at least eight months, you will be in a much better position to plan. Until then, be prepared to adjust things as you may overreach and have to take a step back and try again.

The best rule of thumb for those new to structured training is: If you are not seeing small improvements over the course of several weeks, and you are using the principles presented in this book and training more than eight hours a week, then something is amiss. You may not be recovering well due to extraneous

The starting line of the summer Pierra Menta race. France. Photo: Ulysse Lefebvre

stressors in your life, or the training workload is too high, or the progression is too fast. You need to make adjustments to either your training load or your lifestyle, or both.

Making the Plan

In the following pages we'll lead you through the methods we use to set up a training plan. The tables in chapters 10 and 11 will act as a menu for selecting specific workouts by category to insert into the weekly plan of the various periods building toward a single event or a multievent season covering several months. Event-specific workouts are included and labeled as such where appropriate.

The approach we have taken in the rest of this section of the book is to give example weeks for each of the periods for the different events and for athletes of different levels. These weeks are accompanied by a discussion that explains how to fit them into a plan and how to progress the workouts.

A Review of Workout Categories

Aerobic Conditioning and Aerobic Capacity: Z1, Z2

This training improves your ability to do a high volume of aerobic work, which is best measured by AeT pace. It also supports high-intensity training.

- Multiple hours. Z1 and Z2, low intensity, long duration.
- Pick-ups or strides. Forty-five- to 75-minute Zones 1–2 workout with 6x15 sec to 8x30 sec accelerations up to a relaxed fast pace (spread out over the course of the workout), with a two-minute easy recovery between.
- Steady. Sustained Z2 effort for 30 to 60 minutes.

Aerobic Endurance: Z3

Increases your maximum sustainable uphill pace and extends the time you can sustain that pace.

- Continuous Z3 tempo for 20 to 40 minutes.
- Intervals. Intensity at and just below LT heart rate (Z3). Work periods of 8–15 minutes. Active recovery intervals are two to four minutes. Total work volume is 40–60 minutes.

Aerobic Power: Z4

Trains aerobic and anaerobic systems to their maximum combined capacity. Using interval style with work periods from 30 seconds to 8 minutes and a work-to-rest ratio of 1:1. This is very taxing training, making up less than 10 percent of the annual volume. Intensity needs to be 90-95 percent of maximum heart rate. These are best done on an uphill.

- Recovery intervals need to be sufficient to allow you to complete each repetition at the same pace and heart rate. Total work duration of 15 to 30 minutes.
- 30/30s. See sidebar on page 177.
- High-tempo/high-resistance intervals. One of Kílian's favorites. Two minutes of high-tempo/high-heart-rate running followed by a two-minute active rest, then two minutes of long strides done on foot or skis on uphill terrain. Repeat until you feel pace and heart rate drop off.

Anaerobic Capacity: Z5

Use Hill Sprint or Hill Bounding (see page 181) for specific leg strength/power. Start this in the Base Period one time per week if your general strength is adequate. Done near your maximum intensity on the steepest hill you have available with good footing. The duration of each repetition is from 10 to 30 seconds. Full recovery (minimum of two to three minutes) between reps. Start with 6x10 sec. Add two more reps each week.

General and Max Strength

Use the Core and Max Strength programs in the Transition Period twice per week. Use the Max Strength in the early Base Period twice per week. In the final stages of preparation, use the ME program specific for VK, long skimo, or trail run/race.

Krissy Moehl drinks a ginger soda to settle her upset stomach during an FKT attempt on the Wonderland Trail, Washington. Photo: Fredrik Marmsater

CHAPTER TEN

Transition Period Training

This period is meant as a preconditioning period to prepare you for the specific demands of the Base Period and is mainly important for those without a strong background of endurance training, or those who are new to structured training, or those returning to training after a significant break from training.

Many athletes will find this period valuable, no matter if it is only three weeks for someone coming off a summer running season and moving to skimo training or if it's eight weeks for someone just starting his or her first season of structured training. More advanced athletes with a good feel for their bodies may choose to immediately enter their Base Period. We suggest a conservative approach by anyone in doubt.

Where to Start

If you are used to structured training, these guidelines will help your planning:

If your break from training has been more than four weeks, start week one with about 50 percent of the previous training cycle's average weekly hours. If you are just transitioning your sport focus, such as from running to skiing, with a training break of no more than two weeks, you can start the first week at about 80 percent of your most recent training volume.

If you are new to structured training, then you will have to guess at your initial weekly hours of aerobic training. Here are some conservative targets for annual (fifty weeks) training hours for those with no previous history:

- Juniors (age fifteen and under): 300 total annual hours

- Juniors (age sixteen to nineteen): 450 total annual hours

Transition areas are often messy. Luke Nelson after a run near Stanley, Idaho. Photo: Steven Gnam

Michele Tavernaro runs the Malga Ces Trail in Passo Rolle, Trentino, Italy. Photo: Federico Modica

- Twenty to thirty-five: 400 total annual hours
- Thirty-five to fifty: 350 total annual hours
- Over fifty: 300 total annual hours

   Note: It's easy to get overexcited when starting a new program when motivation is high and you are feeling rested. *Don't!* You should not find the workload challenging during the early weeks of the Transition Period. If you do, you have started too aggressively. It is far better to start too conservatively with a new program. It is easy to raise the load a bit if, after a few weeks, you feel you need more. Coming off the starting line too hard, when you are fresh and excited, means that the accumulated fatigue may not make itself felt until after several weeks when suddenly the "wheels come off" and you are left wondering why. By that time, you might need to take a couple of weeks very easy to get back on track. Obviously, this is not ideal for the overall progression in your training.

   If you are entering your first organized training season, consider undergoing an eight-week Transition Period and making the progression in the workload more gradual. Use these weeks wisely and set yourself up for long-term success.

Weeks	Weekly Aerobic Volume
1–3	Build weeks. Use previous guidance for starting volume. Add 7–10% per week.
4	Recovery week. 50% decrease from week 3.
5–7	Build weeks. Week 5 volume equals week 3 +10%. Then add 5–7% in weeks 6–7.
8	Recovery week. 50% drop from week 7.

Fig. 10.1 General Progression of Training Volume for Eight-Week Transition Period

	Monday	Tuesday	Wednesday	Thursday	Friday	Saturday	Sunday
AM	Off.	Z2, 10% of weekly volume.	Z1, 25% of weekly volume.	Recovery level, 10% of weekly volume.	Z2, 10% of weekly volume.	Z1 or Recovery, 15% of weekly volume.	Long Z1 or 2, 30% of weekly volume.
PM	Off.	Core and general strength.	Off.	Off.	Core and general strength .	Off.	Off.

Fig. 10.2 Sample Building Week in the Transition Period

	Monday	Tuesday	Wednesday	Thursday	Friday	Saturday	Sunday
AM	Off.	Z1, 20% of weekly volume.	Z2, 15% of weekly volume.	Off.	Recovery level, 15% of weekly volume.	Z1, 20% of weekly volume.	Long Z1 or 2, 30% of weekly volume.
PM	Off.	Off.	Off.	Core and general strength.	Off.	Off.	Off.

Fig. 10.3 Sample Recovery Week in the Transition Period with 50% Reduction in Load

- Don't accelerate the training load any faster than 7 to 10 percent per week (in terms of hours, vertical feet, or distance) unless you have been training under a systematic plan for at least a couple of years and have had no more than a three-week layoff from the end of your last training cycle.

- If you have never run consistently for months on end or have not been running consistently during the past three to four months, you will need to be cautious with building running volume. Jumping back to daily running before your connective tissue is ready is a surefire shortcut to injury. Skiers are especially prone to running injuries. They come off the ski season quite aerobically fit but without the special running strength they need to exploit that fitness. To avoid injury, return to running gradually over four to six weeks.

- It is easy to overdo it when just starting a new program. Don't feel like you have to get in shape during the first two weeks.

General Guidelines for Your Transition Period Planning

During these early weeks, there is no difference in training for running, ski mountaineering, or skimo. This period serves as general conditioning. Before launching into more vigorous work, you will be best served by building general strength and fitness. This plan provides a gradual adaptation period. Week 8 is a reduced training load to give your body a chance to catch up before launching into the Base Period—the meat of the training.

Workout Notes for the Transition Period

You'll need to place the workouts into the days that fit your schedule and plan for the required time based on your ability. For some people, a one-hour hike may be long, and for others, a two-hour run may be short. No one can determine this for you.

- One long aerobic capacity–building workout each week. Do this at Zone 1 intensity if your AeT heart rate is within 10 percent of your LT heart rate. Do this at Zone 2 if you suffer from ADS (Aerobic Deficiency Syndrome, see page 46) and your AeT heart rate is more than 10 percent below your LT heart rate. This should leave you tired from the duration, not the intensity. This one workout should be 25 percent of the weekly aerobic training volume.

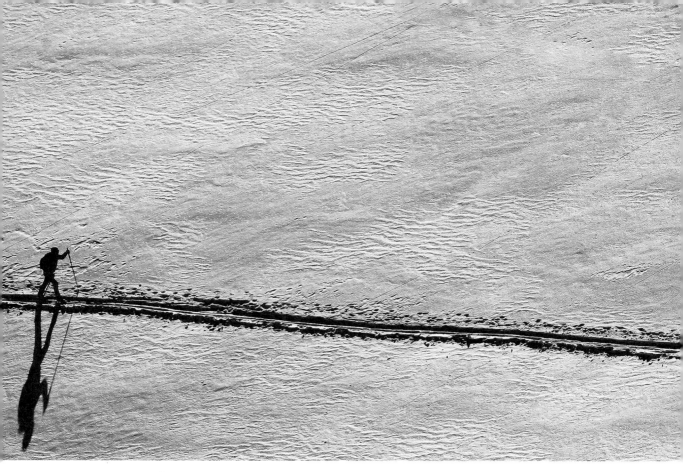

An athlete competing in the Coppa Delle Dolomiti stage race, Brenta Dolomites, Italy.
Photo: Federico Modica

- One or two general-strength sessions each week. Do the appropriate core exercises as a warm-up for these. Select the level of strength to do in the Transition Period by following the strength assessments as detailed in chapters 7 and 8.

- Make up the rest of the volume with easy aerobic exercise at Zone 1 and 2 or Recovery pace.

- All aerobic work should be foot borne: skiing, ski striding, or running and hiking on hilly terrain.

How to Plan Your Race Season

Luke Nelson

Go for what excites you. For me the events that are most appealing are either aesthetic courses—courses in beautiful places—or challenging courses, in terms of terrain or environment. The Rut in Montana is one of my favorite races, and ranking a close second and third are a skyrace in Norway that Kílian Jornet and Emelie Forsberg put on (the Tromsø Skyrace) and the Glen Coe Skyline in Scotland. All three are technical mountain races: they involve moving through mountains and over summits on routes that would be pretty exciting to go do on your Saturday long run. But most people don't go to Norway for their Saturday long run.

You can generalize this out to just about any trail runner: pick the races that inspire you. For me those are technical races like The Rut, but for someone else that might be fifty miles of flat, runnable singletrack. Signing up for a race that inspires you really adds to the motivation of training, and you'll enjoy the event instead of just slogging through it.

Do plenty of Googling. To discover new races, I consult trip reports that runners have either written for sponsors or posted on their personal websites. For me a race needs to be visually stimulating, so sometimes the pictures alone are enough to pique my interest. Another great resource is UltraSignup.com, the major trail race registration site in the United States. Through it, you can find races similar to other races you've done that are in different parts of the country.

Plan early. Depending on the length of the race you're interested in, start thinking about mapping out your calendar as much as a year in advance. And consider having multiyear goals, like picking a pinnacle race you want to do really well at, but maybe you

need a season or two to appropriately build up your fitness and endurance to be successful. I think all too often people sign up for a race on a whim. Sure, you can gut it out, but to have the best experience, start planning and training at a minimum six months ahead, if not longer.

Read the fine print. Physical preparation aside, there's also a practical concern to getting a head start on your planning. With trail and ultrarunning gaining in popularity, well-known races tend to fill up quickly, sometimes within an hour or two of the registration opening. There are lotteries and wait lists and plenty of runners who miss out on spots in events they're gunning to do. If your heart is set on a big-name race, make sure you know the exact time when registration is going to open, and get your name in the second it does.

On top of that, some races require you to have completed another race of a certain distance in order to qualify for the race you want to do. Maybe you need to have finished a 50K to qualify for a 50-miler, or maybe you need to prove you have the technical know-how to tackle a more rugged course. Do your research well in advance, and cover your bases when it comes to these prerequisites.

Balance your races so that they aren't all the main event. Back when I did more racing, my coach Scott Johnston and I would structure my calendar so that not all of the events I signed up for would be my main focus. Instead, I would do certain races as part of my training to get ready for bigger goal races. A good example of that would be in 2016 when I did the Sky Extreme World Series, which included the Norway

Luke Nelson running up what inspires him: technical mountain trails, this time in the San Juan Mountains of Colorado. Photo: Fredrik Marmsater

and Scotland races. To get ready for those longer objectives overseas, I used the US Skyrunner Series in the shorter distances as training. No disrespect to those events, but that year the primary objective was to do well in Europe. The calendar was still full, but I trained up to and through the shorter, US-based races.

Don't pile on the ultras. The strategy of using races as training can be beneficial, but it has to be applied very cautiously. If not, you risk going too hard in the stepping-stone events and getting overtrained. I was racing sky-distance races, which are shorter efforts—much shorter than the pinnacle races I was trying to do. That allowed me to race hard without the same impact as one of the Extreme Series ultramarathons. Had I been trying to do the ultradistances in the US series, it would have been too much, and I would have seen decreasing performance as the season went on. I just can't recover that well every three to four weeks.

It's really helpful to look at what the very best marathoners in the world do: they race two marathons in a year. What makes us as ultramarathoners think we can race six and have top-level performances? It's a reality check.

Have fun along the way. Runners often fixate on race goals, but healthy training can have some really fun events baked into it. Get out into the mountains—and enjoy being out there—as part of the training process for big objectives. Training shouldn't be a grind. People often think of races as the only times when they get together with the community and have a lot of fun, but you can have just as much fun getting together with a group of friends and doing a long run in the mountains on the weekend. That can easily fit into a well-structured training plan. ■

CHAPTER ELEVEN

Introduction to the Base Period

As we mentioned earlier, the sports of mountain running and skimo are complementary both from the seasonal standpoint and because most of the physiological demands are the same. Their training methods share a great deal in common. So it makes sense to address their training in one book. The difference in the approach you choose will depend only on whether you want to focus just on running, just on skimo, or on both. We'll cover all three options in the remaining chapters.

Well over 80 percent of your time and energy expenditure are consumed on the uphill sections for skimo and ski mountaineering, and more than 50 percent for running. Even a few percent improvement in the uphill speed can easily translate into several minutes gained over the course of a long climb. Hence, much of the focus here will be on improving uphill performance. The aerobic base miles (or kilometers) that a runner puts in have their analog in skimo as base vertical feet (or meters). For skiers this means accumulating many thousands of feet (or meters) of Zones 1–2 aerobic work supplemented by some strength and higher-intensity training. While runners' training also needs to include sufficient elevation gain and loss, it also has to prepare them to cover the required distance of their goal event. The takeaway is that the bulk of the training is essentially the same for both sports: time on your feet going up and down mountains has to form the vast majority of your training if you hope to be well prepared for the race season. The following information is intended to help you develop a training plan that suits your goals while considering your training history.

The purpose of the Base Period is to increase your work capacity and improve your fatigue resistance. You build this fitness base so that you can handle more

Vertical-race hero Urban Zemmer competing at the Vertical Kilometer Crepa Neigra in Val di Fassa, Italy. Photo: Federico Modica

278 STEVE HOUSE | SCOTT JOHNSTON | KÍLIAN JORNET

work, and eventually more intense work, which prepares you for the races themselves. You'll do this by using the progression principle that we discussed in earlier chapters: slightly exceeding your work capacity in many workouts, then recovering and repeating this process for months at a time. The progression must be gradual (so your body can adapt) and continuous (without breaks). It underlies the entire plan and its effectiveness. Exercising in a random and sporadic way will not give you the best results.

During much of the Base Period, you will be a little too tired to perform at your best. This is why elite athletes build their base *before* the main competitive period. If you do insert races or significant training events into your Base Period, they should be low priority (C level) and barely exceed what you are typically doing in training. These will then minimally disturb the overall training progression toward your ultimate goal. Recall from the capacity versus utilization discussion (see page 74) that it is just not possible to effectively build capacity (fitness) while trying to maximally utilize it (as you will during races or important events) at the same time. Waiting until December to begin a skimo training program that has to overlap with the racing season will certainly compromise either the training or the race results, or both.

All the plans discussed in this book assume that you want to maximize your performance and are willing to undertake a focused plan for months on end. Neither this book nor the plans in it are intended for those looking for shortcuts.

There are no shortcuts.

We want to once again emphasize the principles that you need to follow: maintaining *consistency* in your training routine while *gradually* increasing the training load and *modulating* the training from hard to easy over days and weeks.

The Low-Hanging Fruit

Train your weaknesses and race your strengths.

– Eddie Borysewicz (famed cycling coach)

As with all training, the Base Period must be individualized to best meet your needs. Heeding Eddie B's sage advice, you need to figure out: What are your weaknesses? What is holding you back from improving? Doing this requires detached analysis coupled with some knowledge. Imparting this knowledge to you so that you can make better-informed decisions is why we focused in the early sections of this book on the fundamentals of training for endurance.

We're going to give you a few tips on how to pick out your weaknesses in a minute, but one sure way *not* to do this is to do in training only the things you are good at or enjoy. What's wrong with that approach? Plenty. We all gravitate

Alyson Dimmitt Gnam logging miles on alpine singletrack surrounded by blooming bear grass in Glacier National Park, Montana. Photo: Steven Gnam

toward doing things we are good at in most areas of our lives. We also avoid things we don't enjoy or are worse at—nobody likes to do things they suck at! This natural tendency often drives us to overemphasize in training the areas where we are already the strongest, while avoiding the things where we have more room to improve. Continuing to make significant gains in your strong areas, year after year, is going to be tough, whereas a shift of training emphasis to your areas of weakness can deliver big results. Here are a couple of common examples:

- If you are stronger (relative to your competitive standing) on the uphills in running races but get dropped on flatter and faster terrain, this would indicate that your aerobic endurance is probably relatively higher than your running economy. A wise training trade-off for this type of runner will be to shift some emphasis to flatter, faster running and technique work.

- If you have a strong downhill skiing background and manage to dominate on the downhill sections of skimo races but lose time on the uphills, then you'd be wise to put more effort into increasing your aerobic endurance.

- If your legs get very sore and your muscle fatigue lingers for several days after a long run or race with a lot of vertical gain and loss, you may need to increase your leg strength and muscular endurance in the Base Period.

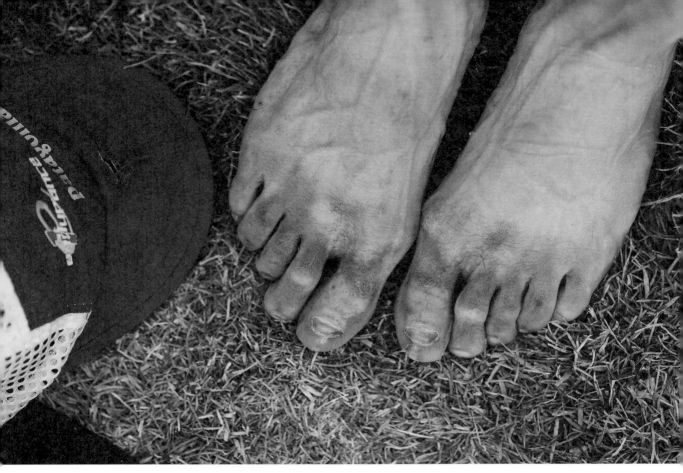

Luke Nelson's feet after running The Rut 50K race in Big Sky, Montana. Photo: Steven Gnam

There is no better proving ground in sports than competition. Examine your racing history: On what parts of the course, or even on what type of courses, are you relatively better or worse than your competitor peer group? The areas where you are worse than your peer group should be the areas you pay more attention to. Beginners in a sport usually make rapid improvements in all areas and quickly see big performance gains. But the better you get, the more elusive those gains will become.

Even professional athletes have limited energy and time. Most amateurs will have quite restrictive time and energy constraints for training. They especially need to make wise use of their training time. The message here is that just running more miles or putting in more vertical meters, while certainly important, may at some point begin to show diminishing returns on the training investment, and the savvy coach and athlete need to be open to changing the training stimuli in order to continue making gains.

The Cornerstone of the Base

For most readers and for all the sports covered in this book, the number one area of training focus must be increasing that all-important aerobic base. Without this base all the rest is mere window dressing. For seasoned endurance athletes with that big base of aerobic work, the training can and must take on multiple dimensions and will therefore become more complex. If you were nodding in recognition as you read the first "low-hanging fruit" example above, you need to recognize that your aerobic endurance is not what is holding you back in races and be brave enough to step away from the safety of training only your strength. This doesn't mean that you stop the aerobic training, but it does mean a re-allotment of training time to include the faster flat running.

While there is no simple rule of thumb for deciding how much time to spend working on running economy or skimo technique, deciding if your aerobic base is big enough for the current Base Period, and when it is most beneficial to include higher-intensity training, is a much simpler task.

The best way to decide how much emphasis you still need to place on basic aerobic fitness versus adding more high-intensity endurance training is to refer back to the Ten Percent Test (see page 91). If the difference between your AeT and LT (in terms of heart rate) is 10 percent or less, you should include up to two weekly high-intensity aerobic endurance sessions in your Base Period. If your AeT-to-LT spread is greater than 10 percent, delay the introduction of Zone 3 workouts and limit the higher-intensity workouts to no more than once a week.

The reason for this distinction is that those with a higher basic aerobic work capacity can handle more intensity, meaning they will recover and benefit better from it. Those with a wider spread still have some low-hanging aerobic fruit to harvest and, while they can surely benefit from the addition of high-intensity training, their gains will never be as great nor as long-lived as for those who have more aerobic capacity.

The strength training in this period plays only a supporting (albeit important) role for the other more sport-specific training. If you do find yourself lacking the basic strength as determined in the strength assessment test in the chapter 7, then you should start with remedial strength training. Those with a better strength base will find the Specific-Strength recommendations useful. But you won't be spending many hours each week in a gym lifting weights in any of our programs.

The Mechanics of Planning

We've gone to great lengths to explain the need for individuality and how you can adjust and monitor your training to get the best results. We emphasized the nuanced gray areas that make coaching more art than science. Now we are about to embark on what we referred to earlier as the "mechanistic" approach. We're going to describe ways to lay out a long-term plan for yourself. Knowing full well that, no matter how pure your intentions, you *will* deviate from this, or any, long-term plan.

Lining Up and Knowing I Would Win

Rico Elmer

I was born in a small valley near the Linth River. Though the mountains there are not high—around 10,000 feet—the valley floor is at 1,000 feet and the summits form a cul-de-sac that traps the moist air coming from the west, so we always have a lot of snow. I started cross-country skiing early, as most kids in the area did. I participated in training and racing from an early age. I raced at the World Cup level in cross-country, but I never really felt at home there. I was not the most stellar technician, and I didn't do well in any important races except when conditions were horrible.

I did my first ski mountaineering races in my early twenties, and when I was twenty-five I started training with a coach, Gregor Hagmann.

At that time the Swiss had a system where an athlete could apply for employment with the Swiss Border Guard and be paid a salary, yet only needed to train … and show results. When I was twenty-six I got this job and I started training full-time. The results came: when I was twenty-nine I won my first major race, the Patrouille des Glaciers. My teammates, Emanuel Buchs and Damien Farquet, and I set a course record.

In those days in the sport of ski mountaineering, there were not too many transitions, usually only one to three per race, and there was a lot of flat skinning. My experience cross-country skiing was valuable in that regard, because I knew how to glide a ski. My cross-country ski training in my youth helped me a lot.

In my first years of training with Gregor I could really feel that I was improving significantly from year to year. Then from 2000 to 2004, I knew at each starting line that, as long as I didn't make a big mistake, I was going to win the race. During that time I didn't

feel I was really improving, I just wanted to hold onto that level as long as I could. In 2006 I felt that I started to lose that really good fitness, that I had been in the sport too long. I was growing tired of it.

My summer training was always a lot of volume. On a typical day I'd wake up and go for a twenty- to thirty-minute run, come back, have breakfast, and then go for my long run of the day. After lunch I'd take a nap, and then go for a shorter one- to two-hour run in the afternoon before doing some core strength training. I often mixed running with roller skiing. Roller skiing is excellent training for ski mountaineering. I did a lot of double-poling on the roller skis.

It's my belief that having a big base is key to succeeding on race day, though there are other puzzles to unlock when it comes to training—including intervals. Intervals were always an important part of my progression. At the end of a race season I would take one to two months completely off from training, and then as the snow started to melt, I'd start to run again. After two to three months of volume, mostly mountain running and roller skiing, I'd start to do intervals. I did all kinds of intervals: 30/30s, pyramids, frog-hops front and back, everything Gregor could invent. I often did intervals during my long workout; never just on a whim though, it was all planned.

In the fall I always did some kind of race—a mountain bike race or mountain running race, but not a ski race—to help get my mind into racing mode, into going as fast as possible.

Eating was also very important. Not to be crazy about nutrition, but to eat enough. I experimented with getting lighter. I am five-foot-ten, and my best

Rico Elmer competing in the three-day Transcavallo World Cup skimo race with his partner Damien Farquet. The pair placed third and won the overall European Championship that season, 2004. Italy. Photo: Rico Elmer Collection

ght was 154 pounds. I went down to 143 pounds at one point, but I wasn't nearly as fast and I was getting sick all the time. I ate a balanced diet while training; I always eat some of everything.

I followed the same routine before each race. If the race was on Saturday, on Wednesday I would do one interval workout, hard but short. Thursday I would do about twenty easy minutes on a bike and then travel to the race. Friday I would go out on my skis and check out the course. During this check I would do two to three quick sprints, each a bit harder, with the last one to get my heart rate to max, just for one minute or less. The night before the race I ate spaghetti with olive oil, just plain. Three hours before the race I ate muesli or bread, and then fifteen minutes before the race I ate just a little carbohydrate again. I could eat almost anything, as long as it was healthy, the morning before a race.

To have a good race, I had to be nervous. At some races I was so nervous my fingers tingled. That was too much. But I always prioritized my races, focusing on one or two each year. ■

Rico Elmer is a Swiss ski mountaineer who dominated the ski mountaineering race circuit in the early 2000s: he won the European Championship of Ski Mountaineering in the team division in 2003 (with Damien Farquet), and he won the individual title at the World Championship in 2004. He has won nearly every major race in the ski mountaineering world, including the Patrouille des Glaciers (1998 and 2000) and the Trofeo Mezzalama (2003). Rico is the former head coach of the Swiss National Ski Mountaineering Racing Team; he coached six-time world (team and individual) champion Florent Troillet.

Tadej Pivk during the Dolomites Skyrace on Sass Pordoi, Italy. Photo: Federico Modica

To reduce the chances for significant deviations and drastic changes to this plan, we've developed some ways that allow you, by referring back to the previous chapters, to build a fairly customized plan and then to make the inevitable adjustments on the fly.

As the earlier sections of this book explained, there is no one-size-fits-all approach to training. Trying to blindly copy the training of a highly successful athlete is almost guaranteed to lead to disappointment and even worse.

To guide you through the mechanics of creating a plan, refer first to the flow-chart below.

Fig. 11.1 The Mechanics of Planning

First select the athlete category that most closely fits your circumstances. The macro plan you assemble in step 2 will help you have an overview of the coming weeks and months without getting mired down by planning the actual days. Use step 3 to create a general daily structure to the weeks. Lay out actual workouts in the weekly structure only one to two weeks ahead. This will save you frequently changing the plan based on unforeseen circumstances and help avoid that "blind adherence" to the plan that we cautioned against earlier.

Federica Biofava charges up a hillside in the Camonica Valley of northern Italy. Photo: Davide Ferrari

Step 1. Choose Your Athlete Category

To start this process, you need to honestly assess what you are bringing to this project.

The needs of the experienced mountain athlete with several seasons of training and multiple races in the bag are quite different from what is needed by those just coming into these sports with the hopes of completing their first 50K running race or trying out a skimo race or two next season, or someone who may have never followed any sort of training program but wants to make the most of a once-in-a-lifetime ski tour. Select the category that fits you best.

- The first, Category 1, is for the beginner and less experienced athlete who needs to *build* a base of fitness.

- The second, Category 2, is for athletes with at least one successful season (preferably several seasons) of training behind them who need to *maintain* and supplement an already-existing base.

CATEGORY 1

Athletes in need of building a base:

- Have not averaged more than 400 hours per year of focused training for running or skimo during the past two years.

or

- Are under the age of eighteen.

or

- Have not, during the previous twelve months, successfully* completed races or events at the distance/duration they are aiming for in the next training period.

If you fit into this category, the single most effective thing you can do is to increase the volume of training you are doing. Ideally you will do this over a long period in your off-season.

Note: If you are training at well below 400 hours per year, then you should expect to spend additional training cycles in this base-building phase of training. This applies especially to juniors and the inexperienced. Do not skip to the Category 2 section too early or you will struggle to handle the workload and may not see improvement.

*Successfully: This means you performed well and you were happy with the result. You achieved or came close enough to the goals you had set for yourself that you were satisfied. You were not destroyed or injured by the event.

CATEGORY 2

Athletes in need of maintaining their base while supplementing it:

- Have trained consistently at over 400 hours per year for at least the past two years. This athlete never really stops training other than short breaks, so his or her base remains high.

and

- Are over the age of eighteen.

and

- Have, during the previous twelve months, successfully* completed races or events at or near** the distance/duration they are aiming for this training period.

and

- Race several to many times during one year.

If you fit into this group, increasing the specificity of your training will yield the biggest gains. This means more training that mimics the demands of the event itself and, to the extent that it does not reduce your Zones 1–2 base training volume appreciably, more high intensity.

*Successfully: This means you performed well and you were happy with the result. You achieved or came close enough to the goals you had set for yourself that you were satisfied. You were not destroyed or injured by the event.

**Near: This means you have successfully completed a race or event that sits in the conventional progression of difficulty or distance as the next step below the targeted event for this training cycle.

Step 2. Select a Macrocycle Plan

In this section we'll lay out a few admittedly idealized (plans rarely work out as planned), longer-term plans such as the ones below. Select the type of plan from this group that best fits your goals and individual needs. We've tried to provide a variety of plans so that you can find one that is right (or close to right) for you. This system allows you the maximum freedom to structure your own plan while giving guidance to help you apply sound training practice to the organization of that plan. The first chart below shows the training progression using vertical gain and loss as a proxy for training load for an athlete preparing for his or her first season of skimo racing. The blue bars represent the weekly vertical in meters and feet.

Above each week is a letter: B (Base), I (Intensity), R (Recovery), S (Specificity), T (Taper), and G (Goal). These letters indicate the week type. You can start to build your plan in a spreadsheet, calendar, or notebook by transferring the workouts from the menu for the appropriate type of week into the days of the week.

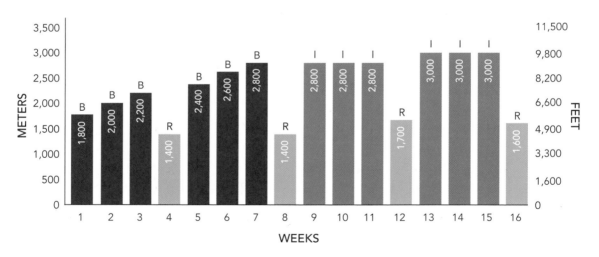

Fig. 11.2 Preseason Skimo Progression, Cat 1 First Season Athlete

This plan is for someone interested in trying his or her first couple of skimo races this season. You should have an average weekly vertical of around 1,500–1,700 meters for the previous eight weeks to support this plan. If your weekly average is lower, reduce week 1 vertical by your percent below 1,600, then continue the progression percentage as shown.

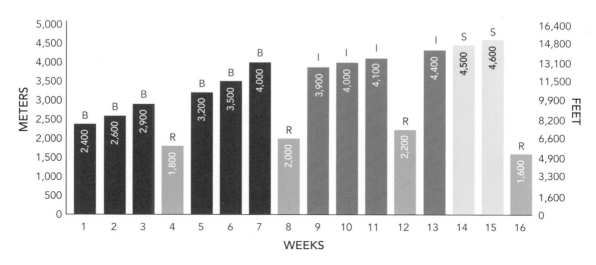

Fig. 11.3 Early-Season Skimo Progression, Cat 2 Athlete

This is for the athlete making the transition from a summer of mountain running who has averaged a weekly vertical of around 2,000–2,200 meters for the previous eight weeks. The plan is meant to end as the full multirace season begins. This plan could also work well for a ski mountaineering goal, such as a hut trip or a grand tour like the Haute Route.

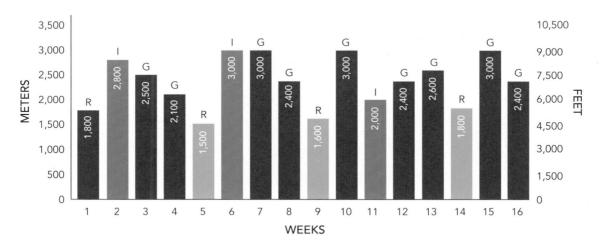

Fig. 11.4 Skimo Race Season Progression, Cat 2 Athlete

This plan is for someone competing in a race series extending from December until April. This plan should be preceded with a plan following close to Figure 11.5.

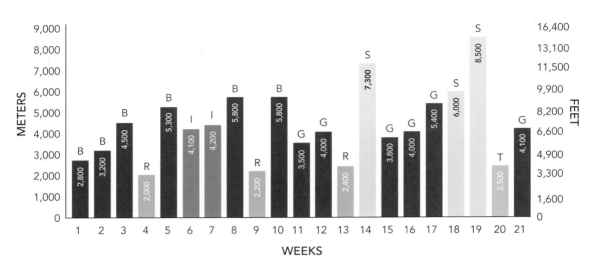

Fig. 11.5 Actual Skimo Training Progression, Cat 2 Athlete

This is an actual training plan for a nationally competitive skimo racer with an end-of-season A priority race in March doing a few C category races for training during the winter. The actual training will probably not follow the plan exactly. Regardless, this athlete achieved personal best results throughout the season. This progression starts in mid-October after a summer of base training. Could be used for races like Patrouille des Galciers and Power of Four.

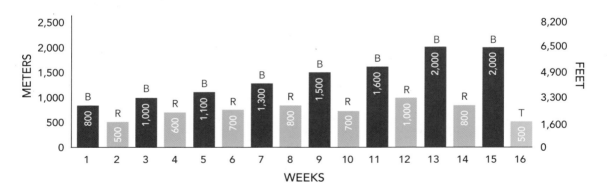

Fig 11.6 Progression in Vertical, Hut-to-Hut Ski-Touring Trip

Here is an example of a progression in vertical meters for someone hoping to comfortably handle a multiday hut-to-hut ski touring trip, such as the Haute Route or Wapta Traverse. This would be the bare minimum for a trip like the Hoch Tirol.

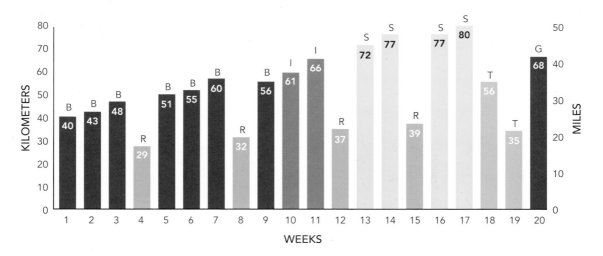

Fig. 11.7 Idealized Plan, Cat 1 First Time 50K Running Race

This is for an athlete targeting his or her first 50K running race. It could also serve as a program for a recreational runner with a personal goal of similar distance.

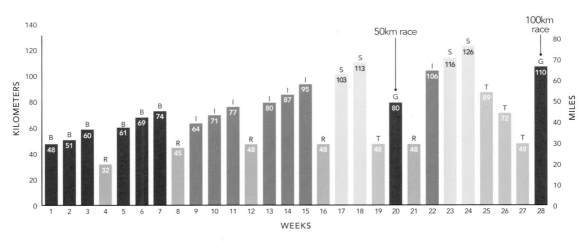

Fig. 11.8 Idealized Progression, Cat 2 Single A Priority 100K Run

This is the idealized plan for an athlete who has a single A priority running race with an intermediate B priority race. This plan could be reasonable for many Category 1 runners during the second season of structured training. It would also be a good plan for a recreational runner looking to complete a personal mountain-running project.

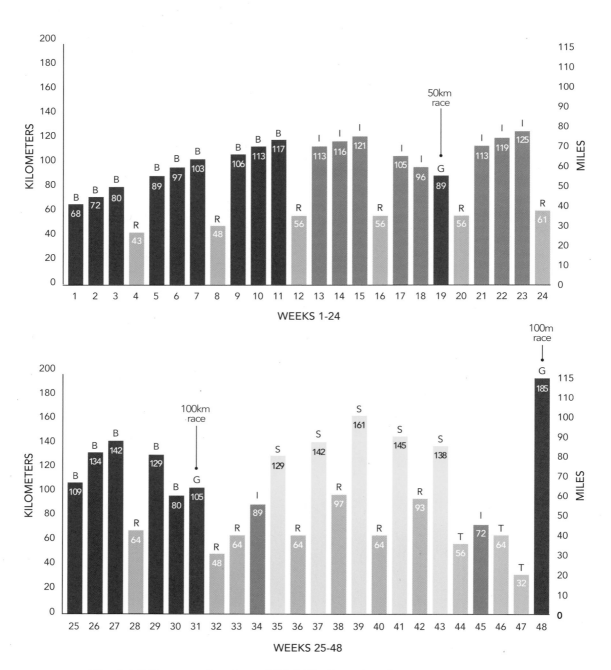

Fig. 11.9 Progression for a 100-Mile Running Race

This is an idealized progression toward a single A priority 100-mile running race with two intermediate B priority races. A plan like this is most reasonable for a Category 2 runner. Category 1 runners may be tempted to rush to these longer distances, but we strongly recommend that you build your running base over a few years of continuous training if you hope to prosper in the long term and avoid career-ending burnout and injury.

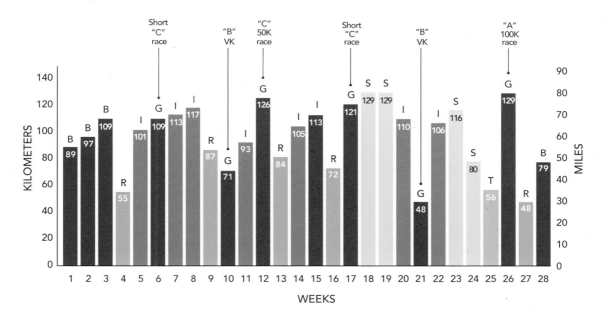

Fig. 11.10 Progression for Cat 2 Runner with a Good Base

This is how a Category 2 mountain runner might approach planning for a spring, summer, and fall of racing. Due to the athlete's high base level of fitness, none of these planned races exceed his or her current capacity. He or she will be able to use several races throughout the season as hard workouts without having to interrupt the normal flow of training. Too many athletes try to accomplish such a season with too small of a base and end up discouraged due to injury and/or exhaustion. We encourage you to take the long view and strive to reach this level over several years of steady work.

Step 3. Pick from the Week-Type Menu

Choose the week type below that matches the letter above the week in your macrocycle plan. The workouts are listed beneath each week heading in the menu below with a description and specific recommendations for implementing the workout. Next, distribute the listed workouts for that week into your plan calendar in a way that fits your schedule using the guidelines that have been given according to the type of workout.

B (BASE) WEEK

These are the foundational weeks upon which all the other training rests. They build aerobic capacity, improving running economy and increasing your strength. The accumulation of time, distance, and vertical in the aerobic base intensity, Zones 1 and 2, is the aim. If you are aerobically deficient (experiencing ADS, see the Ten Percent Test on page 91), then you will do nearly all your aerobic

STEVE HOUSE | SCOTT JOHNSTON | KÍLIAN JORNET

base training in Zone 2. Otherwise, you will use Zone 2 sparingly for no more than 15 percent of total weekly volume and do the base work in Zone 1.

Strength: Two workouts per week. These can be General or Specific, depending on your needs. Use the appropriate strength phase from your strength assessment. Two Core Strength workouts can be done on these or other days.

Active recovery: Include active recovery work on problem areas. Stretch, roll, massage, swim. Be proactive with self-maintenance. Do this at least three times per week.

Recovery workouts: Count this in the aerobic base distance for the week. These can be planned as very light training days after a heavy day. Or any day when you feel "off" after a warm-up and your body is telling you it is not ready to be pushed. These would be days when you would give the workout a C or D grade. Cut the intensity dramatically and shorten the workout if needed. These workouts should leave you feeling better than when you started, either immediately afterward or a few hours later. If they do not help, consider taking the next day off.

Aerobic base workouts: Start your planning by selecting one day each week for your long workout. Aim for between 30–40 percent of your overall weekly distance/vertical on this one run/ski. In lower-volume weeks, the percentage of the overall weekly volume will be higher on this one day. As your weekly volume increases, you may need to make the long day a smaller percentage of the weekly total. Distribute the remaining distance over at least four workouts. These runs will include the warm-ups and cool-downs for Hill Sprints/Bounding and ME workouts. Two of these runs should include some fast downhill running pick-ups. Skimo can also include skiing and roller skiing. Ski mountaineers optionally can include some Ski Striding. See sidebar on ski simulations (see page 313).

Muscular endurance: If muscular endurance is a weakness of yours (see page 240), this would be a good time to begin focused ME workouts. Ski mountaineers, use these workouts once per week in the early weeks.

I (INTENSITY) WEEK

Refer to the intensity guidelines for more details. These weeks introduce higher-intensity training in Zones 3 and 4, which will directly improve your endurance. They supplement the B week training. They do not replace it. If you are aerobically deficient (ADS, see the Ten Percent Test on page 91), then you will do nearly all your aerobic base training in Zone 2. Otherwise, you will drop Zone 2 and do the base work in Zone 1.

Luke Nelson, Chloë Lanthier, and Clare Gallagher run in the Dolomites, Italy. Photo: Eliza Earle

Strength: One Hill Sprint/Bounding workout these weeks. Continue two Core Strength workouts each week. Ski mountaineers, use Hill Bounding.

Active recovery: Include active recovery; work on problem areas. Stretch, roll, massage, swim. Be proactive with self-maintenance. Do this at least three times per week.

Recovery workouts: Count this in the aerobic base distance for the week. Terrain should be less steep. These can be planned as very light training days after a heavy day. Or they can be unplanned and used when you feel "off" after a warm-up and your body is telling you it is not ready to be pushed. These would be days when you would give the workout a C or D grade. Cut the intensity dramatically and shorten the workout if needed. These workouts should leave you feeling better than when you started—if not immediately afterward, then a few hours later. If they do not help, consider taking the next day off.

Aerobic base workouts: Start your planning by selecting one day each week for your long workout. Aim for between 30–40 percent of your overall weekly distance/vertical on this one run/ski. In lower-volume weeks, the percentage of the overall weekly volume will be higher on this one day. As your weekly volume

Riccardo and Giulia Dallio do a snowy aerobic base workout in Val Venegia, Trentino, Italy.
Photo: Federico Modica

increases, you may need to make the long day a smaller percentage of the weekly total. Distribute the remaining distance over at least four workouts. These runs will include the warm-ups and cool-downs for Hill Sprints/Bounding and ME workouts. Two of these runs should include some fast downhill running pick-ups. For skimo, also include ski simulations. Ski mountaineers optionally can include skiing or ski simulations. See sidebar on ski simulations (see page 313).

Muscular endurance: Drop muscular endurance and begin integrating Zone 3 or Zone 4 workouts. Ski mountaineers, move to two times/week.

High intensity: For a full discussion, see page 305. Begin by adding Zone 3 intervals. Start with time in Zone 3 that's no more than 5 percent of your weekly total. Start with duration and overall volume that allows you to recover in forty-eight hours. If you still feel tired legs seventy-two hours later, then cut back on the next workout. When you can handle 10 percent of the total weekly time in Zone 3, begin to replace some Zone 3 with Zone 4. Skimo should use a ski-specific mode. Ski mountaineers, disregard this category.

Previous page: Running through Plaza Geru high in the Camonica Valley, Italy.
Photo: Davide Ferrari

R (RECOVERY) WEEK

The recovery week is intended to act as a consolidation week to allow your body to catch up. Cut to 50 percent of the total volume. The focus here needs to be on recovery first. The purpose of the recovery week or few days is not to add to your fitness bank account, but to get you recovered as well and as quickly as possible so you are ready to start building fitness again. This week should be the most loosely structured so that you can take days off or do especially light training. You want to be feeling like attacking the next week by Sunday. If not, you didn't recover. Insert alternative recovery training like swimming or easy cycling, or any other favored recovery activity. If you are aerobically deficient (ADS, see the Ten Percent Test on page 91), then do nearly all your aerobic base training in Zone 2. Otherwise, use Zone 2 sparingly for no more than 15 percent of total weekly volume and do the base work in Zone 1.

Strength: One Core Strength workout per week. Cut Hill Sprint/Bounding volume in half, doing these exercises late in the week. Ski mountaineers, use Hill Bounding cut in half.

Active recovery: Focus active recovery; work on problem areas this week. Stretch, roll, massage, swim. Be proactive with self-maintenance. Do this at least three times per week.

Recovery workouts: Do at least two workouts in this intensity zone this week. Count this in the aerobic base distance for the week. Terrain should be less steep. These can be planned as very light training days after a heavy day. Or they can be unplanned and used when you feel "off" after a warm-up and your body is telling you it is not ready to be pushed. These would be days when you would give the workout a C or D grade. Cut the intensity dramatically and shorten the workout if needed. These workouts should leave you feeling better than when you started—if not immediately afterward, then a few hours later. If they do not help, consider taking the next day off.

Aerobic base workouts: Aim for a long workout of around 40 percent of your overall weekly distance/vertical. Do this late in the week when you are more recovered. These will include the warm-up and cool-down runs done in conjunction with Hill Sprints/Bounding and high intensity. Do one other workout this week at this intensity of about 20 percent of the total; do the rest in the Recovery Zone. One of these runs should include some fast downhill running pick-ups. Skimo racers can also include ski walking, roller skiing, and Moose Hoofing.

Muscular endurance: Drop or cut by 50 percent.

High intensity: Cut all high-intensity work by half from the last week. Do one workout late in the week. Skimo racers can also include ski walking, roller skiing, and Moose Hoofing. Ski mountaineers, disregard this category.

S (SPECIFICITY) WEEK

This is a week used in the later weeks of your plan to prepare you for the specific demands of your A priority event. For ultrarunners and ski mountaineers, this will come from doing back-to-back long runs/skis. This gives you a similar training effect as doing one very long day by mimicking some of the demands of your event, but it reduces the stress and shortens the recovery time significantly.

For shorter, high-intensity events like a VK or skimo race, this comes from reducing the aerobic base training and adding in more Zone 4 interval work. If you are aerobically deficient (ADS, see the Ten Percent Test on page 91), then do nearly all your aerobic base training in Zone 2. Otherwise, use Zone 2 sparingly for no more than 15 percent of your total weekly volume and do the base work in Zone 1.

Strength: One Hill Sprint/Bounding workout these weeks. Continue two Core Strength workouts each week.

Muscular endurance: Ski mountaineers, continue the ME workout once per week. For runners and skimo racers, cut this workout so that the high intensity can be higher quality.

Active recovery: Include active recovery work on problem areas. Stretch, roll, massage, swim. Be proactive with self-maintenance. Do this at least three times per week.

Recovery workouts: Do at least two workouts in this intensity zone this week. Count this in the aerobic base distance for the week. Terrain should be less steep. These can be planned as very light training days after a heavy day. Or they can be unplanned when you feel "off" after a warm-up and your body is telling you it is not ready to be pushed. These would be days when you would give the workout a C or D grade. Cut the intensity dramatically and shorten the workout if needed. These workouts should leave you feeling better than when you started—if not immediately afterward, then a few hours later. If they do not help, consider taking the next day off.

Aerobic base workouts: If training for a long event, do back-to-back long workouts these weeks. Aim for between 60–80 percent of your overall weekly distance/vertical on these two workouts. Distribute the remaining distance over at least three workouts. These will include the warm-ups and cool-downs for Hill Sprints/Bounding and ME workouts. Two of these workouts should include some fast downhill running or skiing pick-ups. Skimo racers can also include Ski Striding, roller skiing, and Moose Hoofing (see page 313).

If training for normal skimo or shorter runs like VK, double up on the high-intensity workouts.

High intensity: For ultradistance runners, cut all Zone 3 and do only one Zone 4 interval session at no more than the same volume as the previous week. Do this workout separated by at least 72 hours from the back-to-back long runs.

For VK or skimo racers, cut all Zone 3 and add a second Zone 4 interval session separated by at least 72 hours from the previous one, separated by recovery workouts. The total time in Zone 4 for the week should be no more than 15 percent of the previous week.

T (TAPER) WEEK

Tapering is a very individual preference, with some top athletes like Kílian preferring not to taper for races. This is especially true if an athlete is racing often. In that case, too much tapering would result in a drop in fitness over the season. Traditionally the load would be reduced for some days, or even weeks (in the case of very long races), before the event so that the athlete is fresh on the day that counts. How long and how sharply you drop the training load will best be learned through experience. Our example plans will include traditional taper periods. In general, A priority races will deserve a more dramatic taper than B priority races. C priority events will be treated as normal workouts. The training is over once you enter a taper period. You should not try to sneak in some special or new workout in hopes of getting fitter or faster. The time for that is long past. You want to gradually reduce the training load as little as necessary to allow your legs to refresh without losing fitness. That's a tricky balancing act.

Strength: One Core Strength workout per week. Cut Hill Sprint/Bounding by 30 percent from week to week.

Active recovery: Focus on active recovery; work on problem areas this week. Stretch, roll, massage, swim. Be proactive with self-maintenance. Do this at least three times per week.

Recovery workouts: You will be cutting overall training volume during the taper, and all but two recovery sessions will be in this intensity range.

Aerobic base workouts: Aim for a long run or ski of around 50 percent of your overall weekly distance/vertical. These will include the warm-up and cool-down done in conjunction with Hill Sprints and high intensity. One other Zone 2 workout with no more than 10 percent of total weekly distance/vertical. Include a few short, fast downhill runs. Skimo racers, include a few quick-tempo pick-ups.

High intensity: Keep all high-intensity work short with long rests. Overall volume of intensity should drop about 30 percent from week to week. This is just for sharpening.

G (GOAL) WEEK

This is the race week itself. It is part of the taper period but also a time to take good care of yourself. This week may involve travel. Nothing you do this week will make you faster, but many things you could do will make you slower. Rest and relax but be active each day. Too much rest will make you sluggish.

Strength: No strength this week.

Active recovery: Focus on active recovery; work on problem areas this week. Stretch, roll, massage, swim. Be proactive with self-maintenance. Do this at least three times per week.

Recovery workouts: Do only Recovery Zone this week. No more than four days, just to keep the legs loose.

High intensity: Spice two of your workouts with three or four accelerations up to a fun, fast pace for thirty seconds each, with three minutes of easy jogging between. None for ski mountaineers.

Base Period Guidelines

Keep the following principles in mind as you do the heavy lifting of planning. Progression of the training load is one of the most important elements to consider as you embark on this base-building phase of what may be your first structured training plan. Increase the load too fast and, at best, you'll get tired and need an unplanned break to recover. At worst, you'll get injured or become overtrained, which could derail your plan for weeks and even months. Getting

Jacqui Levy and Alyson Dimmitt Gnam, determined to keep their training volume on track, transition to spikes during a ski tour outside of Missoula, Montana. Photo: Steven Gnam

this right means selecting an appropriate weekly vertical and progressing at a controlled rate. No one can tell you what is an appropriate amount of starting vertical. We have suggested some guidelines, but this will depend on all the factors that give rise to the individual response to training: age, training history, genetics, and life stressors. While the weekly vertical progressions shown in the charts are conservative and should prevent overuse injuries and overtraining, do not proceed stubbornly if your body is telling you something is wrong. Listen to your body.

Note: If you are training at well below 400 hours/year, then expect to spend additional training cycles in this base-building phase of training. This applies especially to juniors and the inexperienced. Do not skip to the Category 2 Athlete section too early or you will struggle to handle the workload and may not see improvement.

Progression of the Training Volume (Weekly Vertical and Distance)

While we made some general weekly distance recommendations a few pages ago, below are a few ideas to keep in mind as you plan.

Guidelines for progressing the training load:

- For the smoothest long-term progression, keep distance, vertical, and time increases at 10 percent or less from week to week, except after a recovery week, when you may increase these much more.

- Do not increase distance and vertical for more than three weeks in a row.

- Do not increase distance, vertical, *and* intensity in a single week. Try to increase only one at a time. If you need to increase two of these, then keep the total increase amount to under 15 percent. Example: 10 percent distance increase with 5 percent vertical increase, or 8 percent increase in Zone 3 time with 7 percent increase in distance.

- Do not make distance/vertical increases of greater than 15 percent for two weeks in a row.

- Typically you should follow large jumps (near 15 percent) in weekly distance, vertical, or intensity with a recovery week to allow your body to adapt.

Modulation of the Training Load

In our macroplan examples, we mostly used three weeks of gradually building the workload followed by a recovery week, during which the training load is greatly reduced. The use of a 3:1 build:recovery cycle is not meant to impose an inflexible structure. You may find that your body does best with a 2:1 cycle. This will take some experimentation and you may need to vary this depending on how you are adapting to the training. Do not stubbornly follow any plan without paying attention to how your body is adapting to it (see the overtraining discussion on page 136). Most importantly: You need to build modulation into your plan. Rest *before* you are forced to. Recovery after hard work is when the gains in fitness occur. During recovery weeks, take enough recovery days so that you feel fresh by the end.

Guidelines for modulating the training load:

- Pay attention to your body. Keep a log. Experiment to find what works for you.

- Modulate the vertical/distance in a manner similar to the way the macroplan weeks show. As much as possible, stick to a progression and don't jump around randomly.

- Recovery weeks should drop the training load typically by at least 40 to 60 percent of the last big week's volume. Don't do more than one intensity session.

- If you do not have much experience, especially *successful* experience, with high-intensity sessions, you may need to shift to a 2:1 or even 1:1 weekly cycle to allow adequate recovery.

- If you intentionally use an overreaching period (see page 99), then plan for a correspondingly lighter recovery period, dropping the load by as much as 70 percent.

Vertical

Just as with distance, the amount of vertical feet (meters) you include in your weekly training is going to depend on several factors: the vertical in your goal event, your access to hills and mountains for training, and your training history. For best results, pick your goals according to what you have available to train on, and then train on hills similar to the goal race. Just as with weekly distance, if you are new to these sports, you'll need to start small and build vertical gradually over the whole plan. Whereas if you have a good history of training, you'll start with and maintain a bigger weekly vertical.

Guidelines for weekly vertical:

- If you are new to these sports, start with no more than a third to one-half of your goal event's total vertical in your first week.

- Plan on training a minimum of your goal event's total vertical during two of your late Base Period weeks.

- Main workouts should be done on foot: running, ski simulations, roller skiing, or skiing.

- These big vertical weeks should correspond to the longer distance weeks.

- Cut vertical by a similar amount as distance reduction during recovery weeks (40–60 percent).

High Intensity

While it is fairly easy to prescribe low-intensity training volumes (because more is almost always better), it is much more challenging to prescribe specific high-intensity workouts. The principle of individuality comes into play much more so when speaking about intensity. Your training history will affect how often and how much high-intensity work is best for you to incorporate into each session. If you have a history of high-intensity training, you will understand what an appropriate intensity dosage is and you will be able to recover better from these workouts. If you are new to adding high-intensity workouts into a high-volume base-building period, you will need to be more conservative as you learn how much and how often you can handle them while maintaining a high aerobic volume.

Skimo: High-intensity workouts play an important role in skimo training because the races are generally performed at significantly higher intensities than ultradistance running events. Regardless, high intensity is still a supplement to, and not a replacement for, the basic aerobic work you need. Especially for Category 1 athletes approaching their first skimo season, aerobic (Zones 1–2) vertical base workouts should take priority over intensity. Ideally you will not add higher-intensity workouts until your AeT heart rate or pace is within 10 percent of your LT heart rate, but that is not always practical. (See the Ten Percent Test on page 91.)

Runners: If you are competing at distances for which you have adequate base volume, then adding high intensity will be a valuable tool for increasing performance. However, if you are moving up to a new distance and stepping into new territory, you'd be wise to prioritize increasing the distance and vertical before adding intensity.

The practical reality is that at some point you must begin to add intensity regardless of the state of your aerobic capacity. Begin to add one Zone 3 workout each week when within two months of your first race. Adding intensity should not require reducing the volume of training by more than 5 percent. If it does, you risk losing the aerobic base you have built. Balancing the introduction of intensity into your program is, like most aspects of training, highly individual and can be tricky to do well. Following are some guidelines to help you.

Guidelines for intensity:

- Kílian's preferred way of introducing high intensity is with Zone 3 training. Include one Zone 3 workout per week when you feel like you are handling the Zones 1–2 volume well. While a highly trained athlete may be comfortable with two sessions per week totaling as much as one to two hours in Zone 3, it will take years to build up to this volume. The best practice for Category 1 athletes will be to ease into Zone 3 with one workout a week, with a total of twenty to thirty minutes of Zone 3 done as an interval workout, such as 3x7 or 3x8 min with short, active rest intervals in a 3:1 or 4:1 work-to-rest ratio. If you do not recover well from this workout, then either you were pushing too hard or the overall volume of work was too high. Adjust accordingly and try again.

- The volume of high-intensity training in each week, and within each workout, should increase gradually and not start out too high. Add only as much as you can before it forces you to drop the volume of your aerobic base (Zones 1–2) training by more than 5 percent. If you can't maintain your volume of Zones 1–2 training, you risk having a short peak followed by a drop in performance.

- The type of intensity you add to your program is dependent upon the event you are targeting. Long Zone 3 sessions will serve well for long-distance races. On the other hand, shorter Zone 4 and Zone 5 sessions will be very useful when you are training for a VK or shorter race.

- Ease into intensity training by first adding one weekly Zone 3 workout. Start with about 5 percent of weekly volume in Zone 3. Add Zone 3 volume gradually and not more than 10 percent per week.

- Kílian recommends increasing high-intensity volume only when you are comfortable handling the current volume/intensity mix. Adding intensity too fast is one of the most common mistakes athletes make.

- Drop or reduce Zone 2 training when you begin adding Zone 3 or 4 work to your plan. Shift to more aerobic base work in Zone 1.

- Consider adding Zone 4 intervals to your week only when the volume of Zone 3 has reached about 10 percent of your weekly volume and you are feeling comfortable with that amount—recovering well and not seeing any drop in overall weekly volume.

- Add Zone 4 intervals by gradually replacing the volume of Zone 3 with Zone 4 work done each week. Start with no more than 5 percent of your total weekly volume in Zone 4. If you must drop the overall weekly Zones 1–2 volume by more than 5 percent, just use the Zone 3 more until you feel that is easy to handle.

- If you are new to structured training, start your Zone 4 intervals by doing 30/30s (see page 177) before progressing to longer and more taxing intervals.

Strength

Keep in mind that strength for the sake of strength is not the point. Strength in endurance sports is used only in a way that improves performance and prevents injury. It plays a supportive role. The most effective form of strength training for these sports is muscular endurance. There are a number of ways to improve this quality, which translates directly into improved performance.

The Ghost on the Mountain

Luke Nelson

Rumors on the mountain were spreading. Word among the groomers was that there had to be something on the mountain. Even the long-time cat drivers had expressed concern. I overheard the conversation while eating breakfast in the lodge after a long training session.

"New footsteps appeared each time I passed the steep section under the Sunshine Chair," one groomer said. "Four laps, four different sets of footprints."

Another groomer added, "Footsteps that start out of the blue and then just disappear—so weird. I know it has to be a ghost or something."

I chuckled as I scarfed down hash browns and eggs. It wasn't the first time this season that I had caught wind that the night grooming staff was concerned about a ghost on the mountain. You would think that since I trained late at night or early in the morning, often in the dark, I too would be concerned about the ghost.

But I knew better. The ghost was me.

I had committed to putting in a very focused training block on snow in order to prepare for the upcoming US Ski Mountaineering Championships, and because I had recently started a new job that occupied most daylight hours, I trained in the dark. I trained every day, and most days twice a day. I would park as low on the mountain as possible in order to maximize vert, which put my truck out of sight of the grooming staff. The majority of my training occurred well off of the groomed runs and kept the beam of my headlamp hidden.

Once or twice a week I would do intervals that included a transition from skinning to booting up a steep, groomed run. I would time it so that I would literally race the groomers up the mountain. The competition helped me push the interval harder than I would have been able to otherwise. Because I started the interval skinning and then transitioned to booting, my tracks weren't obvious until I was kicking steps. Well before the cat turned around, I would transition back to skiing and slip into the woods to ski back to the bottom.

Once I heard about the ghost, I may have gone to extra measures to assure that I didn't get spotted during my nightly training ... just to keep the story interesting.

This went on for well over a month until a week or so before the US Championships, when I had planned a time trial up the entire ski area. I popped out of the woods next to the groomer, who was very surprised to see me, and then proceeded to race him to the top of the mountain. It was a close race, but in the end the machine pulled ahead. The cat driver jumped out at the top and waited for me to crest the final climb. He let out a whoop and gave me a high-five, then told me I owed him a beer for how nervous he had gotten about the ghost on the mountain—the ghost he was relieved to see was just me.

A week later I stood on top of the podium in Jackson Hole. The consistent training, even in the dark of night, had paid off. ∎

Luke Nelson running the ninety-three mile-long Greys River Valley. It was minus twenty Fahrenheit when the team started and it stayed cold for the entire trip. Wyoming. Photo: Fredrik Marmsater

CHAPTER TWELVE

Special Considerations for Skimo and Ski Mountaineering

In this chapter we'll give you some ski-specific information to help you get the most from your plan, including example weeks for special situations that arise during the competition season.

The best way to improve your winter skimo results and ski mountaineering experience is to spend a summer running many hours and many thousands of vertical meters in the mountains. While running uphill is similar to skinning, adding ski simulations in your workouts, such as Ski Striding, Hill Bounding, and roller skiing, along with ski-specific muscular endurance during late summer and early fall, to a good summer of mountain running will help your transition into on-snow training.

The main distinction between skimo and ski mountaineering is the tempo and hence intensity of uphill skinning. Due to the weight of the equipment (skis, boots, and pack) needed for ski mountaineering and the potential for breaking trail in deep snow, the arm and leg turnover is much slower than in skimo. This additional weight means that muscular endurance is a bigger factor in determining your performance in ski mountaineering. Ski mountaineer training hence needs added ME work in place of Zone 3 and Zone 4 interval training.

The start the of 27th Pierra Menta in 2012; Tony Sbalbi (no. 29A) finished ninth overall with his teammate, Jean Pellissier. France. Photo: Jocelyn Chavy

Structuring a Category 1 Athlete's Skimo and Ski Mountaineering Plan

The following section includes different example weeks for a Category 1 athlete. These example weeks are meant to be used along with the preceding information on how to plan, monitor, and adjust your training. This structure applies to both skimo and ski mountaineering. Ski mountaineering should emphasize muscular endurance strength training.

Example Early Base Period Week. Category 1

	AM	PM	Comments
Day 1	Rest day.		This can be a good day to take off or use for light recovery activities after a big weekend of training.
Day 2	Strength: use the strength assessment on page 205 to determine what stage of strength is appropriate. Use that workout. Hill Bounding for more advanced athletes.	Optional second workout: upper-body ME (see page 217).	Keep strength workouts separated by 72 hours.
Day 3	Aerobic base: up to 25% of weekly vertical.	Optional second workout: Zone 1 or Recovery. Up to 10% of weekly vertical.	If ADS, use Z2. If no ADS, stay mostly in Z1. If on skis or roller skis, add 8x15 sec quick-tempo uphill with 3 min easy between.
Day 4	Recovery workout: done at Z1 or Recovery heart rate, depending on fatigue. At least 15% of weekly time.	Off.	Done on flat-to-gentle terrain.
Day 5	Strength: General or Specific. If Tuesday is Hill Bounding, then today is ME workout.	Optional second workout: Zone 1 or Recovery. Up to 10% of weekly vertical.	
Day 6	Aerobic base: up to 20% of weekly vertical.	Off.	If ADS, use Z2. If no ADS, stay mostly in Z1. If on skis or roller skis, add 8x15 sec quick-tempo uphill with 3 min easy between.
Day 7	Aerobic base: Zone 1. Done on hilly terrain. Up to 40% of weekly vertical.	Off.	Stay in zone even if it means walking some hills.

Fig. 12.1 Example Week of the Early Base-Building Period

Note: Percentages given in these tables are rough guidelines, not exact amounts.

Ski Simulations

Running uphill bears a strong resemblance to skiing uphill. However, there are enough differences that make it worth exploring more ski-specific movements for your summer and fall training. Cross-country skiers have developed a few dryland ski-simulation movements used for different types of training. We have already discussed Ski Bounding (see illustration below) as a strength exercise. For long Zones 1–2 uphills, use Ski Striding to imitate the longer stride length allowed by the glide of the ski on the snow. For Zone 3 workouts, they use Elghuf (Moose Hoofing), which is a loping, long stride somewhere between Ski Bounding and Ski Striding in intensity.

Fig. 12.2 Moose Hoofing

This type of movement is best described as low-intensity bounding. It is not a run because you are exaggerating the stride length and reaching farther out in front of your body with the uphill leg. It is intended to simulate ski striding up a hill at an intensity you can sustain for minutes rather than the seconds you can sustain actual bounding.

Fig. 12.3 Ski Bounding

Bounding is an explosive, exaggerated stride meant to act as specific strength and power training for skiers. As such it should be used in short and very powerful sets lasting only seconds at maximum power. Strive for maximum time in the air and an explosive push-off.

Fig. 12.4 Ski Striding

This movement is used to simulate skiing uphill and intended for long-duration lower-intensity training. It more closely mimics skiing than does running, but it is best to do it on uphills and then switch back to running on the flats.

Specific Training for a Specific Goal

Javier Martín de Villa

"Why would you want to move to Granada?" A Spanish Mountain Federation manager was helping me with the paperwork that would secure my transfer to the university there.

I explained that I wanted to place top three in the world championships the following year, and that I'd be able to train more effectively in Granada, which is near the Sierra Nevada, than if I continued studying in Madrid.

Trying to be polite, he told me that maybe I was being a little too ambitious. That I should be more realistic about my expectations. His words only enhanced my resolve, motivating me to follow through with my plan rather than abandon it.

That spring, during the 2003 European Championships of Ski Mountaineering in Slovakia, I had finished far below expectations. I was determined to perform better at the 2004 World Championships of Ski Mountaineering, especially because it would take place in the Pyrenees, in my home country of Spain. My coach, Jose, and I collaborated on a plan; something had to change if I wanted to finish strong.

At the start of the summer we reviewed my previous five years of training and analyzed the specific requirements of the 2004 championships. I wanted to prepare in the best possible manner. We knew the date of the event, so we had a time frame for the training plan. We knew I would participate in the vertical and individual races, but not the team race, with the primary goal being the individual race; my focus would be racing from forty minutes to a maximum of two hours. We knew the races would

start at 2,000 meters, so altitude would be a serious consideration. And we knew that the individual race would consist of three to four long climbs with technical downhills, for a combined vertical gain of around 1,600 meters.

Once we had all this information, we mapped out a plan that would build toward the one clear goal of placing well at—and ideally winning—the world championships the following March. But first we had to fit the training into my day-to-day life.

At the time, I was balancing my athletic career with my university studies in Madrid, so I couldn't dedicate all my time to training. During the winter I could rarely escape the city more than three days a week to ski. Now, motivated by this goal race, I made the decision to move to Granada, where I could continue my university studies while living just forty minutes from a ski resort that starts at 2,100 meters and rises to 3,400 meters. That altitude profile was a perfect match for the 2004 world championship course, and I'd be able to increase my number of days on skis.

I tried to accumulate as much volume as possible that summer and fall when I had more time and the days were longer. Once the snow started, my average weekly volume was twelve hours of endurance training (just counting uphill time when skiing), plus two days of strength training.

My coach and I also designed three higher-impact "shock weeks." The first one fell in mid-October, when I went to the annual training camp at Tignes in France with the Spanish national team. The goal was to accumulate the maximum possible volume on skis—twenty to twenty-five hours in a week. This would be the culmination of the high-volume period of my training, and the aim was to have it transfer over to the specific action of ski mountaineering racing.

The second shock week was set for over my winter break from university, and it involved a combination of volume and high-intensity workouts. It marked the start of the high-intensity period, where I focused on race pace and the specific requirements of the goal race. A third and final shock week started with a vertical race and ended with the Spanish Championship; the main goal of this week was to make all my final race-specific adjustments—to fine-tune gear, strategies, and pace.

Poised at the starting line of the world championship individual race in March, I recalled what that Spanish Mountain Federation manager had said to me about my move to Granada. Despite what he believed about my ambitions, I knew that I had to be the best version of myself to get the best outcome.

I came in second place in the espoir division. Denis Trento and I fought to the very end, but about 100 meters from the finish line on the final downhill, we both crashed. He got up before I did and won by seconds. My specific work over the course of the season—both in terms of conditioning and technical training—was critical to achieving this proud result. ∎

Javier Martín de Villa is a Spanish climber and professional ski mountaineer. He has competed in more than 100 international races as a member of the Spanish national team, winning seven international medals including a silver at the world championships in 2004. When not racing, he trains other high-performance athletes, works as a mountain guide, and consults for Dynafit International. He still lives in Granada, which is more than just a great place for training.

The art of the quick transition. Spanish national team members showing how it's done during the Pierra Menta in 2016. France. Photo: Ulysse Lefebvre

Skimo Technical Aspects

Skimo is a sport with a very large technical component, and while fitness plays the main role in performance, ignoring technique will put a ceiling on your race results. Space constraints prevent us from covering skimo technique other than to mention a few areas that require lots of practice:

- Transitions
- Kick turns
- Skin management
- Boot packing
- High-tempo skinning
- Downhill fast skiing

It can be best to first learn how to do these in a low-pressure, low-intensity setting with some coaching. If you can't do them slowly and with control, you will never do them well under pressure and at speed. As you improve these skills, a fun way to add challenge is by finding a short course that includes several of these skills and which takes 10 to 15 minutes to complete. After a nice warm-up you can run through the course at an intensity like Z3 (not maximum)—fast enough to challenge your skills but not so fast as to be exhausting. You want to reinforce *good* technique, so focus on staying in control and allowing your proficiency to develop over a period of weeks and months. Start with one workout per week, doing one lap through the circuit. Then, as you become both fitter and more proficient, add more laps, taking a few minutes of rest between laps, during which you think about where you made mistakes and how you can avoid them the next time.

Example Recovery Week. Category 1

These recovery weeks are vital to long-term progression in training load. The focus is on recovery this week; you are not adding to your fitness base. You want to get recovered as well and as quickly as possible so you are ready to start building fitness again. This week should be loosely structured. By Sunday you should feel like attacking the next week. If not, you didn't recover well enough. Insert alternative recovery training like swimming or easy cycling, or any other favored recovery activity.

	AM	PM	Comments
Day 1	Rest day.	Off.	This can be a good day to take off or use for light recovery activities after a big weekend of training.
Day 2	Recovery workout: do full run at Recovery heart rate. 20% of weekly time.	Off.	Stay in the zone. Done on flat-to-gentle terrain.
Day 3	Aerobic base run: Z2. 20% of weekly vertical.	Off.	
Day 4	Strength: cut your normal strength workout by 50%.	Off.	
Day 5	Rest day.	Off.	
Day 6	Recovery workout: do full run at Z1 heart rate. 20% of weekly time.	Off.	Stay in the zone. Done on flat-to-gentle terrain.
Day 7	Aerobic base: up to 40% of weekly vertical.	Off.	If ADS, use Z2. If no ADS, stay mostly in Z1. If on skis or roller skis, add 8x15 sec quick-tempo uphill with 3 min easy between.

Fig. 12.5 Example of a Recovery Week in the Early Base Period

Note: Percentages given in these tables are rough guidelines, not exact amounts.

The start of any skimo race is a blur of action. Pierra Menta, France. Photo: Ulysse Lefebvre

Example Skimo Precompetition Period Week. Category 1

When you get to within two months of your first competition, the training focus must shift to more race-specific workouts with the inclusion of high intensity in Zone 3. Some points to remember:

- Replace the Zone 2 workouts with one Zone 3. Zone 3 workouts will be stressful.

- Maintain the aerobic base with Zone 1 volume.

- Reduce any leg-oriented specific ME training because of the muscular demands of the Zone 3 workouts.

- Maintain upper-body ME work with one workout every seven days.

- General or Specific (Hill Bounding) and Core Strength can be maintained with one workout every seven to ten days.

- Continue quick-tempo work with pick-ups in one aerobic workout/week.

	AM	PM	Comments
Day 1	Rest day.		This can be a good day to take off or use for light recovery activities after a big weekend of training.
Day 2	Strength: upper-body ME and core. See page 217 in Strength Section.	Optional second workout: Z1 base workout up to 8% of weekly vertical.	
Day 3	Zones 1–3: up to 15% of weekly vertical. With 5–7% in Z3. Warm-up to include 8x10–20 sec quick-tempo with 2 min easy ski recovery.	Core strength.	Use ski-specific mode for Z3 work: ski, roller ski, or ski simulations. Progress from shorter to longer duration. Intervals or continuous.
Day 4	Recovery: done at Z1 or Recovery. At least 15% of weekly time.	Optional second workout: Z1 or Recovery on gentle terrain.	Stay in the zone. Done on flat-to-gentle terrain.
Day 5	Strength: Hill Bounding steeply up.	Optional second workout: Z1 or Recovery. Up to 5% of weekly vertical.	
Day 6	Z1: up to 15% of weekly vertical.		If feeling recovered, OK to add some Zones 3–4 at end as a progressive distance in later weeks.
Day 7	Aerobic base: up to 40% of weekly vertical.	Off.	If ADS, use Z2. If no ADS, stay mostly in Z1. If on skis or roller skis, add 8x15 sec quick-tempo uphill with 3 min easy between.

Fig. 12.6 Example Week for Precompetition Period

Note: Percentages given in these tables are rough guidelines, not exact amounts.

A skin track crosses Pointe du Dard, Beaufortain, France. Photo: Ulysse Lefebvre

Structuring a Category 2 Athlete's Skimo and Ski Mountaineering Plan

The following section includes example weeks for Category 2 athletes. You have significant training experience now; it is our aim that the following information can give new insights and some new tools to modify and adjust what may already have brought you some successes.

Early Base Period

As a more advanced athlete, you have probably spent the summer building a solid aerobic base supplemented with strength training and are well prepared for the skimo-specific work. You will still be wise to dedicate a couple of weeks to a high volume of ski-specific aerobic base training. Kílian likes to do a fall glacier training camp with a high volume of low-intensity, skimo-specific training. He also makes use of roller skis during this period. You may not have the opportunity to hit the glacier in September, but your goal is the same: to spend a lot of time on ski-specific base training.

	AM	PM	Comments
Day 1	Rest day.		This can be a good day to take off or use for light recovery activities after a big weekend of training.
Day 2	Core and ME for upper body and legs. See upper-body and core exercises in Strength Section.	Second workout: Recovery workout. Up to 5% of weekly vertical.	
Day 3	Z1: 15% of weekly vertical. If on skis or roller skis, include 8x15 sec pick-ups with 3 min easy between.	Optional second workout: Z1 or Recovery. Up to 5% of weekly vertical.	Z2 if you suffer from ADS.
Day 4	Z2: long uphill skimo specific. Start with 10% of weekly vertical.	Second workout: Recovery. Up to 5% of weekly vertical.	After at least 6 weeks, you can introduce some Z3 into this workout.
Day 5	Strength: Hill Bounding.	Optional second workout: Z1 or Recovery. Up to 10% of weekly vertical.	
Day 6	Z2: 10% of weekly vertical.	Off.	If on skis or roller skis, include 8x15 sec at high-tempo striding uphill with 3 min easy between.
Day 7	Aerobic base: Z1. Up to 40% of weekly vertical.	Off.	Z2 if you suffer from ADS.

Fig. 12.7 Example Week for Early Skimo Base-Building Period

Note: Percentages given in these tables are rough guidelines, not exact amounts.

	AM	PM	Comments
Day 1	Rest day.	Off.	This can be a good day to take off or use for light recovery activities after a big weekend of training.
Day 2	ME. See page 217 in Strength Section and core strength.	Recovery activity.	
Day 3	Z1 or Recovery. Stay in the zone. Up to 10% of weekly vertical.	Off.	Best if foot borne, outdoors on hilly terrain. But laps in a tall building or time on a treadmill or stair machine can be substituted.
Day 4	Z1 or Recovery. Stay in the zone. Up to 10% of weekly distance and vertical.	Off.	Best if foot borne, outdoors on hilly terrain. But laps in a tall building or time on a treadmill or stair machine can be substituted.
Day 5	Z2 vertical: up to 15% of weekly vertical.	Off.	Best if foot borne, outdoors on hilly terrain. But laps in a tall building or time on a treadmill or stair machine can be substituted.
Day 6	Z1: up to 25% of weekly vertical. Can be Z2 if suffering from ADS.	Off.	Late in the preparation phase, these days should be spent on skis.
Day 7	Z1: up to 40% of weekly vertical. Can be Z2 if suffering from ADS.	Off.	Late in the preparation phase, these days should be spent on skis.

Fig. 12.8 Example of Base and Specific Week for Ski Mountaineer Preparing for Multiday Ski Touring Trip

Note: The ME work is a high priority, especially if you do not get a chance to ski much in the winter. The only difference between the Base and Specific weeks is the overall volume.

The joy of skiing uphill. Photo: Kílian Jornet

Skimo Middle and Late Weeks – Precompetition Period

Start to add high-intensity workouts no later than two months before your first competition.

Some suggestions:

- When Zone 3 volume is 5 percent of weekly vertical, replace Zone 2 workouts with Zone 1.

- Reduce any leg-oriented ME training in the gym because of the muscular demands of the Zone 3 workouts.

- Maintain upper-body ME work with one workout every seven to ten days.

- Do one Hill Bounding and Core Strength workout every week.

- Continue high-tempo work with pick-ups in one aerobic workout per week.

- After four weeks of Zone 3 workouts, introduce some shorter Zone 4 interval training one day each week. If you have little experience with Zone 4 intervals, consider beginning with 30/30s (see page 177). When you first add Zone 4, do it by reducing the Zone 3 time to about 50 percent of the time you are in Zone 4. See how you handle this jump in intensity and adjust accordingly.

	AM	PM	Comments
Day 1	Rest day.		May use for light recovery activities after a big weekend of training.
Day 2	Zones 1–3 ski specific: start with 15% of weekly vertical with 5–7% in Z3.	Recovery workout: up to 5% of weekly vertical.	Z3 can be done as a tempo, progressive distance, or intervals.
Day 3	Recovery workout: at least 10% of weekly time.	Strength: upper-body ME and core.	Stay in the zone. Done on flat-to-gentle terrain.
Day 4	Z1: 15% of weekly vertical. Warm-up to include: 8–10x20 sec quick-tempo with 2-minute recovery.	Recovery: up to 5% of weekly time.	
Day 5	Z1: up to 20% of weekly vertical.	Recovery if doing intervals, otherwise Z1: up to 5% of weekly time or vertical.	Z2 if ADS. Optional: later weeks, add Z4 intervals. Z4 time less than 5% of total weekly volume/vertical.
Day 6	Strength: Hill Bounding.	Z1 or Recovery: up to 10% of weekly time/vertical.	
Day 7	Aerobic base: Z1. About 30% of weekly vertical.		Z2 if ADS.

Fig. 12.9 Example Week for Skimo Late Base/Precomp Period

Note: Percentages given in these tables are rough guidelines, not exact amounts.

Training During Race Season for Category 1 and 2 Athletes

The training outlined above is designed to bring you into racing shape by the early season but still allow for performance gains as the season progresses. Races will serve to build the race-specific speed endurance. If you race often, a real challenge can be to maintain the aerobic base. It is hard to fit in the longer Zones 1 and 2 days, let alone any hard workouts, when you are trying to recover enough to keep racing frequently. You may need a couple of days of tapering, a day of travel going to the race, and a couple of days for travel and recovery after a race before you feel like you can train effectively again. That schedule doesn't allow much time for training between races.

Managing training around racing is challenging, even for the very best. Unless you are at a high level of fitness, trying to squeeze much productive training between races separated by only five or six days, with two days largely taken up by travel, risks reducing the next race's performance.

Some suggestions for the racing season:

- The bigger your training base, the more easily you can manage the intensity of frequent races. This takes years of consistent training to build. Racing too much and too often with a small base will lead to a decline in performance.

- Prioritize your races: A races are the main focus of the season. B races are less important, but you may want a day or two of lighter training before them. C races are those that you use as hard workouts and train through.

- If possible, plan for one or two training blocks of two to three weeks between races partway through the season when you can return the focus to training. You might do this training block around one or two C races or leading into a B race. This will help you maintain your fitness all the way through the season.

- On the following pages we've listed example plans for how you might handle three typical mid-season scenarios.

	AM	PM	Comments
Day 1	Day after last race. Active recovery: stretch, swim, foam roll. Light recovery workout if feeling good.		For volume/vertical, these weeks use average volume/ vertical from mid–Base Period weeks.
Day 2	Recovery workout: 5–10% of weekly vertical.	Core Strength.	
Day 3	Z1: 15% of weekly vertical.	Hill Bounding, 6x15 sec.	Maintain strength through the season.
Day 4	Z2: 15% of weekly vertical. Warm-up to include 8–10x20 sec quick-tempo with 2-minute recovery.	Off.	
Day 5	Z1: 15% of weekly vertical.	Off.	
Day 6	Z4: 10% of weekly vertical. Time in Z4 less than 7% of total weekly volume.	Off.	
Day 7	Z1: 35% of weekly vertical.	Core Strength.	

Fig. 12.10 Sample Training Plan for a Three-Week Break in Race Schedule to Rebuild Capacity

Note: Percentages given in these tables are rough guidelines, not exact amounts.

	AM	PM	Comments
Day 8	Recovery activity.	Off.	For volume, these weeks use average volume in mid–Base Period weeks.
Day 9	Zones 1–3: 15% of weekly vertical. 10% of weekly vertical in Z3.	Off.	Try to do Z3 as long tempo.
Day 10	Recovery ski: 5% of weekly volume on mellow terrain.	Hill Bounding, 6x15 sec.	Maintain strength through the season.
Day 11	Z1: 10% of weekly vertical. Warm-up includes 8–10x20 sec quick-tempo with 2-min recovery.	Off.	
Day 12	Recovery ski: 10% of weekly vertical.	Core Strength.	
Day 13	C or B priority race or Z4 intervals: 15% of weekly vertical. Time in Z4 less than 10% of total weekly volume.	Recovery ski: 10% of weekly vertical.	Do longer cool-down after race.
Day 14	Long Z1: 35% of weekly vertical.	Off.	

Fig. 12.10 Continued, Week 2

	AM	PM	Comments
Day 15	Active recovery: stretch, swim, foam roll.	Off.	
Day 16	Z1–Z3: up to 10% of weekly vertical. 5–7% in Z3.	Off.	
Day 17	Recovery ski: 15% of weekly vertical.	Hill Bounding, 6x15 sec.	Maintain strength through the season.
Day 18	Z1: 35% of weekly vertical.	Off.	
Day 19	Z1 ski: 15% of weekly vertical with 6x15 sec quick-tempo pick-ups.	Off.	
Day 20	Travel day. Try to ski on the course to preview. If not racing, then Z1: 20–25% of weekly vertical.	Off.	
Day 21	A or B race. If not racing, then Z4 intervals: 15% of weekly vertical. Time in Z4 less than 10% of weekly volume.	Recovery ski: 5% of weekly vertical.	

Fig. 12.10 Continued, Week 3

Christina Lustenberger and Tanner Flanagan putting in the track above Rogers Pass, British Columbia, Canada. Photo: Fredrik Marmsater

Scenario One: Recharging the capacity bank account.

If and when you find yourself with a sizable gap (two or three weeks) between races, you'd be smart to drop back and do some basic capacity-building work. This will leave you a bit fatigued, so don't plan an A priority race during the training block. Targeting an A or B priority race or event at the end of this period will require some lighter training for a few days beforehand. This longer break between races will be enough time for you to get in some productive base training and still have time to recover from that training before the next important race.

	AM	PM	Comments
Day 1	Z1 or Recovery pace on gentle terrain. Or recovery activity, if needed.	Off.	Spend additional time on recovery if needed.
Day 2	Z1 or Recovery pace on gentle terrain. Or recovery activity.	Off.	Spend additional time on recovery if needed.
Day 3	Z1–Z4 ski: 15% of weekly vertical. Time in Z4 less than 5% of weekly volume.	Off.	
Day 4	Hill Bounding, 6x10 sec with 2-min recovery between.	Off.	
Day 5	Travel. Easy run or ski post-travel.	Off.	
Day 6	A priority race.	Off.	
Day 7	Long Z1 or Recovery pace before travel.	Off.	

Fig. 12.11 Sample Two-Week Plan for Training Between Important Races

Note: Percentages given in these tables are rough guidelines, not exact amounts.

	AM	PM	Comments
Day 8	Active recovery: stretch, yoga, foam roll, swim.	Off.	Spend additional time on recovery.
Day 9	Z1–Z4 ski: 10% of weekly vertical. Time in Z4 less than 5% of weekly volume.	Off.	Spend additional time on recovery.
Day 10	Z1 ski: 15% of weekly vertical.	Off.	
Day 11	Hill Bounding, 6x10 sec with 2-min recovery between.	Off.	
Day 12	Travel, easy run, or ski post-travel.	Off.	
Day 13	A level race.	Off.	
Day 14	Long Z1 or Recovery pace before travel.	Off.	Optional A priority race.

Fig. 12.11 Continued, Week 2

A competitor during Adamello Ski Raid competition, Italy. Photo: Federico Modica

Scenario Two: Back-to-back A priority race weekends.

These are important races, so you need to be rested going in and then recover well between weekends. There will really be no chance to do capacity-building training during the inter-race week or you will not recover. Maintenance work is all you should plan. Plan a high-tempo workout and an aerobic maintenance session. The rest should be recovery or technique work. There is nothing you can do in such a short window that will make you faster, but a lot of things you can do that will make you slower.

Scenario Three: B/C priority race leading into A priority race.

It can be useful to plan a B or C priority race as a preparation leading to an important race. Treat this race like a hard workout and take a light day on either side of the race; make the race the hard workout for the week. This type of race—where there is little pressure—should allow you to relax and try new strategies and pacing. Since racing experience is invaluable, use these days not only for physical training but for mental training as well. An example two-week period where you are using these low-priority events to build toward an A priority race might look like the following.

	AM	PM	Comments
Day 1	Active recovery: stretch, swim, foam roll.	Spend additional time on recovery.	For volume these weeks, use the average volume in late Base Period recovery weeks.
Day 2	Z4: 15% of weekly vertical. Time in Z4 less than 5% of weekly volume.	Off.	
Day 3	Z1 ski: 15% of weekly vertical.	Off.	
Day 4	Hill Bounding and tempo.	Off.	
Day 5	Travel. Easy run or ski post-travel.	Off.	
Day 6	B/C priorty race.	Off.	
Day 7	Z1 or Recovery workout on gentle terrain.	Off.	Get recovered.

Fig. 12.12 Sample Two-Week Training Plan Before Using B/C Races in Preparation for an A Race

Note: Percentages given in these tables are rough guidelines, not exact amounts.

	AM	PM	Comments
Day 8	Z1 or Recovery workout on gentle terrain. Get recovered.	Off.	For volume these weeks, use the average volume in late Base Period recovery weeks.
Day 9	Short Z4: less than 5% of weekly volume in Z4.	Off.	
Day 10	Hill Bounding and quick-tempo pick-ups.	Off.	
Day 11	Z1 ski: 10% of weekly vertical in Z2, bumping into Z3 if feeling good. Time in Z3 less than 5% of weekly volume.	Off.	
Day 12	Travel. Easy run or ski post-travel to shake out legs.	Off.	
Day 13	A priority race.	Off.	
Day 14	Z1 or short Recovery workout before travel.	Off.	

Special Considerations for Mountain Running

When you plan to undertake a mountain running event, you will probably know its distance and its elevation gain and loss. Knowing this allows you to use a rather formulaic approach to planning a training progression. Understanding that specificity in your training is important, you should also choose training terrain that, as much as possible, models the terrain of your target event.

Volume

Below are general guidelines that may help you set realistic goals. Just because you are able to get through one week for each of these example distances doesn't mean that you will be able to log *consistent* weeks at these levels. To build up to even the suggested 50 kilometers (the minimum covered here), weekly distance numbers can take months of continuous running training progression to achieve.

Recall from the sidebar "How Kílian Records His Training" on page 127 that he records time, distance, vertical, and the technical difficulty of the terrain. You would be wise to copy this system so that you can learn how the combination of these different components affects you.

Recommended Minimum Peak Weekly Distances for Mountain Races

50K race: Before starting a structured training plan, you should be comfortable with regular weeks of 40 kilometers (25 miles). Peak week = 80–88 kilometers (50–55 miles). Average per week for biggest 12 weeks = 50 kilometers (36 miles).

Peter Schlickenrieder runs in the Brenta Dolomites, the Tuckett Hut behind him. Italy.
Photo: Federico Modica

100K race: Before starting, you should be comfortable with the 50-kilometer training loads (above). Peak week = 120–130 kilometers (74–80 miles). Average per week for biggest 16 weeks = 75 kilometers (48 miles).

100-mile race: Before starting, you should be comfortable with the 100-kilometer training loads (above). Peak week = 145–160 kilometers (90–100 miles). Average per week for biggest 18 weeks = 100 kilometers (75 miles).

Of course, being able to sustain (and tolerate) or even exceed peak weekly volumes of training will likely give you better race results.

Seven Recommendations for Trail Racing and Training – Kílian Jornet

I race a lot: I have been doing between thirty and fifty races a year for the last ten years—450 races over the past fifteen years. I don't really prioritize one race over another. I want to do well in all races. But one thing I do is use races to train. It's not that I take it easy during the race; it's that I treat it as intensity work. When I was younger, I did a lot of interval training and strength training, but now I do no strength training and almost no interval training. Instead, I get my speedwork done during races, and when I'm not racing, I do volume. I enjoy volume; it works well for me, and I have a fast recovery so I can assimilate it all.

This is not to say everyone should take this approach. I have been an endurance athlete since I was very young, I worked with a coach for many years, and I studied sports science at university. I have the background to train and race this way.

When people start running (or skimo racing) when they are older, they often train with no structure. There is no long, scientific learning process behind it. And even people who have been running for years can make mistakes in training.

Whether you are new to the sport or are very experienced, take these seven recommendations to heart.

1) Consider the stress of everyday life. People who come late to endurance sports want to start at a good level, but they often fail to take into account the stressors of everyday life. They train a lot on top of work and family obligations, not realizing that when you train something, it's a stress to your body. And this stress needs recovery time.

2) Don't overdo it. Many people work full-time and train on the side because they really love running. Sometimes these runners get better, get a sponsor, and decide to work less and train much more. Then their performance drops and they burn out because they have become overtrained. Just because you have more time to train more doesn't mean you should fill it all with training.

3) Be realistic about your goals and expectations. Setting a goal—whether it's winning a race, finishing in a certain time, or just finishing—is what will motivate you to train. It will motivate you to keep pushing through the hard moments and to improve from them. But be humble about what you can do. Honestly analyze yourself in the beginning—your strong points and weak points, even your work situation, diet, and travel. Do not overestimate yourself. To see if something is possible, look at what you want to do and what you will need to change for that to happen.

If a goal is unrealistic, you probably won't reach it, and that can leave you less motivated. What you see as a bad result may actually be a very good result, it just wasn't your *goal* result. In this case, the problem wasn't your performance, it was that the goal was too high.

4) Be progressive. It is important to understand the progression of training and the progression of distances. These days, people want to do a 100-miler, like it's not enough to do a marathon. Maybe they do one 100-miler and it's okay, they get through it. So they do a second one and maybe get through, and then they do a third one and end up broken for five years. You need to move through 10K, 20K, 30K, and beyond. I didn't start out running 100-milers. I progressed over years of structured training.

5) Prepare for the technicality of a course. It is important to think about variables beyond just distance and elevation. People know and understand those, but they often fail to estimate the technicality of a course—if the tread is soft, grassy, hard, or rocky. We organize a Skyrace near Tromsø, Norway, that has a ridge with some third-class steps, and the downhill is off-trail through a snowfield and rocky terrain. It is not mountaineering, but it is not exactly running. Even if you can run 100 miles with a lot of elevation change, you may not be able to finish a race that is so technically difficult.

6) Train each element, because they are all connected. When it comes to your performance in a race, everything is linked: your physical preparation is linked to your technical preparation, which is linked to your mental preparation and your gear. Each one affects the rest, so they all need to evolve together.

7) Don't take it all too seriously. To keep up motivation, don't take training too seriously. Running and ski mountaineering—these are things we are doing mostly for pleasure and because we like them. It's okay to do things in a serious way, but don't take it too seriously. Train well, but don't make it your whole world. It shouldn't feel like an obligation. That's when it starts to be a problem. I train because I enjoy it.

Traversing the Borders of Pain

Emma Roca

Only two weeks had passed since I'd won the 2014 Leadville Trail 100 in Colorado. Now I was set to embark on the Transalpine Run, a stage race done in teams of two that traverses the Alps of Germany, Austria, and Italy. I would be racing in the mixed category with Gerard 'Blacky' Morales, a fellow member of Team Buff. Together we would tackle eight grueling stages for a total of 293 kilometers and 13,700 meters of gain. It would be an unforgettable experience.

Each year the Transalpine changes direction, with the route in 2014 starting in Ruhpolding, Germany, and ending in Sexten, Italy. The course was as challenging as it was beautiful, taking us over mountain passes as high as 3,000 meters and through lush, dreamy alpine valleys—a wonderful landscape. We ran and walked among snowy mountains, navigated technical trails full of rocks and slippery roots, and traced ridges littered with large blocks of granite. We passed under the Tre Cime di Lavaredo and cut through forests full of mushrooms. We crossed borders that went beyond physical and mental limits. We ran day after day with minimal recovery between each stage.

I had unique insight into the impact this race was having on my body. As runners, we all know that these big efforts stress our systems, but as a doctoral student of biochemistry, I have a more scientific understanding of the biochemical and physiological effects of stage races. During this race, in fact, I was conducting a study for my thesis.

Blacky and I were one of eight mixed Spanish teams who offered up our bodies, blood, and urine in the interest of developing a fuller picture of what happens during a multiday effort like the Transalpine. From before the start to after the finish, we underwent numerous tests to determine to what degree we were recovering—or not. It was clear from the results

that our bodies were breaking down progressively from stage to stage.

You would think that having an intimate knowledge of ultrarunning physiology would somehow translate into a more carefully crafted running practice. Or that after fifteen years of racing ultras internationally and winning world championships, I would know what is best for my body. Sometimes that is not the case. As they say, "En casa del herrero, cuchillo de palo." (In the blacksmith's house, a wooden knife.) During the Transalpine, the crazy competitor in me overruled the logical scientist.

I hadn't let myself recover enough from Leadville, and the pressure of running as part of a team—a team that was gunning to make the podium—placed too many demands on my already overtaxed body. It was especially challenging being a woman in a race with a man. The physical and psychological tiredness flowed easily, and I went through the occasional moment of tension with Blacky. That said, he and I worked very well together overall, with him helping me a lot through each stage.

At the end of the first day, I noticed a pain in my left knee that increased as the days went by. Every morning I looked for a hotel near the staging area that had a stationary bike in its gym so I could warm up. Even then, I started each stage at a half-limp, hobbling until the knee warmed up and I could get into a rhythm that allowed me to finish the stage and even maintain our lead. But the pain at the end of each day was intense: the tears came and I could barely walk. After the competition, an MRI confirmed that I had a stress fracture in the head of my femur—an injury that would keep me immobilized for six months.

We won the Transalpine that year, despite my stress fracture. Perseverance, tenacity, commitment,

Emma Rocca cools off in celebration of her team's victory at the end of the final stage of the Gore-Tex Transalpine Run. Sexten, Italy. Photo: Harald Wisthaler

and competitiveness are great stimulants for me, and in this race they pushed me past the pain and into first place. It took strength and determination to finish and win, even at the risk of exacerbating my injury.

When you live, analyze, and feel all the wear, pain, and impact of the kilometers of a race like the Transalpine—not only physically but also mentally—you ask yourself the obvious question: Why do we keep going when our bodies tell us to stop? I do not have a rational answer to offer. It is true that endorphins exist, and sometimes the suffering in the moment becomes its own reward later on, once you've forgotten just how bad it was.

I know what is happening inside of me during a stage race, and I know how much my body needs to rest, but the experiences I live in an ultra or a long mountain race are priceless mental rewards. I'd rather pay the price that comes with running ultras than miss out on these unique, extraordinary adventures. ■

Emma Roca is a Spanish ultraendurance athlete, professional firefighter, entrepreneur, writer, and mother of three. She is working toward her PhD in biochemistry.

Structuring a Category 1 Athlete's Mountain Running Training Plan

If you fit into this group, the biggest single thing you can do to improve your race performance is to train *more*. Not train harder, just train more hours, accumulate more vertical meters, run more kilometers. That's because your performance in the sports covered in this book is almost entirely dependent upon your basic aerobic capacity to do work. By now you understand that the only way to improve that quality is to do more low- to moderate-intensity training (Zones 1–2). Elevating this basic aerobic work capacity is the key to future success. So, that's where the emphasis has to be placed. There is no shortcut, no secret workouts. You need to first condition your body to handle a lot of training; then later as you become fitter, you can start to layer on higher-intensity work that will allow you to run or ski faster for longer. But right now if you can't run continuously for an hour or two, on mountainous terrain, day in and day out, you do not need to worry about high intensity. This is a bottom-up approach where each subsequent layer of training at higher intensities stands upon the base provided by the levels below and supports the levels above.

For athletes in this category, the need for a very gradual ramping up of weekly volume must be strongly emphasized. The progression of training volume that we suggest (see fig. 11.7 page 291) is on the conservative side for a reason. By far, the most common running injuries are to the lower legs and are the result of increasing running volume too fast. These are typically overuse injuries caused by an accumulation of the chronic stress of impact. The problem with them is that by the time you feel the injury, there is likely to have been a lot of damage done and you may lose weeks to recovery. Avoiding injuries of this type has to be a first priority of any training plan. Once you are injured, no plan will work for you.

The connective tissue in your legs will be slow to adapt to the stress of running; the best advice is to proceed with caution when increasing running volume and intensity. It takes weeks of sustained and repeated running for the tendons and fascia to increase in elasticity and strength to handle the pounding of thousands of impacts each day, each of which will be at least two times your body weight, and much more on the downhills. Patience is a virtue when it comes to increasing running volume. Be kind to your body and allow it time to adapt before demanding too much from it.

A 50K race is a great way to dip your toe into ultras. With that in mind, the first part of this section will address the specific needs of the less experienced runner, presumably with less running history and fewer miles in the legs. For them, a twenty-week plan is what we consider as the minimum training period if preparing for a first-time 50K race.

If you have little recent running history, you'd be wise to precede this program by at least a six-week Transition Period (see page 145). However, if you have been

Urban Zemmer putting a big base to the test on the final section of the 2015 Crepa Neigra Vertical Kilometer Crepa Neigra race in Canazei, Italy. Photo: Martina Valmassoi

regularly running about 20 to 25 miles (35 to 50 kilometers) per week, you can start with week 1. Don't expect optimal results if you spent the winter on the couch and then try to jump right into a 40-mile week. Even if you have been skiing all winter, you'll need at least a short Transition Period to get your running legs back. Otherwise, you may end up injured in a few weeks.

Keep the following critical aspects in mind when designing a training plan. These will help you create good training plans and are discussed in more detail in the Methodology Section.

- You will not really begin running training until you have accumulated about 100 miles (161 kilometers) in your legs. Until then you are just conditioning your legs so that they can handle daily running. It might take some seasoned runners two weeks to hit this target early in their training cycle; it might take beginners at least six weeks.

- Intersperse big training weeks with lower-load weeks so that your body has a chance to absorb and adapt to all the good training of the build period. Do not hold the training load constant for multiple weeks. A lack of modulation will cause stagnation and possibly overtraining.

Running with sheep in Italy is a lot safer than running with bulls in Spain. Mortirolo Pass, Camonica Valley, Italy. Photo: Davide Ferrari

- The principle of specificity as applied here means that you need to run (and hike some steep sections) for training. Biking and swimming are great exercises, but they should not be substitutes for running unless injury necessitates it. These can be effective recovery workouts to give tired legs a break. You should also choose terrain that is as similar to your goal event as possible. If you are going to race on rocky or rough trails, that will demand very different coordination than an event that takes place on smooth trails. Incorporate frequent short sections of fast downhill running to develop the strength and quickness needed, especially on very rough trails.

Example Weeks for Category 1 Mountain Runners

Use the following example weeks to help you understand the general layout of a week's structure.

Previous page: Jeff Browning running past Island Lake, Colorado, during a recon of the Hardrock 100 course. Jeff won this race in 2018. Photo: Steven Gnam

	AM	PM	Comments
Day 1	Rest day.	Off.	This can be a good day to take off or use for light recovery activities after a big weekend of training.
Day 2	Z1: up to 15% of weekly vertical and distance. Z2 if you suffer from ADS.	Core and general strength.	Choose the appropriate strength stage from your assessment.
Day 3	Z2: up to 15% of weekly vertical and distance.	Off.	
Day 4	Z1 or recovery: at least 15% of weekly time.	Optional ME. See page 240 in the Strength Section.	Stay in the zone. Done on flat-to-gentle terrain.
Day 5	Hill Sprints, 6–8x10 sec.	Off.	When appropriate, move to Hill Sprints for strength.
Day 6	Z2: up to 15% of weekly vertical and distance.	Optional second workout: Z1 or Recovery. Up to 5% of weekly vertical.	
Day 7	Z1: up to 40% of weekly vertical and distance.	Off.	Z2 if you suffer from ADS.

Fig. 13.1 Example of an Early Base-Period Week for a Category 1 Mountain Runner

Note: In these early weeks (at least eight weeks) the main goal is to accumulate running time. Keeping the intensity low will allow you to get more distance in. This conditioning period is critical for a successful and injury-free implementation of the rest of the plan. Start work on ME workout for general strength if you are deficient.

	AM	PM	Comments
Day 1	Rest day.	Off.	This can be a good day to take off or use for light recovery activities after a big weekend of training.
Day 2	Z1 or Recovery: up to 10% of weekly time.	Core strength.	Stay in the zone. Done on flat-to-gentle terrain. If still feeling the weekend in your legs, then make this a very easy recovery run.
Day 3	Z1–Z3: up to 15% of weekly distance and vertical. Up to 5-8% in Z3.	Off.	Start with 3x8 min. Increase Z3 volume only as your body allows.
Day 4	Z1: up to 15% of weekly distance and vertical.	Off.	Z2 if you suffer from ADS.
Day 5	Hill Sprints, 6-8x10 sec.	Optional second workout: Z1 or Recovery. Up to 5% of weekly vertical.	
Day 6	Z1: up to 15% of weekly distance and vertical.	Off.	Z2 if you suffer from ADS.
Day 7	Z1: up to 40% of weekly distance and vertical.	Off.	Z2 if you suffer from ADS.

Fig. 13.2 Example of a Late Base-Period Week for Category 1 Mountain Runner

Note: These weeks see the introduction of high-intensity training along with increasing volume. Reduce or eliminate the ME training if and when you start the Zone 3 work.

	AM	PM	Comments
Day 1	Rest day.	Off.	This can be a good day to take off or use for light recovery activities after a big weekend of training.
Day 2	Z1 or Recovery: up to 10% of weekly time.	Core strength.	Stay in the zone. Done on flat-to-gentle terrain. If still feeling the weekend in your legs, then make this a very easy recovery run.
Day 3	Z1–Z3: up to 10% of weekly distance and vertical. Up to 5% in Z3.	Off.	Start with 3x8 min. Increase Z3 volume only as your body allows.
Day 4	Z1: up to 10% of weekly distance and vertical.	Off.	Z2 if you suffer from ADS.
Day 5	Hill Sprints, 6–8x10 sec.	Off.	
Day 6	Z1: up to 30–40% of weekly distance and vertical.	Off.	Z2 if you suffer from ADS. In this week you are doing back-to-back big days to more specifically prepare for longer runs.
Day 7	Z1: up to 30–40% of weekly distance and vertical.	Off.	Z2 if you suffer from ADS. In this week you are doing back-to-back big days to more specifically prepare for longer runs.

Fig. 13.3 Specific Week for the Late Base Period

Note: Use of back-to-back long runs to simulate more of the demands of the actual event.

Structuring a Category 2 Athlete's Mountain Running Training Plan

If you meet that second set of criteria listed on page 287—have done many successful races and been logging a lot of distance and vertical for two to three seasons—you no doubt have established a solid base of training. You may no longer be satisfied with just finishing these races. Or you may be interested in moving up to a longer race, or are looking for ways to boost your performance. You may even be planning on an event that includes much more elevation gain and loss. If so, refamiliarize yourself with the following guidelines.

Moving Up in Distance

If you are planning on moving up to a significantly longer race than you have done, either in the past six months or ever, such as moving from a 100K race to a 100-mile distance, then the way forward is simple: You must increase the volume of running. Instead of maintaining typical weeks of 40 to 50 miles (60 to 80 kilometers) with peak weeks of 60 to 75 miles (100 to 120 kilometers), you will need to gradually build your typical weekly volume into the 70 to 80 miles (112 to 128 kilometers) range with peak weeks of 100 to 110 miles (160 to 180 kilometers).

For racers finding themselves in this position, try to follow a similar volume progression as presented in the example weeks in fig. 11.7 on page 291. Similar to when you were building up to your first long-distance race years ago, concentrate your efforts first on accumulating the volume of training so you feel confident you can cover the distance, and then add intensity sparingly and conservatively.

Refer to the charts on pages 288–293 for idealized volume-progression plans for three different scenarios:

1. A single A priority 100K race with a B priority 50K race earlier.

2. A single A priority 100-mile race with a B priority 100K race earlier.

3. Several C and B priority races leading up to an A priority 100K race.

Racing More Often or Improving Performance

If you are not planning to move up to longer races than your current training base will support, but instead are looking to improve performance or race more often throughout the season, consider the addition of more high-intensity training to your program. This example week will be appropriate for those runners with a solid aerobic base who do not have ADS and can pass the Ten Percent Test (see page 91).

	AM	PM	Comments
Day 1	Rest day.	Off.	This can be a good day to take off or use for light recovery activities after a big weekend of training.
Day 2	Z1 or Recovery: up to 10% of weekly time.	Core strength.	Stay in the zone. Done on flat-to-gentle terrain. If still feeling the weekend in your legs, then make this a very easy recovery run.
Day 3	ME. See page 240 in the Strength Section.	Off.	Use this in place of Z3–Z4 intervals for much of the Base Period.
Day 4	Z1: up to 10% of weekly distance and vertical.	Off.	Z2 if you suffer from ADS.
Day 5	Z1: up to 10% of weekly distance and vertical.	Off.	
Day 6	Z1: up to 30% of weekly distance and vertical.	Off.	Z2 if you suffer from ADS. In this week you are doing back-to-back big days to more specifically prepare for longer runs.
Day 7	Z1: up to 30–40% of weekly distance and vertical.	Off.	Z2 if you suffer from ADS. In this week you are doing back-to-back big days to more specifically prepare for longer runs.

Fig. 13.4 Example of a Specific Base-Period Week for a Category 2 Mountain Runner

Note: This athlete wants to boost volume and simulate the demands of the longer event week.

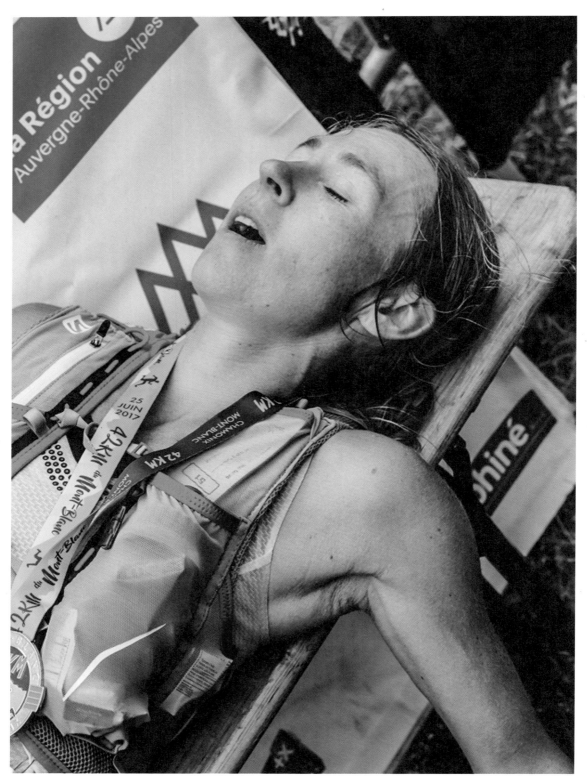

Megan Kimmel tries to recover after winning the 2017 Marathon du Mont Blanc, Chamonix, France. Photo: Martina Valmassoi

	AM	PM	Comments
Day 1	Rest day.	Off.	This can be a good day to take off or use for light recovery activities after a big weekend of training.
Day 2	Z1–Z3: up to 15% of weekly distance and vertical. Gradually add up to 5% in Z3.	Core Strength.	Use intervals, tempo runs of progressive distance here. Increase Z3 volume only as your body allows.
Day 3	Z1 or Recovery: up to 10% of weekly time.	Off.	Stay in the zone. Done on flat-to-gentle terrain.
Day 4	Hill Sprints, 6–8x10 sec along with Z1. Up to 10% of weekly distance.	Off.	
Day 5	Z1–Z4: up to 10% of weekly distance and vertical. After 4–6 weeks of Z3, gradually add up to 5% in Z4.	Off.	Once comfortable with the volume of Z3 (up to 10% of weekly), add Z4 intervals starting with 30/30s.
Day 6	Z1: up to 15% of weekly distance and vertical.	Off.	
Day 7	Z1: up to 40% of weekly distance and vertical.	Off.	

Fig. 13.5 Example of a Late Base-Period Week for a Category 2 Mountain Runner

Note: This athlete wants to run more and shorter races in one season.

NOTES ON ADDING MORE INTENSITY

- The type of intensity you add to your program depends on the event you are targeting. Long Zone 3 sessions will serve well for long-distance races. On the other hand, shorter Zone 4 and Zone 5 sessions will be very useful when you are training for a VK or shorter race.

- In general, use a mix of intensities in the overall plan. Opinions vary widely, but there is no conclusive evidence to support one method over others when it comes to building endurance. Fitter athletes will benefit from longer-duration repetitions (more than six minutes) and higher overall volume of high intensity.

- The volume of high-intensity training in each week, and within each workout, should not start too high and should increase gradually. Add only as much as you can before it forces you to drop the volume of your aerobic base (Zones 1 and 2) training by more than 5 percent. If you can't maintain your volume of Zones 1 and 2 training, you risk having a short peak followed by a decline in performance.

- Drop all Zone 2 training when you begin adding Zone 3 work to your plan. Do all aerobic base work in Zone 1. Zone 2 will be too stressful for most athletes when they begin adding intensity.

- Include one Hill Sprint workout (see page 182) in most weeks to build and maintain specific leg power.

- If you need to improve your muscular endurance (see page 240), begin to add the ME workouts in the early weeks and drop them when you introduce Zones 3 and 4 workouts. Add these workouts after at least four weeks of only Zones 1 and 2 base training. Use them one time per week for eight weeks. The Zones 3 and 4 intensity later will maintain the muscular endurance you build.

- After six to eight weeks of successfully incorporating these Zone 3 workouts, it can be time to introduce some Zone 4 work to the week. Replace some of the Zone 3 with half the volume of Zone 4. Thirty minutes of Zone 3 would be replaced by fifteen minutes of Zone 4. As mentioned above, drop any Zone 2 work when adding Zones 3 or 4 work. All aerobic base maintenance will be done in Zone 1 or even lower at a Recovery effort. Kílian's favorite way to introduce Zone 4 is with the use of 30/30s (see page 177).

Wildlife Rendezvous

Jeff Browning

During Colorado's wild and tough Hardrock 100-Mile Endurance Run, I descended the narrow, rock-strewn Continental Divide Trail as it parallels cascading Pole Creek. It was the middle of a clear and beautiful night, and the moon was waxing gibbous. I was on pace to break the double record—the combined times of the Western States 100 and Hardrock 100, two classic races held a mere nineteen days apart. As I was taking in the gorgeous silhouettes of the surrounding rock formations and the rush of the creek just to my left, I caught glowing eyes in my headlamp to my right.

As with all nighttime mountain running excursions, it's a solid strategy to stop and identify what genus those eyes belong to. I flipped the headlamp to its highest setting—a hundred-meter flood that illuminated not one but two mountain lions lounging on a slab of rock above me. A quick assessment of the situation revealed maybe 30 meters of brush between the trail and where the slab of rock jutted up.

The one in front, the bigger of the two, stood up. I yelled in a deep, commanding voice, "You don't want any part of me!" I then proceeded to keep my light on them and walk down the trail, beating my chest and yelling like a deranged wild man. The big one paralleled me on the rock. Lucky for me, her slab quickly ran out, and the trail curved around a wall of rock that shielded me from their line of vision.

As soon as I was out of sight, I turned and bombed the downhill like I was racing a 10K, all fatigue from 80-plus mountainous miles completely gone. Every 50 to 100 meters, I stopped, turned, and scanned behind me for eyes—nothing. Then I took off again like I'd stolen something. I continued this pattern, with less frequent looking behind me, for the next twenty minutes.

Trail running in wild, mountainous locales is fairly stealthy, especially if you're running solo. It has set me up for some very unique appointments with wildlife, and cats have been a particularly good motivator to get my mind out of the pain cave.

The Stalker and the Stalked

That Hardrock encounter was my third rendezvous with a mountain lion in the night portion of a 100-mile race. The second was uneventful, but the first and most harrowing occurred during the San Diego 100 at mile 97. It had already been a creature-filled night: my pacer, Jesse, and I had marveled at a tarantula on the Pacific Crest Trail at mile 83—our own personal live biology session—and we later followed a stubborn skunk for a quarter mile before he hissed and took off into the tall grass.

Just a mile after Jesse and I sprinted by that skunk to avoid getting sprayed, I caught movement to my left. Something had jumped toward us off a car-size boulder and into the tall grass. I stopped and popped my headlamp to high beam. A cat raised its head out of the grass, maybe 20 meters away. Two green eyes glowed in the night.

"Cougar, cougar!" I yelled to Jesse, to which he frantically replied, "Where?" and quickly, "I see it!"

We began yelling and kept the cougar blinded with our lights. It was within the dreaded pouncing distance; one spring from those powerful hind legs and we'd be dinner. We made our way sideways, walking down the trail with our lights fixed firmly on the cougar. The cat ducked down and disappeared into the tall grass.

"Where is it?" Jesse yelled.

It emerged adjacent to us, paralleling our movements and then crouched under a half-fallen tree. The cat's ominous green eyes watched our every move.

Jeff Browning just after finishing the Run Rabbit Run 100 in the predawn hours. Steamboat Springs, Colorado.
Photo: Fredrik Marmsater

After we'd gained enough distance and finally started to run again, we continued to pause every 40 meters to scan behind us and to our sides to be certain the cat wasn't tracking us. As frightening as it was in the moment, now it's another special story to tell.

Hurdling and Trail Running

Not all of my wildlife encounters have been dangerous. During the Bighorn 100 in northern Wyoming, as I was bombing down to Little Bighorn Canyon, where the trail plunges more than 2,000 feet in 2 miles, the scrub oaks erupted to my right. I'd been fully engaged in the enterprise of negotiating technical terrain, and now I panicked. The sound had my imagination racing through all the possibilities: bear, moose—*I'm gonna die!*

Instead, a marmot came scurrying out and intersected my path at top speed. I screamed like a three-year-old who just lost a cookie and hurdled the critter without breaking pace. With my heart rate spiked, and relieved that it wasn't a bear, I shouted over my shoulder as I descended: "You scared the crap out of me!"

Head Protection Needed

One of my favorite wildlife encounters is also one of my most bizarre experiences in ultrarunning. I was pleased to be leading the Cascade Crest 100 in central Washington at mile 52. Running up Keechelus Ridge at dusk, I was buzzed by a barred owl about three feet over my head. The owl swooped up into a fir tree and stared down at me with those big, wise eyes. A line immediately came to mind from the children's book *Sam and the Firefly* by P.D. Eastman, which I regularly read to my young kids at the time. I quoted Sam the owl's nightly call to action: "Who? Who? Who wants to play?" Chuckling at my wit, I proceeded to run up the road.

As soon as my back was turned, the owl dive-bombed me and clawed the back of my head—*whap!* My chin flew to my chest, and I instinctively checked my head for blood. I guess he did want to play! I aimed a few handfuls of gravel around where he was perched, and he flew off. I continued up the road, but constantly looked over my shoulder for signs of Sam.

Running in big mountain landscapes and backcountry wild places is meditative and special, but understanding the dangers is also important—especially when it comes to wildlife. It's important to research the types of wildlife you might encounter where you will run and the strategies for dealing with those creatures. Run like hell, back away slowly, or hurdle the marmot. Whatever the encounter, knowing how to act is the first step in walking away safely with a good story to tell later. ■

Jeff Browning, aka 'Bronco Billy,' is a professional ultrarunner and online endurance coach. He loves the flow and solace that running in big, wild landscapes offers. Embracing the space (but never the carnivorous wildlife) is what has kept him running and competing in ultramarathons for nearly two decades. You can find out more about his coaching services or running escapades at GoBroncoBilly.com or follow him on Twitter and Instagram @GoBroncoBilly.

Moving Up in Vertical

The amount of vertical feet (or meters) you include in your weekly training is going to depend on several factors: the vertical in your goal event, your access to hills and mountains for training, and your training history. For the best results, select your goals according to what you have available to train on, and then train on hills similar to the goal race.

If you've been counting on the vertical meters in your weekly training to build the specific strength you need, but are feeling that your legs are the weak link, consider adding a period of ME training to your program.

NOTES FOR WEEKLY VERTICAL

- Begin your vertical progression with no more than a half of your goal event's total vertical in your first week.

- Incorporate muscular endurance work into the plan from the start. Keep it up as long as you are seeing gains. See page 240 in the Strength Section for more details.

- Plan on training a minimum of your goal event's total vertical during at least two of your precompetition-period weeks.

- These weeks should correspond to the bigger distance weeks.

- Do not increase distance, vertical, and intensity in a single week. Try to increase only one at a time. If you need to increase two of these, then keep the total increase to under 15 percent. Example: 10 percent distance increase with 5 percent vertical increase, or 8 percent increase in Zone 3 time with 7 percent increase in distance.

- As with distance, increase vertical no more than 10 percent in consecutive weeks, and no more that 20 percent in a four-week span (three building weeks followed by a recovery week).

- Cut vertical by a similar amount as distance reduction during recovery weeks (40–60 percent).

	AM	PM	Comments
Day 1	Rest day.	Off.	This can be a good day to take off or use for light recovery activities after a big weekend of training.
Day 2	ME and core strength. See page 240 in the Strength Section.	Recovery activity.	
Day 3	Z1 or Recovery. Stay in the zone. Up to 10% of weekly vertical.	Off.	Best if foot borne, outdoors on hilly terrain. But laps in a tall building or time on a treadmill or stair machine can be substituted.
Day 4	Z1 or Recovery. Stay in the zone. Up to 10% of weekly distance and vertical.	Off.	Best if foot borne, outdoors on hilly terrain. But laps in a tall building or time on a treadmill or stair machine can be substituted.
Day 5	Z2 vertical: up to 15% of weekly vertical.	Off.	Best if foot borne, outdoors on hilly terrain. But laps in a tall building or time on a treadmill or stair machine can be substituted.
Day 6	Z1: up to 25% of weekly vertical. Can be Z2 if suffering from ADS.	Hill Sprints, 6–8x10 sec.	Best if foot borne, outdoors on hilly terrain. But laps in a tall building or time on a treadmill or stair machine can be substituted.
Day 7	Z1: up to 40% of weekly vertical. Can be Z2 if suffering from ADS.	Off	Best if foot borne, outdoors on hilly terrain. But laps in a tall building or time on a treadmill or stair machine can be substituted.

Fig. 13.6 Example of an Early Base-Period Week for a Category 2 Mountain Runner

Note: By incorporating an ME workout, this athlete is aiming to complete a goal event with much more vertical than has been typical for this runner.

The Happiness Factor

Emelie Forsberg

I do not run to compete. I do not train to win races. I run because it brings me joy.

I came into the world of racing later than most. I was very active as a child, doing all kinds of sports, but I stopped everything when rock climbing stole my heart when I was fifteen years old. After that, I devoted all my free time to climbing—first trad and later sport. Running and skiing were still there for me as old friends, providing my endurance training, but I identified as a climber.

It was not until I was twenty-two that I realized that running had become my new passion. I was a devoted runner; I loved it so much. Now it wasn't climbing I built my life around, it was running. On foot, I explored the mountains surrounding where I lived, worked, and studied.

The simplicity of running appealed to me: I loved that I could just grab my shoes and go out to get some fresh air, clear my mind, and be in nature. I circled mountain massifs to see what was on the other side, and I headed up unfamiliar trails, curious where they would take me. I ran up to and around summits. I ran to see how many kilometers my legs could cover.

I did maybe two races every year, and I liked the racing because I met so many people who loved the same thing I loved. And I enjoyed pushing myself a little bit harder than I would have done if I was alone. I never thought that one day I would be a professional mountain athlete. I was just doing what gave me so much happiness: running (plus skiing in the winter when I couldn't run in the snowy mountains).

When I was twenty-five, I slipped on a banana peel into the world of full-time racing. I had just joined the Swedish Salomon team (Free shoes! Race fees!), and the international team invited me to a training week, which led to me trying my first international race: the 2012 Dolomites Skyrace.

I was amazed at how many runners showed up for the event. I was a little nervous at the start and tried to follow two strong ladies up the first climb. I was third to the summit, then first across the finish line with a new course record. I loved every step of it and wanted to do more.

The decision to become a professional runner was not easy for me. I was almost finished with my biology studies when I got the opportunity to travel the world running races. I chose the running, and it worked. But I was and always will be conscious of why I'm doing this: my top priority is to not lose the happiness—the feeling I had when I chose to build my life to be able to run. It was not for winning a race, it was for loving my life.

For me racing has never been and will never be the number one thing. To win a race is big, but it's not everything. This is only my approach. I have met many athletes whose priority is to train toward the goal of winning "A" races, no matter what. I admire their determination.

We all need to find our own way to keep the motivation to train, because in the end, that is what makes us stronger. For me, racing should be fun. But I won't sacrifice my health and happiness for it. It's a luxury for me, and it's fun to push myself to be the strongest version of myself. ■

Emelie Forsberg *is a devoted lover of mountains, a small farmer, a proud vegan, and an avid baker.*

Emelie Forsberg turning up the happiness factor on her way to first place in the 2017 Pierra Menta with partner Laëtitia Roux. Photo: Jocelyn Chavy

Glossary

1RM: See One-Rep Max.

ADENOSINE TRIPHOSPHATE (ATP): A molecule that acts as an energy-transfer medium within each cell. It is one of the end products of cellular metabolism. ATP supplies the energy for muscle contractions when its chemical bonds are broken. ATP is synthesized using the energy released when the macronutrients in food are metabolized. ATP is continually being broken down and remade via the metabolic processes. The rate at which ATP can be resynthesized determines the rate of work of which the human body is capable.

AEROBIC BASE: The physiological state in an endurance athlete brought about by extensive training at low to moderate intensities. This training enhances the ability of the trained muscles to produce energy aerobically and especially using fat as the primary fuel. This training makes up the vast majority of an endurance athlete's annual training volume. It supports the higher-intensity training by allowing the athlete to recover faster from intense training and races.

AEROBIC DEFICIENCY SYNDROME: A condition common in endurance athletes who spend too much training time doing middle- to high-intensity efforts, which causes an increased development of the anaerobic glycolytic metabolic pathway and reduced development of the basic aerobic metabolic pathway in the affected muscles. If this training state persists long enough, the athlete will see a lowering of his or her Aerobic Threshold.

AEROBIC METABOLISM: In our usage, we are referring to the cellular respiration process that takes place within the mitochondrion and whereby the end products of the breakdown of fat, carbohydrate, and protein are combined with oxygen to produce ATP. It is the primary energy-production pathway for endurance events lasting more than about two minutes.

AEROBIC THRESHOLD (AET): The uppermost intensity of exercise where the production of ATP begins to be dominated by glycolysis rather than by the oxidation of fats. At this point, blood lactate begins to rise above the resting level. By convention, a blood-lactate concentration of about 2mMol/L (millimole per liter) is indicative of AeT. Another marker of the aerobic threshold is the depth and pace of ventilation. When conversation can't be maintained at a normal cadence, the First Ventilatory Threshold (VT1) has been reached. VT1 corresponds closely to the AeT. This is an important physiological marker of intensity for endurance athletes because it marks the upper level of the most important training zone to use in developing aerobic capacity, the cornerstone to all endurance activities lasting over two minutes. The marker is very trainable and will move higher as measured by both speed of movement and heart rate. Top endurance athletes can have an AeT that is within 10 percent (and less) of their lactate (or anaerobic) threshold.

ANABOLIC: The metabolic process of combining smaller molecules into larger ones. The synthesis of protein that results in new structures within the body is an example of anabolism. Hormones that stimulate the metabolism of protein synthesis are known as anabolic steroids. Training has its effect due to the anabolic process stimulated by the training bouts themselves.

ANAEROBIC METABOLISM: The metabolic chemical reactions that take place without oxygen as one of the reactants. In terms of exercise, it refers to the cellular respiration process that takes place outside the mitochondrion but within the muscle cell, whereby energy is produced to fuel muscle contractions without the use of oxygen. Two types of anaerobic metabolism occur. For very short (ten seconds or less) bouts of very high-intensity exercise, high-energy phosphate fuels stored in the muscle cell as ATP and creatine phosphate (CP) can be used to produce energy for muscle contraction. For longer-duration, high-intensity exercise, the breakdown of glucose through anaerobic glycolysis provides the energy for ATP synthesis. When the requirement for muscle power is greater than can be met with aerobic glycolysis, the shortfall will be made up by anaerobic glycolysis. Lactate is a byproduct of anaerobic glycolysis and can be used as a marker of intensity of exercise.

ANAEROBIC POWER ENDURANCE: Endurance of maximal effort sustainable for less than sixty seconds. This method comprises a tiny segment of the overall volume of an endurance athlete's annual training. However, it is useful for developing Sport-Specific Strength because it requires the recruitment of a much larger muscle mass than normal, extensive, endurance training.

ANAEROBIC (LACTATE) THRESHOLD (LT): The lowest intensity of exercise at which the production of lactate exceeds the muscle's ability to take up and utilize that lactate as fuel in aerobic metabolism. Above this intensity, lactate levels in the blood begin to rise. The greater the intensity above the LT, the greater the rise in blood lactate.

AUTONOMIC NERVOUS SYSTEM: The part of the nervous system responsible for control of the bodily functions not consciously directed, such as breathing, the heartbeat, and digestive processes.

BASE PERIOD: The training period wherein the athlete focuses on building work capacity in the fundamental components that make up the event being trained for.

BIOGENESIS: The production of new organisms from existing ones. Mitochondria undergo biogenesis as the means of increasing both their size and number within the cells.

BODY WEIGHT: The resistance to movement provided only by a person's own body weight (such as a pull-up or a push-up).

CAPACITY TRAINING: Training that improves the *long-term* performance *potential* of the athlete.

CAPILLARY: The smallest of the body's blood vessels. The cross section of capillaries is on the order of the size of a red blood cell. They transport the blood, along with the nutrients and oxygen that it carries, into intimate contact with the organs and muscles.

CARBOHYDRATE: An organic compound made up only of carbon, hydrogen, and oxygen. In terms of dietary makeup, the carbohydrate group comprises mainly grains, fruits, and starches.

CARDIAC OUTPUT: The amount of blood being pumped by the heart in one minute. It is the product of the stroke volume as measured in liters per beat and the heart rate as measured in beats per minute.

CATABOLIC: The metabolic process of breaking larger molecules into smaller ones for the release of energy. Extensive catabolism of the body's protein structure can have a debilitating effect.

CATALYST: A substance that increases the rate of a chemical reaction by lowering the activation energy required for the reaction to take place. The catalyst is not consumed in the reaction. Biochemical reactions are catalyzed by enzymes.

CIRCUIT: A strength workout where an athlete completes one set each of several exercises in quick succession before returning to the first exercise and repeating the circuit. Can be repeated multiple times with various rest periods as needed for different training effects.

CONTINUITY: Maintaining a regular schedule of training with minimal interruption.

CORE: Vernacular for the musculature of the torso. The core is referred to as the critical link between the shoulder girdle and the pelvis. All athletic movements involve the core in either a static, stabilizing role or in a dynamic role of transmitting motion.

CORE STRENGTH: Strengthening of the core musculature in both its static and dynamic roles is critical for all athletes. Many exercises exist for core strengthening by either isolating the core or by directing forces generated in the limbs through the core to an opposing limb or resistance from gravity.

CREATINE PHOSPHATE: Also known as phosphocreatine, abbreviated PCr or CP, this is a highly bio-available source of high-energy phosphate stored in skeletal muscles. The CP reserve is small, lasting only five to eight seconds of an intense effort. The CP can anaerobically donate a phosphate group to ADP to form ATP for muscular contraction. During periods of low-intensity exercise, excess ATP can be used to resynthesize CP by giving up a phosphate group to the creatine to form CP by a process known as phosphorylation. This continual give-and-take mechanism allows CP to replenish and be available for repeated bouts of high-intensity work.

CYTOSOL: The intracellular fluid in which the various cell structures live. Glycolytic metabolism takes place in the cytosol. Aerobic metabolism takes place within the mitochondria, which in turn lie within the cytosol.

DURATION: The length of time of an exercise bout or training session.

ECONOMY: The energy cost of locomotion. This varies with speed and modality. For example, high running economy on the flats does not directly translate to high running economy while running steeply uphill.

ENDURANCE: The ability to resist fatigue during exercise. For high-intensity exercise, endurance is measured in minutes, whereas in low-intensity exercise, endurance is measured in hours or even days. Duration is inversely proportional to intensity. Proper endurance training helps an athlete increase the time to fatigue at a given intensity.

ENZYME: Biological catalysts responsible for enabling the myriad chemical reactions that sustain life. As with other catalysts, they accelerate the chemical reaction by lowering the activation energy of the reactants and are not consumed during the reaction. In some cases, they speed up the reaction by more than a million times.

FAST-TWITCH (FT) FIBER: A type of muscle fiber that is on the higher-power end of the fiber spectrum. These fibers contract more rapidly and with greater force than their slow-twitch relatives. They are larger in cross section, have lower mitochondrial density and lower-density capillary beds suffusing them, and rely more heavily on glycolytic metabolism for ATP production. They have less endurance than the slow-twitch fibers, but a certain class of FT fibers, called FTa, can be trained for more endurance.

FAT (DIETARY): A diverse group of chemical compounds that are insoluble in water. Fats can be categorized as saturated, unsaturated, and trans fats. The chemical bonds in fat allow it to store almost twice the chemical energy per unit of mass than carbohydrates and protein. Because of this, fats provide a large reservoir of energy for low- to moderate-intensity exercise.

FREQUENCY: The number of times each week that an exercise routine is completed.

FUNCTIONAL ADAPTATION: One category of changes to the human body as a result of the recurrent systematic stress of training. The adaptations to training are categorized in two general ways: functional, which relate to the function of the various body systems; and structural, which relate to the body's structures.

GENERALIZED ADAPTATION SYNDROME (GAS): The predictable way the body responds to stress as described by Canadian-Hungarian endocrinologist Hans Selye (1907–1982).

GLYCOLYSIS: The metabolic process that breaks down glucose (a form of sugar derived from carbohydrates) into pyruvate and ATP. Glycolysis is an anaerobic process. The end product of glycolysis, pyruvate, can enter the mitochondria and undergo further aerobic metabolism if the aerobic capacity is sufficient. Pyruvate can also be a metabolic dead end when the aerobic capacity of the muscle is insufficient. In this case, the metabolite lactate accumulates with negative consequences to endurance. Glycolysis is the primary energy supply for ATP synthesis in high-intensity exercise because glycolysis proceeds at a faster rate than the breakdown of fats.

GRADUALNESS: Adaptation to a training stimulus takes time and occurs in small increments. Rapid increases in training load cannot be accommodated long term. A successful training plan gradually progresses the training load over weeks and months in a systematic way, avoiding large and unmanageable jumps.

HEMOGLOBIN: Abbreviated Hb or Hgb, this is the oxygen-carrying molecule in red blood cells.

HOMEOSTASIS: A stable equilibrium state in an organism. Correct training disrupts homeostasis, resulting in adaptations that allow the body to handle similar training loads better in the future.

HYPERTROPHY: In strength training, this is the training method that induces muscle growth. The increase in muscle volume can be caused by increased sarcoplasmic volume or an increase in the contractile proteins.

INDIVIDUALITY: The need to account for the individual athlete's genetics, training history, lifestyle, etc., when designing training.

INNERVATE: To supply with nerves.

INSULIN: A hormone central to regulating carbohydrate and fat metabolism in the body. Insulin causes cells in the liver, skeletal muscles, and fat tissue to absorb glucose from the blood. In the liver and skeletal muscles, glucose is stored as glycogen, and in fat cells, it is stored as triglycerides.

INTENSITY: Intensity is a measure of the rate of energy consumed by the body. Intensity determines the preferential fuel the muscles use. It also determines the kind of adaptations that will be caused by the training. Common measures of intensity include heart rate, perceived exertion, blood lactate levels, and percentage of VO_2 max.

INTERVAL TRAINING: An endurance training method whereby, within one workout, bouts of higher intensity are separated by rest intervals. This allows the athlete to handle a higher volume of high-intensity training with less fatigue than when doing a continuous high-intensity effort of the same duration.

KREBS CYCLE: Also known as the citric acid cycle, this is one part of the aerobic metabolic process that takes place within a cell's mitochondria and results in the production of ATP.

LACTATE, LACTIC ACID: A chemical product of glycolytic metabolism in muscle cells. It is immediately dissociated into lactate and a hydrogen ion (H+). Lactate then has two main pathways available to it whereby it can be used as fuel: 1) It can be converted to pyruvate, which can then enter the Krebs cycle of aerobic metabolism; 2) It can be converted to glucose in the liver by the process of gluconeogenesis. The release of the hydrogen ions can have the effect of lowering the blood's pH (or increasing its acidity). If this continues without adequate buffering, it results in a burning sensation in the muscles and a forced slowing of the pace.

LACTATE BALANCE POINT: The point where lactate production is equal to lactate removal. This is considered the point of maximal intensity that can be maintained for a long duration of many minutes without a subsequent rise in blood lactate level. Also frequently referred to as the lactate threshold (LT), or the maximal lactate steady state (MLSS). This metabolic point has a direct relation to the time to exhaustion at VO_2 max intensity and, as such, bears strongly on the endurance of an athlete. It depends largely on the ability of the active muscles to oxidize lactate. Hence, the aerobic capacity of the slow-twitch muscle fibers, along with the lactate shuttle process, is largely responsible for endurance at high-intensity levels of exercise.

LACTATE SHUTTLE: A mechanism, identified in the early 1980s by George Brooks, a professor of integrative biology, where lactate is moved out of the muscle cell where it is being produced and into slow-twitch muscle cells where it can enter into the aerobic metabolic pathway to be used as fuel in the synthesis of ATP. This mechanism explains the importance of the Aerobic Base in supporting high-intensity training. The greater the aerobic capacity of the ST fibers to take up and utilize lactate, the more and longer high intensity can be sustained.

LACTATE THRESHOLD (LT) (see Anaerobic Threshold): The highest intensity at which lactate removal is matched by lactate production. Above this intesity lactate begins to accumulate rapidly. Any intesnity above the LT will be unsustainable. The higher the intensity, the less time it can be sustained.

LIPOLYSIS: The metabolic process of breaking down long-chain lipids or fatty acids into Acetyl CoA that can be used in aerobic metabolism for the synthesis of ATP.

LOAD (WEIGHT): The amount of resistance used. For the transition period, athletes should use a load 50–75 percent of their one-rep maximum. For the max strength period, they should use a load 85–90 percent of their one-rep maximum, or enough to allow only five reps.

LOCAL MUSCULAR ENDURANCE (see Muscular Endurance): The concept of training relatively small muscle groups for endurance without imposing a large load on the cardiovascular system. This effect is accomplished by making the muscular load high through added resistance. This causes the aerobic capabilities of the high-power muscle fibers, which are responsible for the movement, to be the limit on exercise, not the cardiovascular system's ability to supply oxygen to those muscles. The fatigue from this sort of training will be localized to that small group of muscles alone.

MACROCYCLE: From conventional sports, a period representing one complete cycle of training resulting in the preparation for a major event. In competition, this period will usually coincide with an annual cycle of training, hard competition, and the regeneration/recovery necessary before embarking on another annual cycle. It is possible to have two macrocycles in one year.

MAXIMUM LACTATE STEADY STATE: See Lactate Threshold.

MESOCYCLE: A period of training, usually weeks long, during which the training is targeting one or a few physiologic qualities.

METABOLISM: In general usage, this refers to all chemical reactions that occur within an organism. Relative to sport performance, we are mainly interested in the energy production necessary to yield ATP molecules and produce muscular work.

MICROCYCLE: A period of training that is repeated several times during a Mesocycle. Typically one week in length.

MITOCHONDRIA: The tiny (0.5–1 micrometer) organelles within all animal cells responsible for the majority of ATP production. Due to their crucial role in cellular energy production, they are often called the powerhouse of the cell. In exercise, we are mostly interested in the mitochondria in the muscle cells, which undergo adaptation resulting from training.

MODULATION: The variation in training load. Can indicate changes in both day-to-day and week-to-week training loads from light to heavy.

MOTOR UNIT: A group of muscle fibers and the motor nerve that fires them.

MUSCULAR ENDURANCE (ME): Shortened from Local Muscular Endurance (see that definition). The ability to do repeated muscular contractions of the same kind against a resistance. The muscular endurance is not limited by cardio-vascular endurance but rather by localized muscular fatigue. In many athletic undertakings, such as running a VK race, the limitations of performance will be largely determined by the local muscular fatigue. As such, the maximal sustainable output, or endurance, is linked directly to the athlete's local muscular endurance in the primary propelling muscle groups.

MUSCLE FIBER: Also known as myocyte or muscle cell, this is an elongated multinucleus cell in human skeletal muscle tissue.

MUSCLE FIBER CONVERSION: Muscle fibers respond directly to the training stimuli imposed upon them. Chronic training of a particular type over many months has the effect of changing the muscle fiber's characteristics. Multi-year studies indicate that prolonged endurance training will result in improved endurance of the faster-twitch fibers within an endurance-trained muscle.

ONE-REP MAX: The maximum load an athlete can lift for one repetition of an exercise movement.

ORGANELLE: A part of the internal cell structure. In our use: Mitochondria.

OVERREACHING: A method used to temporarily apply an excessive training load to the athlete. Can be as short as one to two days or up to a week-long training camp. Needs to be done in a controlled way when the athlete has minimal life stress. Used occasionally by high-level athletes. Must be followed by a significant recovery period.

OVERTRAINING: A condition common in endurance athletes where training bouts are no longer followed by Supercompensation. No matter the length of the recovery window, the athlete's performance degrades. This is a serious condition that needs dramatic intervention.

PARASYMPATHETIC NERVOUS SYSTEM: The part of the involuntary nervous system that serves to slow the heart rate, increase intestinal and glandular activity, and relax the sphincter muscles. Associated with the rest and digest or vegetative states.

PERIODIZE: A structured organization of training used in all modern sports to allow the athlete to focus time and energy on developing one or a few desired training adaptations.

PH: The measure of the acidity or alkalinity of a substance. Used in chemistry and biology to indicate the relative acidity of a compound.

POLARIZED TRAINING: A term used to indicate a training intensity distribution where training volume is dominated by low intensity (80 percent) and high intensity (20 percent) with relatively little moderate intensity; used predominately by elite endurance athletes. This is in contrast to a distribution of intensity that places most volume in the moderate/middle intensity, which is common with lower-level athletes.

POWER: Equals work divided by the time to complete the work. Stated another way: The rate at which work is done. Often confused with energy or work. The crucial differentiating element of power from work or energy is the measure of time in the denominator.

PYRUVATE: One of the end products of glycolytic metabolism that can take one of two metabolic paths: 1) entering the mitochondria and undergoing aerobic metabolism if there is sufficient aerobic capacity in the muscle cell; or 2) accumulating in the cytosol of the cell and being converted to lactate.

RECOVERY TIME: The rest interval between sets of the same exercise or between different exercises when using a circuit or in interval training.

REPETITION OR REP: One complete exercise movement cycle. One pull-up movement would be one rep. One two-minute running bout in an interval workout would be one rep.

SET: A group of repetitions. One set can contain from one rep to many, many reps in the case of muscular endurance training.

SLOW-TWITCH (ST) FIBER: A class of muscle fibers that have greater endurance than their fast-twitch neighbors. The slow-twitch fibers are endowed with more mitochondria, denser capillarization, and higher levels of aerobic enzymes. They are smaller in cross section and contract with less force than the fast-twitch fibers. They have a higher concentration of myoglobin, so appear more red than FT fibers.

SPECIFICITY: Training that mimics the demands of the sport in most ways.

SPORT-SPECIFIC STRENGTH: Training that imposes muscular loads in a sport-specific manner that are higher than those used in the actual event.

STRENGTH TRAINING: Any one of several methods of training directed at improving the contractile qualities of the muscles.

STROKE VOLUME: The volume of blood ejected from the heart with each contraction of the cardiac muscle. This is a highly trainable quality. Endurance training leads to an increase in stroke volume up to a point that is probably largely determined by an athlete's genetics.

STRUCTURAL ADAPTATION: The changes to the body's protein structures brought about by chronic training loads.

SUPERCOMPENSATION: The post-training period during which the parameter that was trained rises to a higher performance capacity than it had before the training.

SYMPATHETIC NERVOUS SYSTEM: A part of the nervous system that serves to accelerate the heart rate, constrict blood vessels, and raise blood pressure. Associated with the fight-or-flight response.

TAPER: To reduce the training load significantly after a training buildup to allow the body to reach a higher level of performance.

TRAINING EFFECT: Indicates, in a qualitative way, how an athlete's body reacts and adapts to the various forms of training stimuli.

TRAINING LOAD: A term used to describe, in a quasi-quantitative way, the type and amount of stress imposed by a single workout or period of training: the Training Load causes the Training Effect. They both depend on the type, the intensity, and the volume of work done in a training bout.

TRAINING STIMULUS: A bout of exercise designed and executed so as to encourage certain adaptations to occur.

TRIGLYCERIDES: A type of fat within the blood that facilitates the transfer of energy either to or from the adipose fat stores of the body.

UTILIZATION TRAINING: Training that improves the *near-term* performance *results* of the athlete. Utilization training is commonly prioritized during the buildup to the competition period or the targeted event. This training models the specific demands of the event an athlete is training for.

VENTILATORY THRESHOLD: A notable shift in breathing depth and rate that indicates a change in cellular respiration, and hence metabolism. Useful as a real-time indication of the intensity of exercise. Exercise science recognizes two ventilatory thresholds: VT1, which corresponds to the Aerobic Threshold, and VT2, which corresponds to the Lactate Threshold.

VK: A race involving an elevation gain of one vertical kilometer on steep terrain.

VO_2 MAX: The measure of the maximal aerobic power an athlete can develop. Measured by comparing the rate of inspired and expired oxygen during a multistep exercise test to voluntary exhaustion.

WORK: From physics. Work equals force times the distance over which the force is applied. An example would be that a 50-pound (20kg) weight lifted 10 feet (3m) has had 500-foot pounds (60kg/m) of work done to it.

Index

Page numbers in italic indicate photos.